To Mr. JR Lind

With Warmest Regards

From A.D. Chisholm.

VEIN OF IRON

VEIN OF IRON

The Pickands Mather Story

BY

WALTER HAVIGHURST

THE WORLD PUBLISHING COMPANY

CLEVELAND AND NEW YORK

Published by The World Publishing Company
2231 West 110th Street, Cleveland 2, Ohio

Published simultaneously in Canada by
Nelson, Foster & Scott Ltd.

Library of Congress Catalog Card Number: 58-14330

FIRST EDITION

Iron seemeth a simple metal, but in its nature are many mysteries . . . and men who bend to them their minds shall, in arriving days, gather therefrom great profits not to themselves alone but to all mankind.

—JOSEPH GLANVILL, 1668

Contents

PROLOGUE—1883   9

Part I. MEN AND IRON

   1. North to Marquette   15

   2. Shipwreck at Sunset   19

   3. Echo From Landy's Pit   30

   4. Lines in a Ledger   36

   5. Stampede to the Gogebic   51

   6. The Long Ladder   65

   7. The Giant Range   73

Part II. THE NEW CENTURY

   8. Arrived and Cleared   85

   9. Men of the Menominee   103

  10. The Strewn Shore   112

  11. Last of the Mine Mules   119

  12. Smoking on the Dynamite Wagon   129

  13. Second Generation   136

  14. River of Iron   144

  15. The Tallest Oak   156

CONTENTS

Part III. TRADITION AND CHANGE

16. The Silent Years   165

17. Shadow of a Man   174

18. At Mid-Century   182

19. The New Fleet   193

20. Operation Hardrock   204

ACKNOWLEDGMENTS   217

INDEX   219

Prologue—1883

A<small>T THE</small> beginning of February 1883 the skies were heavy over Cleveland. After three days of pouring rain the Cuyahoga left its banks. Acres of lumber floated onto Lake Erie, oil tanks exploded, and fire broke out in the industrial flats. Day and night oil flames flickered on the river and a haze of smoke crept up the hills.

On a gray February morning Samuel Mather, a slight, quick-striding man of thirty-one, turned off Superior Avenue into Water (now West Ninth) Street. Around him sounded the life of the city, the hammering of hoofs on cobblestones, the grind of wagon wheels, the puffing of trains from the Union Depot at the foot of the street. When he entered the parlors of the Cleveland Iron Mining Company the noise faded. On his desk was a letter from Ishpeming, L. S. Mich.

Lake Superior was distant then, a remote northern land of promise, like the Alaska of a later generation. But it was a familiar country to the Cleveland iron merchants. Samuel Mather carried scars from a mine explosion at Ishpeming. After many seasons in the North his father, Samuel Livingston Mather, had become president of the Cleveland Iron Mining Company and a leader in the industry. Young Samuel Mather had a thorough knowledge of the iron-ore locations in the Marquette hills and he knew the men of the district. With two of them, Jay C. Morse and Colonel James Pickands, he had discussed a venture in the iron business, the forming of a new company.

The letter on his desk was from Jay C. Morse; it accompanied

a contract with the Argyle Company and referred to 1,800 tons
of ore to be transferred to "Pickands & Co." Wrote Morse:

> You will find the concern made Pickands & Co. I advised this.
> Both you and myself are actively engaged with the Cleveland Co.
> If when Col. and I arrive in Cleveland you think the name
> should be different, say Pickands, Mather & Co. we can make
> the change, but for the present the concern's name is Pickands &
> Co. Please notify the Commercial agents of the existence of this
> firm. Notify them of a capital of $300,000. I am afraid this will
> not be enough but we must have that amount to start with.

There were many frontiers in America in the years following
the Civil War. A young man could feel the pull of the homestead lands beyond the Missouri, the lead and silver camps of the
Rockies, the cattle ranges of Wyoming, the silver mines of Nevada
and the gold mines of California, the green valleys of Oregon.
Cleveland was most aware of the northwestern frontier on Lake
Superior, a dark wild district where a pioneer generation had
opened the copper mines on the long trap range of the Keweenaw
Peninsula and had traced the oval iron formation in the blunted
hills above Marquette. Cleveland men had followed the iron.
They had developed mines and forges; they had opened trails,
cleared roads, and built a railroad from Marquette Harbor to the
iron locations around Negaunee and Ishpeming. In the Marquette Range they had their special portion of the American
frontier, with its own rigors, demands, and promises.

There were two great resources in the Middle West, coal in
the Alleghenies and iron ore in the hills of Lake Superior, and
the Great Lakes waterway could bring them together to create the
American steel industry. Cleveland lay between the two resources
and on the vital waterway. Already Cleveland men had made
their city the capital of the iron-ore trade. Now, in 1883, a new
company was entering the lists.

Two weeks later, in mid-February, came another letter from
Ishpeming. This time Morse suggested that the new firm include
Samuel Mather's name.

> If you are going to be active in the business your name should
> appear. I only supposed you were going to devote a portion of
> your time to the new concern, but I am glad you have decided
> to go in and I believe the Col. and you can make a concern that

we will be pleased with. I question if I had better appear in that concern. . . . Perhaps I had better be a special.

Already Morse had many interests in the North. While serving as general agent for the Cleveland Iron Mining Company he had reached into other mining firms, iron furnaces, shipping, supplying, and banking. In the new firm he became a "special" and roving partner, bringing new interests to the company from a distance.

That spring the iron trade listed the firm of Pickands Mather & Co., a name which would become familiar from the blast furnaces of Pennsylvania to the mines of Lake Superior. Behind it were three Ohio men, each drawn to the magnetic promise of the North, who had met in the frontier district of Marquette. While they were launching their company a Scottish author and scientist, Samuel Smiles, wrote of iron as "this extraordinary metal, the soul of every manufacture, and the mainspring, perhaps, of civilized society." They came together from diverse backgrounds but they saw in the iron hills a common future.

PART I

Men and Iron

Sing to me the source of metals,
Sing the origin of iron,
How at first it was created.
        —*Kalevala*

PART I

Men and Iron

Sing to me the source of metals,
Sing the origin of iron,
How at first it was created.
              —*Kalevala*

CHAPTER I

North to Marquette

IN DECEMBER 1863 after the battle of Missionary Ridge, the 124th Ohio Volunteer Infantry was camped at Clinch Mountain in eastern Tennessee. Like the rest of the Army of the Cumberland the regiment was plagued by camp fever and measles, along with the routine diarrhea—"Tennessee quickstep"—that came from drinking river water. They had few tents and meager clothing; with feet muffled in rags they dragged up wood to keep the fires burning. One of their officers, Lieutenant Colonel James Pickands, mixed a soft soap of lye and ashes so they could bathe their blackened hands and feet.

In the same season the 103rd Ohio Regiment had marched out of Knoxville to join the Fourth Army Corps. In mud and cold they moved slowly, pushing the Rebels back to Bear Station. At the end of December they fell back to Strawberry Plains. In their dreary camp men from Cleveland and Akron talked of seeing old friends in the 124th at Clinch Mountain. One of them, Captain Henry S. Pickands, hoped to find his brother.

On the night of January 6, Captain Pickands warmed stiff fingers at the fire outside his tent. Then on a box by candlelight he wrote a letter to his mother in Cleveland. It was a cheerful, vivid, expressive letter, telling about a meeting with his younger brother who outranked him by two grades.

> . . . I mounted a horse and started to find the 4th Corps, which I learned were encamped some eight miles from us. The roads were wretched, the day cold and blustery. I got lost in the woods and on the wrong road, but finally by perseverance and hard riding I found Hazen's Brigade and the 124th. Jimmy was

seated by a log fire in front of his quarters as I rode up and dis-
mounted, and you may imagine the meeting was a joyful one.
He looked weatherbeaten a little but in splendid health and good
spirits. There was no use in talking of returning to camp that
night—

The brothers, separated for nearly two years, talked about
Akron and Cleveland and the Presbyterian manse they had grown
up in, about their father and mother and sisters, about their
younger brother Sammie of the 1st Artillery Regiment who had
died of fever in West Virginia; James Pickands on leave from his
own regiment had brought the body home to Cleveland. They
talked of the uncertain future, of what they might do when the
war was over. In the morning they rode to Strawberry Plains
together, two gaunt and rangy men on mud-splashed horses, still
talking. James Pickands, twenty-two years old when he was commissioned Major in the 124th, had a young soldier's ardor and
idealism; he had thought of a career in military service, but now
that dream was past.

   . . . Jim has got glory enough and sore bones enough with
sleeping on the hard ground, and is quite as desirous of getting
inside a suit of plain clothes and having cooked meals and a bed
to sleep in as his older brother. His high notions of regular service
have all subsided, and we found ourselves talking of a small business house with "Pickands Bros." over the door, or a small farm
in the country and I don't know how many more absurdities.
But strange things happen sometimes, and who knows—we may
realize it yet. . . .

Far ahead of them as they parted in the winter morning was
the fulfillment of those fancies, when James Pickands would be
Mayor of Marquette and Henry Pickands Treasurer of Schoolcraft
County and they would be launching an iron business on the
remote shores of Lake Superior. But now they returned to the
hazards of war. Even after the peace at Appomattox the perils
were not past. Entraining at Raleigh, the 103rd regiment was in
high spirits, until the cars plunged down an embankment in the
Alleghenies. Henry Pickands, then a major, escaped without injury. The 124th fought through the spring of 1864 at Dalton,
Resaca, and at New Hope Church, where in the assault on
General Cleburne's division Colonel James Pickands was badly

wounded. He returned to the regiment in time for the Battle of Nashville, and was commissioned full colonel before they were discharged.

Back in Cleveland Colonel James Pickands, like countless other soldiers, had his picture taken before he put away his uniform. It shows a stalwart, seriously handsome young man with dark eyes, a long straight nose, a dark mustache, and short chin whiskers above the double row of brass buttons on his tunic.

Cleveland, with 70,000 people at the end of the war, was a busy city, schooners and steamers crowding the river mouth, mills, furnaces, elevators, oil refineries spreading in the smoky Cuyahoga basin, a big new Union Depot at the foot of Water Street, carriages rolling past the mansions of Euclid Avenue, visitors thronging the splendid new Kennard House at St. Clair and Bank streets with a Moorish fountain, copied from the Alhambra, bubbling in its lobby. On St. Clair and Water streets were the offices of the iron merchants, dealing in Lake Superior ore. The Civil War had boomed the iron industry, which went on growing after the war was past. Two hundred thousand tons of ore came down the Lakes in 1865; three years later the shipments exceeded half a million. Red-stained schooners lined the Cleveland docks, with horses hauling up the buckets and stevedores trundling wheelbarrows to the stockpile. In the summer of 1865 James Pickands got inside a suit of plain clothes and went to work in the Cleveland office of Brown & Co., iron merchants. This Cleveland firm, a partnership of Fayette Brown, general agent for the pioneer Jackson Mine in the Marquette district, and his son, Harvey H. Brown, represented two of the largest mining concerns on Lake Superior.

Negaunee, Ishpeming, Michigamme were familiar names in the Cleveland iron offices. The old Chippewa words had the sound of a strong and primitive country, and Lake Superior itself was one of the magnetic names in America. Seven hundred miles away a man could feel its challenge and promise. In the spring of 1867 the Pickands brothers, perhaps remembering their talk on a winter night in Tennessee, sailed north to Marquette and the iron country.

Already there and well established in iron enterprises was another young Civil War veteran from Ohio. After discharge from his regiment Jay C. Morse went into the employ of the Cleveland Iron Mining Company in Cleveland. Soon he was sent north as general agent, or business manager, of the Cleveland Mine at Ishpeming. An abrupt, aggressive, tireless man, he soon knew every mine location on the range and every steamer and schooner that sailed into Iron Bay. He had two offices, one on the bay in Marquette, another at the mine pit fifteen miles inland. He knew every bump and stump on the road to the Cleveland Mine and every jolt and jar on the Iron Mountain Railroad. He also knew every enterprise in this bustling district—dynamite-blasting in the hills, ore trains clanking down the grade from Negaunee and Ishpeming, tugboats prodding schooners into the docks at Iron Bay. He soon had a hand in all that business. One of James Pickands' first friends in Marquette was Jay C. Morse. When Pickands talked about opening a hardware store they became partners.

James Pickands at twenty-eight was starting with no money but with great energy, a bold imagination, and boundless belief in the future of the Lake Superior country. At Bluff and Front streets, with Jay Morse helping him to find customers, he opened a hardware business, selling mining machinery, implements, and supplies. But he already had hope and expectation of something more. Within a year he was "Sole Agent for Marquette and Pacific Rolling Mill Iron." Soon he had a stone warehouse on the lake front—it still stands at the corner of Lake Street and Superior (Baraga) Avenue—and a large branch store beside the mines at Ishpeming. When his brother became an ironmaker, managing the Munising and Bay furnaces, Colonel Pickands took on a pig-iron agency. Until 1870 the railroads and mines burned wood, but as the hardwood forests thinned and steam-driven machinery increased in the mines there was a growing market for coal. Colonel Pickands began a fuel business, bringing coal from the Lower Lakes in the holds of ore freighters. It gave the carriers a two-way commerce, and Pickands saw a brightening future for the vessel trade. Each year in this yeasty country brought new developments and fresh opportunities. Marquette was a far-off frontier town, with granite boulders studding the harbor and steep streets ending in a wall of forest. But sometimes standing on the dock at daybreak, Colonel Pickands saw the future lighting the land like a sunrise.

CHAPTER 2

Shipwreck at Sunset

JAY C. MORSE was a small man with a large capacity for action. Darkly weathered, with heavy black hair and mustache and sun-squint lines around his eyes, he had an outdoors look and his eyes roved like a hunter's. He spoke briefly and to the point. Restless and untiring, he seemed everywhere at once—in the offices at Negaunee, the mines at Ishpeming, the docks at Iron Bay. One day a summer shower halted loading at the docks while a string of vessels waited for cargo. When Morse appeared he wanted to know why the men were sitting under the trestle. Because of the rain, they said. "Rain?" the agent asked. "What rain?" He looked up at the wet sky, held out his dripping hands, and declared the rain was over. He got the men out and the cargoes loaded. Then, his clothing drenched and mustache dripping, his face lit up like a lamp. He loved to get things done.

Opportunities jostled a young man in the iron country. Soon Jay Morse was up to his stocky shoulders in mines, furnaces, shipping, and supplying. He was general agent for the Cleveland Iron Mining Company, the Marquette Iron Company, and the McComber Iron Company, secretary of the Bancroft Iron Company and for a time manager of the Bancroft Furnace, president of the Lake Superior Powder Company, a director of the Marquette bank, and a partner in James Pickands & Co.; he ran the McComber business from a desk in the Pickands store. Marquette was a young man's town and Jay Morse had risen fast in a few busy years. Before he was thirty a vessel was named for him, the steam tug *Jay C. Morse* built in Buffalo in 1867, designed for towing schooners through the rivers and ore barges down the

Lakes. It was like Morse, short, deep-drafted, charged with energy.
It steamed up to Lake Superior that summer, and it brought the
first misfortune in Jay Morse's successful life.

When the new vessel reached Marquette in mid-July 1867,
he went down to meet Captain Atkins and inspect the craft. She
was a sturdy vessel, 79 feet long and 18 feet wide, with a nicely
curved deck rail and a tall black stack. To celebrate her arrival
Morse invited a party of friends for a sunset ride on Iron Bay.
Forty-one persons came aboard at seven o'clock; they were the
leading families of Marquette, including the Ely brothers and
their wives, the Calls, the Maynards, and the Honorable Peter
White. That evening the vessel's normal crew of nine was reduced to four, as the cook and the off watch stayed ashore. In
radiant evening light they steered past the trestle docks and between the anchored schooners, past Lighthouse Point and the
Rocks and the mouth of Dead River with sunset warming the
cliffs of lumber at the sawmills. Past the headland of Presque Isle
stretched the great cold lake and the broken lifeless shore, with
the sun sinking beyond the dark height of Sugar Loaf. Through
golden water under the colored sky the wheelsman steered for
the passage inside Partridge Island. Two women sitting on the
forward rail made a nice silhouette against the sunset. In that
beauty and serenity, running at thirteen miles an hour, the *Morse*
struck granite. It shook her like a powder blast and lifted the
bow out of water.

The women on the rail were hurled into the sea. Jay Morse
and the wheelsman, Joe Roleau, leaped in and seized them while
they floundered. Captain Atkins, thrown from the bridge wing
when they struck, lay injured on the lower deck. The two men
were hauled aboard with the shivering women. Then the wheelsman heard a cry and saw Darius Gardner Maynard in the water.
Roleau slashed a rope at the taffrail and threw a plank toward
him. The light was failing now and a cold wind ruffled the sea.
Up from below came the engineer and the fireman; water was
pouring in and the fires were drowned. When he heard Gard
Maynard call again the wheelsman leaped into the numbing sea.
He swam toward something bobbing in the water. When he
reached it there was only the plank. Joe Roleau threshed on
toward shore.

Over the dark water beyond Middle Island, the excursion
party saw a steamer's lights. It was the *Metropolis,* on her run

from Duluth to Marquette. From the *Morse's* deck they shouted and clanged the ship's bell, but the lights of the *Metropolis* slid on past Presque Isle Point. As water washed the railing they climbed to the upper deck. Northward over the dark sea the ghostly aurora streamed up through the stars.

Numb and gasping, Joe Roleau pulled himself out of the water and stood on the rocky shore. It was six black miles to Marquette, through dense woods and the Dead River swamp. He started going. Once in a while he caught the glimmer of the lighthouse. It guided him while he groped through thickets and splashed through the swamp. He swam the Dead River, took a bearing from the lighthouse gleam, and plunged into the woods again.

It was an hour past midnight when he reached the sleeping streets of Marquette, and it took another hour to raise Captain Bridges of the tug *Dudley* and his engineer. While steam was building in the boilers they crept over Iron Bay and made for Partridge Island. They found the *Morse* half awash, with a huddle of people around the smokestack on her upper deck. They were all there—all except Gard Maynard. When Mrs. Maynard put her hands on Roleau's shoulders, pleading for word that he had saved her husband, the wheelsman could not answer. Fifteen years later Colonel Pickand's niece, Helen Goodwin, married the nephew of Gard Maynard, whose grave is the cold unresting sea. Lake Superior does not give up its dead.

In the first gray light of sunrise Captain Bridges took the rest aboard the *Dudley,* leaving the *Morse* wedged on the rocks. They got back to Marquette at seven o'clock, just twelve hours after the excursion had begun. Overnight Jay Morse carried some new lines in his weathered face.

A week later the tug was worked off the rocks and towed to Marquette Harbor. With canvas stretched across the broken bow and pumps working fore and aft, she was towed through the Soo and down to Saginaw, the nearest dry dock. When she came back to Lake Superior again the *Morse* was sold to the Hebard brothers, two English lumbermen who ran big sawmills at Pequaming on Keweenaw Bay. Forty years later, finished with the log-towing business, the *Morse* was sold down the Lakes and went into service on the River Rouge below Detroit.

One of the Morse business interests was the Bancroft Iron Company. The first pig iron on Lake Superior was made by

Stephen R. Gay, a Berkshire ironmaster from Massachusetts, who
came to the Marquette wilderness in 1857. He found there a few
small forges for the smelting of iron ore. One of them had been
built by Edward K. Collins, owner of a famous line of trans-
Atlantic steamships, in association with some Marquette men.
As an experiment Gay leased the forge of the Collins Iron Company at Negaunee and converted it in two days at a cost of two
dollars into a minuscule blast furnace. It turned out pig iron, and
Stephen Gay began a career as ironmaker on Lake Superior. His
son-in-law, a young man named Van Cleve, became James Pickands' partner in Pickands, Van Cleve & Co., the branch hardware store that Colonel Pickands opened at Ishpeming.

In 1860 Stephen Gay built for Peter White and Samuel L.
Mather the big Bancroft Furnace in a clearing on Dead River,
four miles from Marquette. The next year it shipped 2,400 tons
of pig iron. It was a steady producer of first-grade iron when
Morse became its manager, and its success led him to an interest
in the Bay Furnace on the lake shore opposite Grand Island. The
Bay Furnace was designed by L. D. Harvey, another ironmaster
from Stockbridge, Massachusetts, who had previously built the
Pioneer Furnace at Negaunee. By 1870 ironworks were scattered
from the Dead River to Grand Island, forty miles east of Marquette, and inland for as deep as twenty miles, so that today a
hunter may come upon old charcoal ovens in a belt of hardwood
and the ruins of old forges by the rivers. Each of the furnaces
was built at some point of vantage, in a stand of hardwood, or
beside an ore body, or near a bed of limestone.

The huge hardwood forests around Grand Island Bay attracted furnacemen. Two big furnaces were there, the Munising
Furnace built in 1868 and the Bay Furnace two years later. Henry
Pickands became manager of these properties. Still unmarried, he
boarded in the little woods town of Onota in Schoolcraft County;
he was elected County Treasurer in 1875. For years he traveled
the rough roads between the offices, the furnaces, and the mines,
doing business with his brother and his brother's partner.

When men of the Cleveland Iron Mining Company took over
the McComber Mine, at the southern edge of Negaunee, Jay Morse
became its manager and the Pickands brothers invested in its future. They pushed production, taking out nearly 40,000 tons in
the next year, 1873. Believing the McComber ore would make
spiegel iron, a lustrous metal with a high content of manganese,

they loaded fifty tons on a scow in Marquette, sailed it over to Furnace Bay, and produced, in their second try, a handsome run of speckled iron.

For a few seasons Henry Pickands lived a rugged, lonely life in this Hiawatha country bordered by the pictured rocks, a fantastic shore line carved by centuries of wind and water. The land was haunted by old Chippewa legends of the gods of thunder and lightning who lived in caverns on the broken shore. Now the darkness was lit with furnace flames, but when the blast died down the ancient banners of the northern lights streamed across the winter sky. Here amid beauty and solitude, between the dark woods and the shining water, Henry Pickands was learning the mysteries of iron, a knowledge he would soon carry to the busier land at the foot of Lake Michigan.

In 1877 the Munising and Bay furnaces were closed down. It was clear by then that the manufacture of iron belonged on the Lower Lakes, close to supplies of coal and limestone, in the midst of industrial markets. In the woods the old arches and chimneys were left to sun and snow and silence. Slowly they softened with deer moss and lichen; in time they came to look like ruined chapels in the forest. Henry Pickands sailed down the Lakes (he *returned* to Michigan, the papers said) and built charcoal furnaces at Bangor and Fruitport on the southwestern shore of Lake Michigan. He took time to go to Cleveland in September 1878 to be married to Marion Louise Haskins. Then he was back at Bangor, sending the first pig iron to be used by the Northern Chicago Rolling Mill for conversion into Bessemer steel. The iron industry was becoming centralized, and Chicago was one of its centers. With the backing of his brother's new firm, Pickands, Mather & Co., Henry Pickands went to Chicago to form a partnership with William Liston Brown, a founder of the Menominee Iron Company and a pioneer in the development of the Menominee Range. Within a few years Pickands, Brown & Company were the leading iron merchants on Lake Michigan.

One of the Cleveland men who spent summers in Marquette was John Outhwaite, a director of the Cleveland Iron Mining Company and a dealer in iron ores. English by birth, he had come to Cleveland in the 1840's, a trained chemist and metallurgist, and his interests soon drew him to Lake Superior. He became a founder of the Cleveland Iron Mining Company; he and Samuel L. Mather were its largest stockholders. By 1870 John Outhwaite had spent many seasons in Marquette, taking his family with him. There Jay Morse and James Pickands became acquainted with the Outhwaite daughters. When he sailed to Cleveland in June 1870 to marry Caroline Martha Outhwaite, James Pickands became a brother-in-law of Jay Morse, who had already married an Outhwaite daughter. Iron was a family business in those years, with fathers, sons, brothers, and the husbands of sisters and daughters in a complex of partnerships. Now Pickands and Morse had double ties of business and family. In years to come Colonel Pickands would name his youngest son for his partner and brother-in-law.

By 1870 James Pickands, bringing his bride to Marquette, had put down roots like a northern maple. Soon he sent for his parents and his sisters. They arrived in June of 1873, steaming through drift ice in Iron Bay and watching the hills of Marquette grow above the harbor.

The Reverend James D. Pickands, seventy-one, could look back at a long, full life. After graduation from Princeton he had served Presbyterian parishes at Lowville, New York, Wilmington, Delaware, Akron and Cleveland, Ohio. Coming to the Western Reserve in the early years, he had seen a frontier develop into a complex society. But he did not look back; now he looked around him at the new frontier of the North. Each day he walked from the family house on Arch Street down the hill to the harbor, past the iron, coal, and lumber offices, and his son's warehouse. He watched the ore trains on the trestle, the cargo flowing into the vessels' holds, men loading lumber, iron, graphite, slate, and brownstone. Then he marched back up the hill, a straight-backed man in a black coat and white chin whiskers, stabbing the plank road with his walking stick. At his desk in a strong upright hand he kept a record of the northern seasons, snow flurries in September, then blue skies and the maple forests flaming; deep snow in October; on February 9, 26 degrees below zero, three days later 30 below. For a solid month, that first winter, it was zero or colder. On April 15 a blizzard, heavy drifts of snow and the temperature plunging.

The second winter was mild, with little snow until mid-March. Then a two-day blizzard, and another snowstorm on the fourth of April. On that day "our son James elected Mayor of Marquette by a handsome majority." A week later another blizzard raged day and night, and son Henry came in after two days' struggle by wagon and on snowshoes from Onota twenty-five miles away. It was a strenuous country and an exhilarating one. From his desk he peered out at the granite outcrop behind the house and the snowy woods around it, woods that went on west, unbroken, for five hundred miles.

As snow swirled at the window the old man was writing a sermon, a metaphysical-theological discourse solid as the bedrock in the winter woods. "Is Matter Eternal?" All is change, decay, and dissolution, he began his answer to that timeless question, but the Mind of God endures. God is and always has been *immanent* (in-dwelling) in nature. The Infinite Mind, the bedrock reality, creates the ideas that take shape and substance in our fleeting world. He concluded: "If we recognize the divine immanence we shall not think Paul's language too strong—'In him we live and move and have our being' or as the Greek poet has said, 'We also are his offspring.' "

While the old dominie was thinking in these timeless terms, his son, just down the icy hill, was busy with things of this world —boiler plate and bar iron. And by coincidence when the sermon appeared in the *Marquette Mining Journal* the back of the page was filled with an advertisement:

James Pickands & Co.
Wholesale and Retail Dealers in
HEAVY HARDWARE
RAILWAY AND
MINING SUPPLIES

including Bar Iron, Boiler Plate, Sheet, Hammered and Swede's Iron, Black Diamond and Drill Steel, Plate Blister and Sleigh Shoe Steel also Crow Bars, sledges, striking hammers, Railroad Picks, Mine Picks, Strap-back Shovels, Axes, Sand Barrows, Blocks and Cordage, Rubber Hose Fittings, Gas and Steam Fittings, Blacksmith Tools, etc.
HARD AND SOFT COAL

The most lasting matter was on James Pickands' shelves, while his father wrestled with the word *eternal*.

People bring character to a place, and amid the stumps and boulders of Arch Street was a high-minded, reverent, idealistic household. While her father reflected on Plato and the Apostle Paul, Miss Caroline Pickands compiled a "Scrapbook of Poetry," beginning with the motto:

He liveth long who liveth well
All else is thrown away.

A realization from Emerson's essays: "We live in a new and ex-
ceptional age. *America* is another name for opportunity," and a
reminder from John Hay: "Who would succeed in the world
should be wise in the use of his pronouns: utter the You twenty
times where you once utter the I." There was room in this scrapbook for the strange beauty of the North. "Sun dog. A peculiar
appearance of the sky resembling a small piece of a rainbow, but
perpendicular, seen at sunrise or sunset, not far from the sun. Is
said to be a sure sign of rain. (I saw one when on L. Michigan,
July 11, 1879, C.S.P.) " Then comes another kind of observation.
"One cord of wood will make fifty bushels of charcoal, which is
sufficient for the production of ½ ton of pig iron." Iron was in
the Pickands household.

Miss Caroline Pickands opened a private school, reclaiming an
old shanty across Arch Street. Years later a Marquette writer,
Carroll Watson Rankin, wrote an appealing book, *Stump Village,* picturing the little school half-buried in snow, a wall of
cordwood inside the door, and the children sitting on plank
benches around the iron stove. When the public school was built
on Arch Street, Caroline Pickands took charge. Two of her pupils
became famous, Frederick Eugene Wright, with the United States
Geological Survey, and Alfred V. Kidder, an archaeologist who
explored the cliff dwellings of Arizona and New Mexico. Alfred
Kidder grew up with excavations; his father managed the Champion, Angeline, and Volunteer mines in the hills beyond Ishpeming.

Colonel Pickands and his wife lived at the corner of Bluff
and Front streets, now the site of the Marquette Post Office. Their
windows looked down on the railroad dock, at the foot of Main
Street, where horses plodded on the planks hauling buckets of
Pickands coal out of a schooner's hatches. As the business grew
James Pickands set up a battery of Figure 4 rigs (they looked like
a lofty 4) run by a coughing donkey engine. When that became
inadequate the firm moved to a new dock at the foot of Spring
Street, equipped with clamshell hoists. There they handled coal
for the Cleveland-Cliffs Iron Company as well as on their own
account, supplying railroads, mines, and commercial and domestic users throughout the range.

The Panic of 1873 spent itself somewhere below the Soo, and the iron business went on growing. That year, though prices fell, the Marquette mines shipped a record total, over a million tons of ore. Through the seventies production stayed near the million figure, rising to a million and a third in 1880. In 1890 it would pass three million. Marquette men breathed a bracing air.

On the hill where the mansions of Ridge Street stood among the maples there were people of congenial tastes and varied talents, drawn together by business interests and interrelated by birth and marriage—the families of Peter White, Alfred Jopling from England, Edward Breitung from Germany, the Hewitts, Longyears, Maynards, Calls, Spears, Pickandses, and Morses. Their lives had a zest of pioneer endeavors, of occasional visits to Cleveland, Detroit, Chicago, and then the return to their sharp northern seasons. In November the bay froze fast, snow covered the red-stained docks, and the harbor lay white and still. For six months in the wintry town life was enclosed and self-contained. Then came programs in Mathers' Hall, lectures on geology, history, and Indian legends, concerts by the Marquette Vocal Society and the Swedish Quartette. There were dinners and teas in the big houses on Ridge Street, sleigh bells shaking in the cold bright air, the Snowshoe Club setting out in colored mufflers and mittens for the woods of Presque Isle. An unexpected ardor marked this faraway colony, enhanced and heightened by its remoteness. The favorite Marquette stories were of Peter White and John M. Longyear bringing the mail by dog sled from the Soo, and of the arrival of the little steamer *Napoleon* ten days before Christmas 1850 with food and clothing for the winter. Now trains ran through the woods to Escanaba, Green Bay, and Chicago, but Marquette people still loved the feel of being winter-bound. They exulted in the great snows of 1881 when the telegraph wires were down and no train moved in the buried country north of Green Bay. Their newspapers were still dated from L. S. (Lake Superior) Michigan, mail came addressed that way, and a man going to Cleveland or Chicago spoke of returning to the United States. The North was still a land apart, and Marquette was its capital.

Every day in the winter of 1882 Colonel Pickands walked out Ridge Street where his new house was going up across from Peter White's mansion. It was a large frame house, handsome for the time, with broad bays looking toward the harbor and tall gables up among the maple branches. Nine fireplaces, each with a different pattern of fluted columns and carved molding, rose to the ceiling; the openings were framed in Low tiles from Chelsea, Massachusetts. Past the porte-cochere a curving driveway led to a stable screened by birch trees; it had room for teams, sleighs, carriages, and servants' quarters.

This was a home for a growing family. Colonel Pickands had three sons to romp in the halls and slide down the walnut banisters. Ample, friendly, welcoming, it promised a fullness of life—the living room ruddy with firelight while dusk came on, children lying on the floor picking out nutmeats from a wooden bowl, a woman at the piano playing old English melodies, a man coming home to this fulfillment in the early winter dark. But the happiness was brief. They moved in on a cloudless day in May, when the maples were budding and the birches made a mist of green. That evening the rooms were rich with perfume and cigar smoke, the boom of men's voices, and the rustle and laughter of women. The next day Martha Pickands fell ill. In a week she was dead and the big new house was desolate.

Marquette is something like a New England town planted in a distant place. It has deep shadows and it keeps its memories. Some of its memories have passed into legend, like the moving of the Longyear mansion, stone by stone, to Brookline, Massachusetts, because a railroad spoiled its view of Marquette Harbor. The legend of the Pickands house says that the family moved in before the plaster was dry, that Martha Outhwaite Pickands died of pneumonia, and Colonel Pickands never entered the place again. The record is that Martha Pickands died of spinal meningitis which came without warning. A few months later Colonel Pickands moved to Cleveland to develop the new firm of Pickands Mather & Co. Business brought him back to Marquette, but he never entered the house on the hill. Yet the legend says that he built in Cleveland, in his house on Kennard Street, an exact duplicate of the Ridge Street mansion.

The Marquette house was sold to a lumberman and is now the home of Mrs. Frank B. Spear. It has a kind of fame, with its picture in collectors' magazines, because it contains a collection of six hundred bells from forty countries in the world. There are Japanese temple bells, hotel dinner bells, school bells, ship's bells, sleigh bells. The smallest is a Chinese costume bell on a string of beads, the largest is the big brass bell of famous old

Engine 26 of the Lake Superior & Ishpeming Railroad Co. On the high shelf in a tall cabinet is one of Father Baraga's altar bells, used in the Indian Mission on Keweenaw Bay, with the Lorraine cross at its top. Beside it is a tiny silver bell for a lady's garter.

Mrs. Morse was not in Marquette for her sister's funeral. In October 1881 Jay Morse had sailed for Europe with his family. His wife and daughter spent two years abroad, while Morse returned for the new season in the mines. Fortunately for Colonel Pickands 1882 was a busy year.

The Marquette ore formation curved like a fishhook around Negaunee and Ishpeming, with the shank reaching westward past Lake Michigamme. In 1872 the Marquette, Houghton and Ontonagon Railroad pushed west to the old trading post of L'Anse. The road was built with difficulty; spring freshets washed out seven trestles in the gorges, but they were raised again and docks were built in the fine harbor at L'Anse. The railroad spurred exploration through the western portion of the range. Colonel Pickands and Jay Morse formed a company to develop a mine near Boston Lake where a narrow outcrop of specular hematite promised to widen underground. In January 1880 work began, axmen clearing timber, fires burning at the edge of the cutting, log chains clanking, and the breath of horses smoking in the bitter air. The Boston Mine shipped 6,000 tons that season.

While the first Boston ore was thudding into cargo holds the partners formed the Taylor Iron Co.—again Jay Morse, president, James Pickands, treasurer—and leased a location on the railroad ten miles southeast of L'Anse. The Taylor Mine, in Township 49, Range 33, was the westernmost development in the Marquette district. It shipped a thousand tons in 1880. A year later twenty-five workmen opened 200 feet of a deposit 25 feet wide, and the location showed promise.

In 1882, with each of their two mines producing 15,000 tons, Pickands and Morse were planning future operations. But another future opened. That summer a young man from Cleveland, Samuel Mather, proposed a three-man partnership to deal in iron ores.

CHAPTER 3

Echo From Landy's Pit

B<small>Y</small> 1883 the name Mather was already established on Lake Superior, and Samuel Mather was well acquainted in the Marquette district. His father, Samuel Livingston Mather, had been a founder of the Cleveland Iron Mining Company thirty years before, and his younger half brother, William Gwinn Mather, would soon become vice-president of the company. As a boy in the Civil War years Samuel Mather had come to Marquette with his father. His fascination began when he saw the mules prodded off schooner decks to swim ashore. He liked the commotion in the mines, the hearty life in the boardinghouses, the whole north country, and the iron business. In the summer of 1869 he went on his own, taking a job as timekeeper in the Cleveland Mine at Ishpeming. He was enrolled at Harvard College for the fall.

The Mathers were a famous family, brilliant, individualistic, wide-ranging in their activities since the Reverend Richard Mather had left an English parish at Toxteth Park near Liverpool and come to Massachusetts in 1635. In England, when it was reported that for fifteen years Richard Mather had not worn a surplice in his pulpit, one of the church officials declared: "It had been better for him that he had gotten seven bastards." He did bear seven sons, of whom the youngest was named Increase—"because of the never-to-be-forgotten increase, of every sort, wherewith God has favored the new country." Another of his sons was Timothy Mather, progenitor of the Ohio Mathers of the nineteenth century. That branch came west following an investment in the Connecticut Land Company's Western Reserve; in 1843 Samuel Livingston Mather, grandson of the purchaser of Ohio lands, journeyed to Cleveland to sell the property. When he heard reports of a discovery of iron ore on Lake Superior, his future swung in a new direction. In 1850 he was one of a group of Cleveland businessmen who organized the Cleveland Iron Mining Company. He made extended visits to the Marquette district and introduced his sons to the iron business. Now his older son was at Ishpeming in the summer of 1869.

A slight, wiry, observant youth, Samuel Mather went to work in the confusion of drilling, blasting, sledging, shoveling, men and mules toiling in the cut, a switch engine pushing dump cars past. There on July 14, the day after his eighteenth birthday, he swung a sledge at the edge of Landy's Pit in the Cleveland Mine. Officially he was a timekeeper, but he had a boy's zest for a sledge hammer. While he raised the sledge a blast went off below, a premature explosion of black powder. The sound reverberated in the hills, and while the echoes faded the last crumbling rocks slid into Landy's Pit. When they lifted Samuel Mather from the avalanche he had a fractured skull, two broken arms, and a fractured spine.

Iron mining a century ago was a dangerous trade in a difficult country. Samuel Mather, too badly injured for the long trip to Cleveland, lay for weeks in the Ishpeming hospital. Because of the spinal injury he lay on his side, and the left arm, long in bandages, stiffened permanently. Throughout his life he carried that sign of the miner's hazard, though few people knew of his affliction. As a young man he rode horses and climbed mountains. In 1895, after a visit to Mount Hope, New York, he organized the Cleveland Golf Club and introduced that sport to his friends.

In 1869 his injury required a long convalescence, first in Ishpeming and then in Cleveland. After two confined years, needing new scenes and new interests, he went abroad. During the summer of 1872 he boarded in a professor's home in the German city of Hanover, learning languages, walking the cobbled streets of the old *stadt,* and at evening noting in his diary the day's encounters. He was a good observer; in a few words he caught the essential character of a scene and its people. Then to Paris where he walked the streets and boulevards, from the Bois to the Bastille, from Montparnasse to the northern outskirts of the city. With two new friends, George Pendleton and Charlie Lang, he walked in Switzerland, through the high valleys of the Engadine and the Bernese Alps, as he would later take his sons tramping through the Swiss and Italian passes. After a winter in Italy, a spring in Spain, and an English summer, he was back in Cleveland, ready to begin his career. He thought himself too old for college, and all the Mathers knew that there are other kinds of education. "Travel," wrote Francis Bacon, "in the younger sort is a part of education, in the elder, a part of experience." Samuel Mather was impressionable enough to make travel a part of his mind and character. In the fall of 1873 he entered his father's business in the old office of the Cleveland Iron Mining Company at the corner of Water (now West Ninth) and St. Clair streets.

The Lake Superior trade was growing, with long new steamships loading greater cargoes. In 1868 the *R. J. Hackett* had appeared on the Upper Lakes. She was a new kind of vessel, 211 feet long, with engines aft, navigation quarters in the bow, and an unbroken hold for cargo. The next year the *Forest City,* 213 feet long with a beam of 33 feet, was built as her consort. (This oddly elegant term was commonly used for tow barges.) Here was the new system—not a tugboat hauling schooners through the rivers and letting the wind take them on the open Lakes, but a steamer with one, two, or three tows plodding on her week-long haul.

In 1874 came the *V. H. Ketchum.* She was a wonder on the Lakes, twenty feet more keel than anything afloat, longer than most dock facilities in the seventies, and later, when Pickands Mather bought shares in her, becoming their first marine investment. But new docks were on the way, and men were talking of iron ships, still longer, broader, and deeper, to bring bigger cargoes down to the hungry mills. Already the old tandem locks at the Soo, built in 1855, were inadequate for the traffic. In 1875 Congress appropriated funds for a new lock, 515 feet long and 80 feet wide. By the time the Weitzel Lock was open, in 1881, the Marquette Range was shipping a million and a half tons of ore and the rich new Menominee was adding three quarters of a million. West of the Menominee, in the wilds beyond Gogebic Lake, explorers were following signs of another ore body. In these years Samuel Mather visited the Marquette district. He knew Jay Morse and the Pickands brothers; he talked with geologists and engineers. He saw more growth ahead.

In October of 1881 Samuel Mather was married to Flora

Amelia Stone, daughter of Amasa Stone who had built the Lake Shore and Michigan Southern Railroad. They went abroad on a leisurely wedding journey, following autumn down the Mediterranean shore. In January at Sorrento they visited Samuel Mather's favorite aunt, Constance Fenimore Woolson, a novelist and descendant of James Fenimore Cooper, in her villa above the Bay of Naples. Miss Woolson had grown up in Cleveland, with girlhood summers on Mackinac Island. She had visited logging camps, mining towns, and Indian missions in the North. On her terrace at Sorrento she kept asking about the Lake Superior country that her nephew knew. She had written tales of miners, priests, and soldiers in that country, and her novel *Anne* was then appearing serially in *Harper's Magazine*. A tale of old Mackinac "between blue Lake Huron with its clear air and gray Lake Michigan with its silver fogs," it pictured the fort on the hill, Indian campfires on the shore, and black forests framing the snowbound straits. In sunny Sorrento, writing beside her lemon tree on the terrace, Constance Fenimore Woolson remembered the dark north country. She saw it as romance and her nephew knew it as commerce, yet many of their feelings were the same.

On this trip Samuel Mather began the collecting—paintings, ceramics, bronzes, tapestries—which eventually enriched the Cleveland Museum of Art and other institutions. At Granada he commissioned a painting for his father; as a young man Samuel Livingston Mather had gone to Spain on a sailing ship and he kept a love of that country. Travel was always a tonic to the Mathers. Back in Cleveland in the spring Samuel Mather presented the painting to his father and returned to his desk in the Iron Trades Building.

That summer in Marquette he talked with Jay Morse and James Pickands about the old mines and some new ones, and about prospects in new districts. There was much to talk about. The 1880 Congress had passed tariff legislation protecting the iron industry and stimulating all forms of the manufacture of iron and steel. The Bessemer process was making a market for ores once discarded in the pits. In the mines new methods were coming into use. Power drills were increasing production in the workings and hastening exploration for new deposits of ore. Cornish pumps were installed as the pits and shafts drove deeper, and new hoisting machines brought up the ore from mining levels underground. In 1881 the new lock was open at the Soo and canal tolls were abolished; traffic had a new freeway past the age-old St. Marys rapids. In this year, 1882, the historic *Onoko*, the first iron bulk cargo freighter on the Lakes, slid off the ways in Cleveland. Nearly 300 feet long, with a 3,000-ton capacity, she signaled a new speed, size, and efficiency in the transport of iron ore. This summer explorers were marking out a whole new iron district beyond Gogebic Lake; and north of Lake Superior men from Marquette and the East were forming a company to build docks at Two Harbors, Minnesota, lay a railroad to Vermilion Lake, and open up the iron of the Vermilion Range. Some of the old mines in the Marquette hills were now abandoned and the furnaces were crumbling in the forest. But the steel age was just beginning.

The three minds meshed in their discussions—Morse practical and immediate, Pickands far-seeing and habitually hopeful, Mather questioning, considering, and then going beyond the others in his projection of the future. They were naturally drawn into a balance of character and temperament, and especially drawn together were Pickands and Mather. These two men were unlike in many ways. Colonel Pickands, twelve years older, was big, easy, confident, experienced. Mather was slight, intent, habitually shy, and thoughtful. One had begun without money and had made his way by resourcefulness and imagination; the other had advantages from the start. Perhaps the differences made them choose each other.

At the end of the summer they discussed a new venture. For each of them it was a natural, perhaps an inevitable time. Restless Jay Morse, with his hands deep in hematite, was eager to operate on his own account. After his wife's death Colonel Pickands had lost his closest tie with Marquette; he was reaching for new and absorbing pursuits. Samuel Mather, now married and with ten years' apprenticeship behind him, was ready to run his own risks and seek his own goals.

That fall Colonel Pickands sold his hardware business and left an agent in charge of the coal dock at Marquette. In the next year Morse resigned his agency with the Cleveland Iron Mining Company and Samuel Mather withdrew from his father's business. In Cleveland in the spring of 1883, they announced the partnership of Pickands Mather & Co., dealers in pig iron and iron ore.

It was a time of rapid developments. Yet the new ships and docks and mining shafts were but details in a larger context that Samuel Mather saw. He saw that the iron business had reached an end and a beginning: an end of personal, separate, piecemeal operations and a beginning of integrated companies with resources enough to extend from exploration to manufacture. The industry reached from the ore beds in the northern forests to the coal fields of the Alleghenies. It required companies capable of skillful, efficient, and co-ordinated operations all the way from the mines of Lake Superior to the mills of the Ohio Valley.

This reasoning was soon borne out by the consolidation of various small and separate interests into integrated companies. Having been in the commission business for thirty years, Hewitt and Tuttle became in 1884 the partnership of Tuttle, Oglebay and Co.; it would become Oglebay, Norton & Co. in 1889. In 1885 the partnership of M. A. Hanna & Co. (now The M. A. Hanna Company) was formed from the old Rhodes & Card iron-ore and pig-iron agency; it brought new interests and energies to the former firm. In 1890 Samuel Mather's father died while completing plans for the merging of the Cleveland Iron Mining Company with the Iron Cliffs Company.

Pickands Mather & Co. had both family and business relationships with the Cleveland Iron Mining Company, and Samuel Mather retained a financial interest in the organization. The new firm began close to the older one. Their first business was done in the parlors of the Cleveland Iron Mining Company on Water Street. Here they got their mail, kept their books, and received their first callers. They composed a telegraph code for company business. In the code the partners' names fell into the H's: Pickands was *Hackney,* Mather was *Haddock,* Morse, *Haggard*—not a heroic set of terms. But the firm name, Pickands Mather & Co., became *Hickory,* and that held better promise. They wanted to win their share of the business, and they hoped to grow. No one could then foresee that in seventy-five years the company would employ more than ten thousand people in a chain of properties and operations from Rabbit Lake, Minnesota, to Wabush Lake in Labrador.

When ice went out of the Lakes in April and the shipping season began, they moved into offices of their own, two small rooms in the new Grand Arcade, across from the Kennard House on St. Clair Street. Through their windows came the cries of stevedores and the rumble of ore buckets in the river basin.

CHAPTER 4

Lines in a Ledger

PICKANDS MATHER & CO., always conservative, began with an understatement, announcing themselves as dealers in pig iron and iron ore. Samuel Mather could have sold iron ore without a partnership; the new organization was more than a commission house. From the start the company was a mining, shipping, and commission firm, with interests extending from mineral exploration to blast furnaces. It was headed toward a broad range of services for the steel industry: the management of lands, mines, ships, and docks, and the marketing of iron ore, pig iron, coal, coke, and ferroalloys.

While Colonel Pickands and Samuel Mather opened their Cleveland office, Jay Morse remained in the North where he could be close to developments. Never a sedentary man, he would be a roving partner, working at a distance, and from a distance bringing new interests and undertakings to the company.

Morse had a mind like a dip compass, always turning toward new iron locations. Ten years earlier, while the East was numbed by the Panic of 1873, he had joined in the rush to buy lands in the new Menominee district, sixty dense miles southwest of Marquette. In November 1873 he had bought the Isabella lands in dark woods on the dwindling Iron River; two years later he acquired the Riverton tract a couple of miles upstream. It was a deep, lost country then, its only habitation the hut of a squatter who ran a trap line on the Paint and Iron rivers. In 1879 came a German lumberjack, young Frederick Mueller, who filed a pre-emption claim on a quarter section and built a cabin on the east bank of Iron River. To keep Mueller company the old trapper brought him a young beaver, just taken out of a pond. Mueller kept the pet under his bunk, feeding it birch bark and poplar leaves. Each morning the beaver waddled down to the river for a swim and then came back to the cabin. In this domestic life it soon grew fat and lazy.

An old Indian trail crossed the river near the cabin. In the summer of 1880 Mueller watched a procession of timber and iron hunters splashing through the stream and heading into the hills. Some of them asked about belts of pine and hardwood and about red outcrop on the ridges. That year brought a land-office business in Iron River lands, and restless Jay Morse sold his holdings, including the site of the town of Stambaugh, to some speculators from Escanaba, Michigan. Fred Mueller sold his quarter section and took his beaver to a quieter location on Little Hagerman Lake. Some years later the Delta Mine shaft was opened on the site of Mueller's cabin and six million tons of hematite came out of the Riverton lands that Morse had surrendered. The west end of the Menominee was slow in developing, and Morse could not wait. He was never too late in any venture, but at Iron River he was too early.

In 1883 the savage name Gogebic, which to the Indians meant "Trembling Ground," came to mean the lure of mineral lands. Some fortune hunters talked of gold and silver—there was the Wakefield Gold and Silver Mining Company organized by George Miracle—but the real riches lay in iron ore. Geologists had found iron-ore outcrops and had outlined a continuous iron formation paralleling a long ridge of hills, the dwindling of the great trap range that runs down from the rugged Keweenaw Peninsula. For fifty miles from Penokee Gap in Wisconsin this formation could be followed along the gnarled hills, with concentration showing up most frequently in a narrow belt extending twenty miles east from the Montreal River.

Already legends were gathering on the Gogebic. A blue-eyed, blond-bearded geologist, Raphael Pumpelly, after exploring around the world had grasped at fortune on Newport Hill above the site of Ironwood; young Lanfear Norrie had left a clerkship in the Bank of England to search for a great mine in the wilderness; a long-haired hermit, wandering into Rockland from his hut on Gogebic Lake, had startled the barroom loafers with some chunks of russet rock. It was the hermit, old Dick Langford, who "discovered" the range. He led an unemployed mining captain five miles west from Sunday Lake where an upturned birch tree had uncovered a mass of rich red hematite. It was the site of the famous Colby Mine.

In Ishpeming Jay Morse went to see an old friend, Joseph Sellwood, a veteran of the Keweenaw copper country and a former captain of the New York and Cleveland iron mines. Sellwood was running a store and was thoroughly bored with it. He was a mining man by nature—from the age of nine he had worked in the deep tin mines of England, coming to America in the wave of migration after the Civil War. A big man with iron-gray hair and a walrus mustache, he had a quick and roving mind, and his heavy-lidded eyes could gleam like a miner's lamp at the end of a tunnel. Now Sellwood and Morse, acting for Pickands Mather & Co., took up the Colby location in the Gogebic hills. Preliminary work had been done on the Colby Mine by the Cambria Iron Company of Johnstown, Pennsylvania, but they refused to accept the conditions of the lease. Then the Penokee and Gogebic Development Company, in which Pickands Mather had invested, took a twenty-year lease on the property and subleased it for three years to Pickands Mather. Time was short. Quickly Sellwood began moving men, machinery, and supplies into the wild Gogebic country.

Early in 1883 in their rooms in the Grand Arcade in Cleveland, the new partners hired an office boy named Henry Dalton. He was a Cleveland youth, the son of a West Side druggist, who had left a grocery store for the livelier outdoor job of checking cargo on the ore docks. Colonel Pickands found him there, took an immediate liking to him, and brought him into the office. In years to come Henry Dalton's name would travel the Lakes on a freighter five times as big as the vessels of his boyhood. To keep their books the partners hired a young man named Amos Pelardy. The staff was completed when they added strapping young William McLauchlan as pig-iron salesman. McLauchlan was a powerful man, swarthy as an Indian, with heavy features and coarse black hair. In a few years he became a famous salesman.

Far from the ferment on the new Gogebic Range, the Cleveland office was all too quiet. The partners had two small mines, the Boston and the Taylor, in the western portion of the Marquette district. That year the Boston shipped 20,000 tons and was nearly exhausted; the Taylor hit bottom in the middle of the season. Pickands Mather prospects were dim in the Marquette district, where the best properties were already in established hands. The year was further darkened by the suffering and death of Samuel Mather's father-in-law. For years Amasa Stone had brooded on a disaster on his Lake Shore and Michigan Southern Railroad. Four days after Christmas 1876 the Pacific Express was pounding west along Lake Erie through a raging snowstorm. As it crossed the Ashtabula gorge the main span of the new iron bridge collapsed. Ten cars plunged into the gorge and burst into flame. A hundred holiday travelers were killed, fifty others mutilated. The bridge had been built on a design developed by Amasa Stone and the disaster crucified him. After years of remorse and torment he took his own life in May of 1883.

Before the year was over the bookkeeper left the discouraged firm and young Henry Dalton took that job, doubling as office boy. There was talk of disbanding the partnership as they scraped bottom in their Marquette mines. But they had some property on the Potato River at Upson, Wisconsin, a result of their investment in the Penokee and Gogebic Development, and there was the lease on a hilltop where a hermit had seen some exposed hematite. Near Upson, Wisconsin, field men of the United States Geological Survey had noted a lean magnetic ore, the first hint of a new iron range, and Jay Morse was on the heels of the hermit. Perhaps next year would be a different story.

The figures that Henry Dalton recorded for the North and South Vein Colby Mines were:

1884	1,022 tons
1885	84,302 tons
1886	257,432 tons

By then the Gogebic was a frenzy of new fortunes and in Cleveland the firm was moving into larger quarters.

The lines in a ledger are mute, until their meaning comes through. These lines meant struggle, hardship, hope, toil, and accomplishment a thousand miles away. In 1884 two pony trails threaded the dark Gogebic country, leading in from Lake Superior at the mouths of Ironton Creek and Black River. Over those trails, through twenty miles of wilderness, came all the supplies and equipment for the early mines—the spades, shovels, sledges, anvils, axes, chains, blocks, and tackle. There was a file of pack mules splashing through the swamp and plodding over the trap hills, each with a wheelbarrow lashed to the saddle. Then on the tent-scattered, stump-studded Colby hillside, amid the clash of shovels and horse-drawn scrapers, a file of men trundled the barrows in the gouged-out pit. Soon the mine would go underground, but the first ore was there for the scraping. With a racket of saws and hammers a mine office, boardinghouses, shops, and stables went up on the hillside. Captain Harry Roberts kept the drills boring in, the powder blasting, and wheelbarrows moving up the runways. In October 1884 the Milwaukee, Lake Shore and Western Railway, spurred on by Morse and Sellwood along with other pioneer mining men who saw the promise of the Gogebic, entered the corner of Ontonagon County. That fall the first Colby ore was shoveled into lumber wagons and hauled to the railroad. It went on flatcars to Milwaukee, where it was loaded into barges for the long lake run to Erie, Pennsylvania.

The next year the railroad pushed through to Ashland, and Lake Superior had a new ore port. Now ore trains hurried through the hills to dump their loads in the trestle docks. Men stampeded into the Gogebic; the towns of Hurley, Ironwood, Bessemer, and Wakefield sprang up in the woods; and mine shafts probed into the ore bodies, all the way from the Potato River to Sunday Lake. In 1887 Joe Sellwood built a mansion, "the most unique structure in the West," on Colby Hill. It was a rambling many-roomed lodge of Norway pine, rough as the forest outside, polished and gleaming within. It had broad fireplaces against the Gogebic winter, thick carpets that drank the heavy tread of explorers' boots, and deep chairs to invite a man just in from the jolting trails and tote roads. Its wide windows looked down, past the road stained red by the ore wagons, to the lusty town of Bessemer.

For a few seasons Joe Sellwood drove his matched team through the valley, a red-dusted buggy in the summer and a high sleigh when the roads were white. He had opened the Puritan and Brotherton mines; he had also organized the Gogebic Powder Company and built a bank at Bessemer. Once a month on a mud-splashed horse his cashier galloped out of Bessemer with a sack full of payday money for the mines. When Joe Sellwood moved on to Duluth, his mansion became a clubhouse for mine officials and a guest lodge for visitors. Years later Samuel Mather and Henry Dalton made it their headquarters on inspection trips to the range.

Down the Lakes went the rich Gogebic cargoes. They averaged 60-65 per cent iron, with 2 per cent silica and .03-.04 per cent phosphorous—all well within the Bessemer limit, and the furnacemen were clamoring for Bessemer ore. To carry the tonnage Pickands Mather bought additional shares in the *Ketchum* and new interest in the steamers *Robert R. Rhodes* and *Samuel Mather*, both of them wooden vessels, 246 feet long, built in Cleveland in 1887. The *Rhodes* had a roomy forward cabin with a square pilothouse and square portholes; she had a clear cargo deck with masts fore and aft and a tall black stack at her stern. The *Samuel Mather*, the first of four vessels to bear this name, had three masts and topmasts for auxiliary sail and twin black stacks for her twin boilers. She had cabins fore and aft and a deckhouse amidships, housing the lamproom and quarters for the firemen. She towed the barges *Red Wing* and *Newcomb*, under canvas. On the *Mather* they ran the halyards to steam winches and made sail with a clatter, but the barges used manpower. Over the water came the old halyard chantey:

> They paid us off in Liverpool,
> Ronzo, boys, Ronzo—

In those years the fo'c's'les were full of shellback sailors from the coast. The first *Samuel Mather* had a short life. In a thick November fog in 1891 off Point Iroquois in Lake Superior she collided with the steamer *Brazil* loaded deep with ore. She sank like a stone.

In Cleveland the firm, steadily acquiring new holdings of iron ore, moved to larger office space, first in the Merchants Bank Building at Superior Avenue and West Sixth Street; then, in 1888, into the new Western Reserve Building on the corner of Superior and Water. This building, designed by Daniel H. Burnham and built by Samuel Mather, was a landmark in downtown Cleveland. A "towering" eight-story structure, it looked over the busy river basin and out to the newly completed Cleveland breakwater. The building's rotunda was decorated with Italian marble, its hallways were lined with mosaics and tile. Along with the neighboring Perry-Payne Building, it housed shipping and iron-ore companies. At first Pickands Mather occupied the fifth floor; soon they took over the seventh floor also, with the firm's legal counsel, Hoyt, Dustin and Kelley, on the floor between.

Pickands Mather had taken root in the rich Gogebic Range.

Meanwhile, at the other end of the long transportation route they had acquired interests in the Wheeler Furnace Co., the Struthers Furnace Co., and the Ohio Iron and Steel Co., all near Youngstown. It was the beginning of a long-continued and growing P. M. interest in the steel industry in the Mahoning Valley. In the pioneering 1850's furnaces in that district had been the first users of Lake Superior ore; since then their progress, in capacity and efficiency, had kept pace with the growth of mining in the North. The furnace interests would soon be consolidated, as separate mining interests were then being merged into strong and resourceful companies, and there would be close links between them.

Pickands Mather had also increased its coal business, handling all the production of the Essen Coal Company in the Pittsburgh district. Into the Pickands Mather organization came a Cleveland banker, William Parmalee Murray, a man as imposing as his name, to head the Coal Department. A huge man and a great sportsman—he was the first president of the Cleveland Athletic Club—he had a passion for trotting horses; every Friday afternoon he drove his sulky in harness races at the Gentlemen's Driving Club. Big as he was, he looked at home in a sulky, his feet braced and his hands stretched over the flying hoofs. His other excitement was coal, a nineteenth-century industry that in a single generation had grown to vast proportions. In 1850 a hundred thousand cords of wood were burned yearly in railroad locomotives, but coal had been tried and proved efficient, and the great coal mines of the Ohio Valley were being opened up. Since then coal had become the fuel of the iron age, and W. P. Murray was directing coal docks, coal cargoes, coal and coke sales all the way from Pennsylvania to Minnesota. Already the Pickands Mather policy had taken shape—a policy of keeping control in the hands of a senior partner while giving encouragement and support to department heads. The company was growing in directions indicated by the talents of its executives. In 1893 Henry Dalton, W. P. Murray, and William McLauchlan were admitted to partnership in the firm.

While her husband was deep in developments on the Gogebic, Mrs. Jay Morse returned from Europe, and Marquette welcomed its fine lady in her long green gloves. But she fell ill suddenly, as her sister had done two years before, and she died in 1884. More restless than ever Morse went to Chicago with an idea in his head. With the financial backing of his partners he organized the Illinois Steel Company (its code name was "Hercules"), combining Union Steel, in which Pickands Mather had a solid interest, with Joliet Steel and the North Chicago Rolling Mills. Already associated with Henry Pickands' firm of Pickands, Brown & Company, Pickands Mather now had a double stake in the Chicago iron and steel industry. Morse stayed in Chicago, as president of Illinois Steel, for ten years. Then he retired and moved to the South. He retained his Pickands Mather partnership until 1898, spending his summers in Cleveland but only occasionally appearing in the company offices.

Lines in a ledger— In 1884 came new accounts: the Minnesota Exploration Company and the Chandler Iron Company. During the 1880's Lake Superior was one of the most exciting regions in America, with discovery on discovery and men hurrying from one boom district to the next.

At the far end of the vast cold lake in the woods town of Duluth lived the veteran surveyor and explorer George R. Stuntz. In the rugged back country, on the wilderness shores of Vermilion Lake he had met a wandering man named North Albert Posey who was trying to teach the Indians blacksmithing. Posey gave him some chunks of hard blue hematite from the Vermilion hills. In Duluth Stuntz showed the ore to his friend George Stone, and when Stone moved to Philadelphia he carried the word to financier Charlemagne Tower. Seventy years old, with his fortunes made, Tower grew interested reluctantly. He sent a geologist to look at the region, and then he grew excited. He formed the Minnesota Iron Company, bought title to the iron lands, and issued 80,000 shares of stock. Some Marquette men came in, including Edward Breitung and the Ely brothers. Against legislative, financial, and engineering difficulties the company proceeded to map out the Duluth, Mesabi and Iron Range Railroad, to link the Vermilion wilderness to Lake Superior. Mining began, with supplies hauled in by sled through the winter woods; and railroad crews chopped out a swath through cedar swamps and over granite ridges. It was a prodigious task and it cost staggering sums of money. When Tower had sunk three million dollars, they borrowed from banks in St. Paul, Chicago, Boston. They had reached the end of their resources, with the monthly payroll due, when Pickands Mather came in with capital enough to finish construction of the railroad, dock, and port facilities. Immediately the great Soudan Mine began shipping.

The Soudan Mine was named by a big, full-bearded mining engineer, Don H. Bacon, for the African Soudan where Chinese Gordon had drawn the world's attention by his defiance of the Berber tribesmen. A year earlier Bacon had succeeded Jay C. Morse as manager of the Cleveland Mine at Ishpeming; now he had joined the new Minnesota Iron Company, the first organization to begin iron mining on a really extensive scale, and he soon became its president. A classical-minded man and an ardent traveler, he later named many Mesabi mines for Mediterranean islands—Malta, Minorca, Corsica, Elba, and the rest. He had a flair for heroic names, though his own name in the Pickands Mather code book was "Hazel."

At the start the Soudan Mine consisted of seven small pits, named for six investors and the State of Montana. When the first car was loaded someone planted a small fir tree, like a flag, in the bed of ore, and so began a tradition. Since then it has been a custom to thrust a tree into the first ore shipped from any location; that jaunty talisman leading the first train down to the docks signifies the birth of a new mine and the beginning of its growth. The Soudan ore body is deep, and mining soon went underground. To work the deepening drifts Captain Elisha Morcom brought up a crew of miners from Quinnesec, Michigan, on the Menominee. They came in March 1884 by bobsled, over the old Vermilion Trail that had been brushed out by gold seekers after the Civil War. Vermilion gold was a chimera but it opened the way for the iron hunters. Six months later the railroad was completed and it brought more Michigan miners to the Vermilion woods. In the late 1890's there were eighteen hundred men in the maze of drifts deep underground and the Soudan was yielding half a million tons a year.

The Ely brothers, with Cleveland offices at West Sixth and Superior, were the original agents for the Minnesota Iron Company, but in 1887 the agency passed to Pickands Mather. With it came seventeen-year-old Samuel E. Bool, a lad of English birth who after some schooling in Cleveland had learned bookkeeping for the Ely firm. He kept the first ledgers for the Minnesota mines. While the Soudan was sending its steel-blue hematite down the Lakes, other Vermilion shafts came into production. During the early years of the twentieth century Sam Bool rode to work, in the Western Reserve Building, on horseback, making a brave appearance in his street clothes and an English saddle on a well-groomed mare. In 1923 he became a Pickands Mather partner, concerned with the firm's financial operations.

Over at the village of Ely, about twenty miles east of the Soudan location, Joe Sellwood had arrived in time for a new strike. For the Minnesota Iron Company he directed exploration of the Chandler property. The Chandler Mine began as an open pit, shipping 54,000 tons in 1888. Ten years later it produced 800,000 tons and was the wonder of the North. The Zenith Mine at Ely, opened in 1892, ran up staggering losses before it became profitable. In later years Pickands Mather took over its operation. It has produced over twenty million tons of purple hematite.

Back in the Menominee district in Michigan in 1889 Pickands Mather crews were prospecting the Walpole strip between the famous Chapin and Pewabic mines near Lake Antoine and the town of Iron Mountain. It should have been a good location, but the test pits were barren. So they went forty miles north to Gilbert Lake beyond Crystal Falls (of all the ranges the Menominee has the most scattered ore bodies) and bought an exploration on the banks of the dim and winding Hemlock River. They moved in their equipment and made a camp, and soon found a hard red hematite, non-Bessemer, with 2 per cent phosphorous and 5.5 per cent silica. In Cleveland in 1888 brilliant young Samuel T. Wellman had invented a revolutionary open-hearth charging machine, which put an end to the slow, laborious, and hellish hand method and began the swift development of the open-hearth process of steelmaking. It made a hungry market for non-Bessemer ores. In 1891 they opened up the Hemlock Mine and loaded the hopper cars on a new spur of the Chicago and Northwestern Railroad. The Hemlock ore rolled through the Menominee woods and onto the high docks of Escanaba where sailors were singing:

> They let down the chutes and the thunder did roar
> As they emptied their pockets of red iron ore.

At the Hemlock location a gang of woodsmen surveyed a quarter section, chopped out a crisscross of streets, and began building the town of Amasa. It is a somber name—in Hebrew it means "burden"—and the original Amasa, a captain in the army of Israel, was murdered in one of the bloodiest passages of the Old Testament. In Cleveland Samuel Mather's second son was born in 1884 and named for his late grandfather Amasa Stone. Now in the deep woods up Hemlock River a hopeful new town was named for the seven-year-old boy. In later years long-striding Amasa Stone Mather would visit the mine, winning everyone in sight. No man was more beloved on the range than Amasa Mather.

Lines in a ledger. The Hemlock River Mining Company:

1891	35,531	tons
1892	65,459	tons
1893	11,323	tons
1894		
1895	949	tons
1896	94,645	tons

Behind the lines were the braying of mules and the boom of blasting powder, the deepening shaft, the tunneling and stoping, the flicker of candles in the drifts, the smell of manure and mule feed in the dark, the clatter of hoofs and the rumble of tramcars. Then a three-year quiet in the mines, the ore forgotten in the ground until the tide of business rose again.

The year 1893 brought panic from the East. The market code words came: first *Mansion*—Market is declining; then *Methodic* —No buyers at present prices; finally *Methodist*—No buyers at any prices; and the mines were closed in midseason. The logging camps were empty and the sawmills silent. For three years the miners drew in their belts and hopefully planted potatoes and turnips in their stumpy clearings. Fortunately the country had fish and game.

Things change quickly in America. Revival came like a wind in the spring of 1896, and another set of code words passed between the Cleveland office and the northern mines: *Mermaid*—How is feeling in the market? *Messiah*—Market now strong. *Milestone*— Everything at the mine working smoothly. *Missionary*—Shipments must be increased. *Miracle*—Prospects for large shipment tomorrow are good.

In the period of depression fortunes were acquired by men who believed in the future. Scores of independent mines were absorbed and consolidated into larger companies. During the idle years Pickands Mather gathered in new properties, and in 1899 they formed the Menominee Exploration to enlarge further their holdings in the district. This organization became The Verona Mining Company with its Caspian, Bengal, and Buck-group mines, which have produced twenty million tons of ore.

Developments came crowding in the 1890's. For millions of years iron had waited in the old worn hills which the Indians called "Mesabi," and for a generation men had known of an iron formation along that long ridge of granite, though reports of the geologists promised no commercial ore. Still some men were stubborn in their belief in the Mesabi—notably Peter Mitchell of Ontonagon and John Mallman and the seven Merritt brothers of Duluth. They slogged through muskeg and hacked their way into the woods, leaving charred campsites and raw test pits behind them. At last, digging into half-frozen ground in the fall of 1890, the Merritts struck rich ore at Mountain Iron. The next year a couple of woodsmen showed them iron in the roots of a fallen tree. That became the site of the historic Biwabik Mine. Its operators dredged up the ore with steam shovels and sent it down to the high docks at Two Harbors. In the next half century, while scores of new mines probed into the vast iron reservoir of the Mesabi, Biwabik produced twenty-five million tons of soft brown hematite.

New mines required new ore carriers. The Minnesota Steamship Company was organized in 1889 to carry the ore of the Minnesota Iron Company. Its first officers included Jay C. Morse, president, James Pickands, vice-president; Samuel Mather was its president in the late nineties. Through this decade Pickands Mather operated and enlarged the company's M fleet. To the original *Manola, Mariska, Maruba,* and *Matoa,* they soon added the steamers *Marina, Masaba, Maritana, Mariposa, Maricopa,* and the barges *Manda, Martha, Magna, Maia, Malta, Marcia,* and *Maida.* With these vessels to fuel, the company built a coal dock at the mouth of the St. Marys River at Detour. Loaded with bunker coal, it served their own ships and scores of others. New vessels added to the Pickands Mather fleet in the early 1890's were the *Kearsarge* and the *Victory.* In 1895 the firm assumed management of the American Steel Barge Company's fleet of seven whaleback steamers and twenty barges.

With mines, ships, docks, and furnaces, the company had men at work and materials moving all the way from Vermilion Lake to the Mahoning and Monongahela valleys. Heading the Ore Department, as it was then known, was James H. Dalliba, who became a partner in 1898; he was succeeded in 1905 by tireless George Beaumont. The Cleveland office was a nerve center, co-ordinating operations and directing the flow of financial and administrative energy. Decisions in the meeting room sent cargo thundering into scores of vessels and opened up the earth almost a thousand miles away.

By 1895 Colonel Pickands was failing in health and vigor, though he retained his buoyancy and his infectious enthusiasm. Samuel Mather passed through the halls almost oblivious of surroundings: he was revolving long-range plans and prospects, and he dealt with men and movements beyond the reach of his colleagues. Henry Dalton, with a detailed knowledge of every department and a memory of every major transaction, was the man in charge. Intense, hard-working, conscientious, Dalton was secretly called "the ramrod," but his associates admired his thoroughness and proficiency and his capacity for boring in. They also admired his shrewd foresight and his vision of things to come. One day standing on the hill above the busy Ashtabula River, he looked away from the twisting, crowded channel, pointing to the lake front at the river mouth. "The harbor of the future," he said, "will be out there." His words were remembered when the new docks pushed out in sheltered water between the long breakwalls. It was Henry Dalton, more than distant Samuel Mather or failing Colonel Pickands, who gave the office its tone of dignity, reserve, and conservatism. An "English atmosphere" some called it, though there was a very American dispatch in its operations.

Henry Dalton was the father of two sons, who died in infancy of scarlet fever. After that his affection reached out to his colleagues, who recognized the simple, kindly, sweet-spirited man beneath the formal manner. He was both practical and charitable. As Colonel Pickands could never refuse an old soldier, Henry Dalton could not turn away from a good cause. For years he insisted that the company's broom business—brooms for the docks, the ships, the furnaces—be given to the Society for the Blind. A religious and abstemious man, he was tolerant of other men's indulgences. He was often reminded by his younger associate Harry Coulby to keep a supply of fine cigars for his callers—the most frequent of whom was Coulby himself.

The other office callers, steel men, shipping men, engineers, and bankers, were received with a courtly courtesy. Old John Fairfax, an ex-slave from Virginia, had been a bell boy at the

Kennard House before Colonel Pickands brought him to the company office. He had a wise, sweet face, a gentle manner, and a smile like a sunrise. He received visitors with a grace they never forgot. In a firm that prized seniority, with its senior partner receiving a willing deference, John Fairfax became the senior porter and he occupied a special place.

Against the wishes of everyone else John Fairfax arrived at six each morning, climbed six flights of stairs before the elevators were running, and welcomed the office staff. One of his duties was to meet the telegraph boy and deliver the messages. Unable to read or write, he learned to scrawl a "signature" and he studied the names on the envelopes while the messenger read them. If he made a misdelivery no one ever let him know it.

Before the teletype and the long-distance telephone the company used its own private code, in the interests of confidence and economy. It was an extensive code with a vocabulary of some 3,000 terms, largely developed by Henry Dalton. Some of the code words were bizarre, some almost symbolic, and more than a few showed a glint of humor. James Pickands & Co., the original business, was *Historic*; S. P. Ely, a sometimes reluctant associate, was *Hamper*; M. A. Hanna & Co. was *Hosiery*. *Macaroni* meant "Market is rising." *Sweatiness* was "Arrange to work Sunday to unload her." *Foolishness* meant "Freight rate includes handling." *Sassafras* was "Unless we are smarter we will lose sale." In the code book hearty, horsey W. P. Murray had the delicate name *Halcyon,* and strapping Bill McLauchlan, tireless storyteller at the company dinners, was *Hamlet*. It must have amused McLauchlan to sign *Hamlet* to such a message as *Odious Jezebel*— "We will hold offer open until you hear from Cleveland Rolling Mill Co.," or *Hercules Garrulous Inebriate*—"Illinois Steel Company complain that Cary Empire ore they are receiving contains much rock. Remedy this immediately."

In 1896 a message went to all the mines, docks, furnaces, and vessels, and to scores of companies associated with Pickands Mather. Not in code, it was a straight laconic message—Colonel Pickands was dead. Failing for a year, he died, aged fifty-seven, in sleep at his home on Kennard Street in Cleveland. He had taken a trip to Bermuda, felt improved on his return, and spent a few days in his office; now he was dead. He left three sons, Joseph in Colorado Springs, Henry traveling abroad, and Jay M. at home. Joe Pickands was a foot-loose, roving man who would never take to business. Henry would assume his father's partnership and carry on the family name. Jay, after his course at Yale, would come into the office for the brief span before his sudden death in November 1913.

Colonel Pickands' death brought newspaper editorials and resolutions from mining, vessel, and furnace companies all the way from Duluth to Buffalo; the day of his funeral every vessel on the Lakes carried its flag at half-mast. Jay Morse resigned his partnership two years later, in 1898. But the relationship of Morse and Pickands was to be once more complicated. In the 1870's they had married sisters. In the eighties both their wives had died. In 1887 Colonel Pickands had married Seville Hanna, Mark Hanna's sister. A few years after the death of his partner and brother-in-law, Jay Morse would marry his widow. Then the stepmother of the Pickands' sons would become their aunt. It was a complex partnership.

At the time of Colonel Pickands' death, his brother Henry Pickands retired from his iron business in Chicago. He went to live in the Southwest, in Arizona and California. Several years he devoted to travel, spending long seasons in Europe, Asia, and the Hawaiian Islands. When he died in Chicago in 1901, he left no children, but his nephew and namesake had become a Pickands Mather partner. The dream of two young soldiers in a bleak camp in Tennessee—of a small business house, somewhere, with "Pickands Bros." over the door—had been fulfilled in the mines and mills of America.

CHAPTER 5

Stampede to the Gogebic

I F SAMUEL MATHER had gone to college as he planned in 1869, he would have heard some memorable lectures on ore deposits. That year at Harvard a striking young geologist named Raphael Pumpelly began teaching the first mining course in America. He had just three students, but he kept them fascinated with his huge frame draped over the lecture stand, his golden beard and sea-blue eyes, and with rambling accounts of mineral explorations in Corsica, Arizona, Japan, Siberia, and on the wild shores of Lake Superior. He was a profound geologist but not a pompous one; he especially liked a story of how a famous copper mine was discovered by a pig. A solitary settler on the Keweenaw Peninsula, out looking for his pig, heard a squealing from between the roots of a tree. He pulled the pig out of the hole, and with it the first chunk of copper from the Calumet and Hecla location, which became the richest copper mine on earth.

Pumpelly was just thirty-one, but he had already explored and prospected around the world. Educated in Europe, first drawn to geology in Corsica, trained in the Royal School of Mines in Freiburg, Germany, he had taken up a mineral exploration for the Japanese government and had crossed the Gobi Desert and the steppes of Tartary. Back in America in 1867 he was planning to buy some Agricultural College land scrip—at sixty cents an acre—and to look for mineral locations, when another project beckoned. The Lake Superior Ship Canal Company, having secured a land grant to build a canal across the Keweenaw Cape, hired him to manage the selection of 200,000 acres in northern Michigan. The company wanted a search for gold and silver, but Pumpelly convinced them that their best prospects lay in white pine and iron ore.

That winter in the Oriental Hotel in Lafayette Place, New York City, Pumpelly sat over maps, surveyor's records, and geological reports of the Upper Peninsula. In May he arrived at Marquette where he outfitted some timber cruisers and sent them into the wilderness. As his assistant he hired a young German geologist, Hermann Credner, who had already explored in the Marquette district. With Credner and four Indians in two canoes he started up the Michigamme River in search of iron ore.

When they reached the near limits of the canal company's grant, far up the Michigamme, they met another canoe. Out of it stepped Jack Armstrong, a veteran explorer who was looking for pine. For a thousand dollars he offered to lead them to a large outcrop of specular and magnetic ore. Pumpelly agreed; in a mixed pine and hardwood forest they found the outcrop with evidence of an extensive ore body. Toiling through tangled blowdowns and cedar swamps, they came out at Lake Antoine, near the future site of the Menominee district's Chapin Mine, and made a base camp for surrounding explorations. Following magnetic attraction, they selected a belt of land running for twenty miles along the ore formation. Like any geologist Pumpelly was seeing two landscapes, the one he hacked his way through and another, a million years before, when the Menominee cliffs were the coast of a heaving Cambrian Sea that slowly laid its sandstones over great blocks of limestone and iron ore.

The next spring Pumpelly returned to Lake Superior bringing with him Duke William of Württemberg, who wanted to see the American frontier. The seventy-year-old duke proved to be a good man in the woods, accepting without complaint the misery of a wet camp and travel through bogs and windfalls. Now Pumpelly had an audience more responsive than a half-breed canoeman. Drying his long legs beside a campfire, he talked about geology, astronomy, archaeology, his life with shepherds and bandits in Corsica, his journey through the Gobi Desert in midwinter, his love of vast and lonely places. This season he chose lands west of Gogebic Lake in a region that showed rare iron outcrop but frequent dippings of the compass needle. This was to become the Gogebic Range, about half of which (the grant was limited to odd-numbered sections) he selected for the canal company.

In Boston at the end of the summer of 1869, Pumpelly was married, and that fall he began teaching. One year ended his college career. On a spring night some Harvard boys set off a powder blast on the porch of the house where the Pumpellys were boarding. It was done to spite the landlady, but it resulted in a severe shock to Mrs. Pumpelly. To give her the benefit of an outdoor life and to seek his own fortune, Pumpelly went back to Lake Superior. He arranged to prospect for two Boston investors.

In Marquette the Pumpellys outfitted a sailboat and voyaged to Bayfield. From there they went into the Gogebic district to look at lands adjoining the tract Pumpelly had selected for the canal company. Leaving his wife with an Indian woman, Pumpelly and his colleague, Major T. B. Brooks, made a magnetic tracing of the iron formation. It did not seem to indicate merchantable ore. On their way back Pumpelly saw from a hilltop smoke walling the whole horizon to the south and east. This was the first week of October 1871 when the great fire was sweeping the forests of Oconto County and when at the foot of Lake Michigan, two hundred miles farther south, Chicago was burning to the water's edge.

That day an Indian came over the trail with a message for Pumpelly—a telegram from Boston instructing him to make no more land purchases. It was a rebuke of his judgment, and Pumpelly climbed alone to the top of the Gogebic ridge. Sitting on a quartzite upthrust, he looked over the vast sweep of forest, giving way at last to the far cold waters of Lake Superior. In his mind was the geologist's realization: this was the oldest sedimentary rock in the world, the first land mass thrust up from the primordial sea. Along with that grave thought he revolved the problem of land purchase. Then his eyes caught a fleck of yellow staining the rock he sat on. It might mean nothing, or it might mean iron oxides in the overlying formation. On an impulse he decided to claim a two-mile tract along this range. He was sitting on Newport Hill above the site of Ironwood.

In the season's first snow Pumpelly tramped back to the base camp and found his wife embroidering moccasins. At Bayfield they took the last steamer of the season, crowded with drunken quarrymen, to Marquette. There he bought two miles of the range adjoining the quartzite ridge. It was the first purchase of even-numbered sections in the district—the odd sections were already

claimed by the canal company. For twelve years the silence of
the Gogebic went unbroken. When his Boston friends tired of
waiting on their investment, Pumpelly, then making a mineral
survey for the Northern Pacific Railway, bought their interest.
On his land there were opened up in 1886 and 1887 small workings that later became parts of the Newport and the Geneva mines,
both now the property of the Mauthe Mining Company, operated by Pickands Mather. Although Samuel Mather missed Pumpelly's lectures at Harvard, he caught up with him on the
Gogebic.

Ten years after Pumpelly's exploration, two men, wholly
unlike each other, wandered through the country. One was the
bearded old hermit Dick Langford, who talked to himself in a
hut on Gogebic Lake and roamed the forest like an outcast
Indian. The other was moose-tall, elegantly accoutered young
A. Lanfear Norrie of New York and London. Educated in England, Norrie had become a clerk in a London bank where one
day he had a dream that he should come to America and discover
a great mine. He came to Marquette in 1881 and clerked in the
land office of John M. Longyear. When his father sent him a
grubstake of $25,000, Norrie set out with a file of axmen to clear
trail and packmen to carry his tents, clothing, and an assortment
of English boots (size 15), to prospect the Gogebic country.

About this time Dick Langford wandered into Rockland,
Michigan, with some chunks of russet rock that caught the eye
of an unemployed mining captain. Langford was not interested
in mines, but he took Captain Nat Moore to the hill five miles
west of Sunday Lake and pointed to pure Bessemer ore in the
roots of an upturned tree. This became the historic Colby Mine
which started the rush to the Gogebic Range.

Meanwhile Norrie was in the field. Though he knew nothing
of geology or mining he had hired an able prospector, Canadian-
born Captain James R. Wood, commonly called "Iron" Wood,
whose name would soon be given to a pioneer town on the range.
They had a summer lean-to camp on the Montreal River; when
winter came they built a log camp under the wooded hillside. It
was the beginning of Ironwood. Within a mile of camp on the
dense forest edge they discovered the famous Norrie Mine.

Into the new country came another legendary man. Attracted
to Lake Superior for his health, John M. Longyear had already
made a fortune in iron and timber lands. Now he was in the

Gogebic, exploring the lands of the Lake Superior Ship Canal Company and shrewdly entering for himself sections adjoining the company's grant. In the fall of 1882 he visited the Norrie camp, and went on to the explorations on the sites of the Colby and Tilden mines. In a clearing left by some explorer he dug up new potatoes; early snow had protected them in the ground and they yielded a crop each season. To go with this delicacy there were bass from Gogebic Lake—"the best black bass fishing in the world." It didn't remain that way, as heedless woodsmen caught hundreds at a time and left them rotting on the bank.

The State geologist, Dr. C. Rominger, had come into the district from the Menominee, and finding some barren test pits east of Sunday Lake, he said he could carry away all the iron ore on the Gogebic in his hat. But the next year Captain Nat Moore showed him the Colby location and Rominger grew excited. Before the rush began Longyear and Frederick Ayer of Boston filed a claim to the Ashland location in Ironwood. The Ashland Mine, opened in 1884, had shipped a million tons by 1890. Then it was taken over by the Hayes Mining Company, organized by two long-bearded Hayes brothers, the "prune kings" of California. The Gogebic drew men from the farthest corners of the country.

The year 1884 began a land rush unparalleled in the history of the north country. The Colby Mine was producing rich red ore, and the State geologist had issued a luring report. Pulled by that twenty-mile-long magnet of the iron-bearing hills, men poured into the wilderness. In 1885 there were two thousand miners between Sunday Lake and the Montreal River. Seven mines were then producing and scores of other sites were under option. Each location had a noisy camp—axes thudding, timber crashing down, powder blasting in the rock, men and mules scraping away the overburden. On the rivers sawmills were snarling through pine and hardwood, turning out lumber for new railroad beds, new towns, new mine works. Over the range scrambled other prospectors, without lease or title but hoping to find an ore bed and to take an option. A pickax jutted from the pack on their shoulders, they carried a dip compass in hand, and when they slept on the granite ground they dreamed of soft deep hematite. They toiled alone in the deep woods, hacking at the frozen earth in winter or slapping at stinging, sticky swarms of mosquitoes and bleeding from the furious little wounds of the black flies. Now their old test pits, softened with raspberry vines and deer brush, pock the woods from the Potato River to Gogebic Lake, with trees growing up on the piles of earth beside them. There are few Indian mounds in this dark country, but hundreds of mounds cover the dreams of the iron hunters.

For three years the prospectors swarmed in, drawn by reports of "a continuous series of deposits of ore unparalleled in magnitude." It was an unparalleled frenzy in the North, with new companies organizing in Ashland and men in Milwaukee, Racine, and Chicago bidding up the shares when there was only a windlass and a well bucket on the location. Most of the mining companies were formed by men of little means and small experience. Prices rose and fell with every rumor. Hundreds of speculators paid fantastic prices for stock that was worthless; others bought options on forties that contained nothing but a beaver dam in a reed-choked river. In 1887 there were 184 companies on the Gogebic Range. Two years later fifteen companies were left. The boom collapsed like an empty tent. Only the sturdy companies with substantial property remained.

At several points along the Gogebic Range modest outcrops of ore were found, and the first tonnage from these places came out in wheelbarrows, buckets, or horse-drawn scrapers and wagons. Then shallow drifts were sunk and the ore bodies were mined out through underground openings. Year by year the mines deepened, with shafts generally sunk on the footwall paralleling the dip of the iron formation. In later years these inclined shafts would be abandoned and replaced by shafts sunk vertically in the footwall, with long horizontal drifts leading into the iron formation. Deep underground mining required more skill and capital than most small companies possessed. Supervisory costs were as large for a single mine as for a group of properties. So, in course of time group management came into the district. Hanna, Oliver, Oglebay, Norton & Co., Republic Steel Corporation, The Steel and Tube Company of America, and Pickands Mather & Co. had sizable operations. In the interim the other companies, with the exception of Oglebay, Norton, either mined out or disposed of their interests, and Pickands Mather became the dominant producer in the district.

During the five-year fever, the Gogebic towns sprang up, and for a while they were the most famous, or infamous, towns of the North. Hurley and Ironwood, on either side of the dark

Montreal River, and Bessemer were the first lusty settlements. Settlers trekked in over the brushed-out path of the railroad; the towns were building while section crews leveled the road-bed and laid the track. Along the Montreal River grew great tracts of pine. Both iron and timber fed the new settlements, sawmills screaming on the river and powder booming in the hills. From logging camps in the woods men stampeded into Hurley every spring with a winter's pay in their pockets and pent-up hungers in their blood. Hurley was a good-time town, with gambling, girls, and piano music, with rows of saloons, variety shows, and amusement halls. After the wooden shacks and slush ice, the frozen skid road and the cavelike bunkrooms, Hurley was a logger's paradise. In camps from Duluth to Escanaba men talked about the Silver Street saloons—the First Chance Bar at the river, Jim Bartlett's Frogpond Saloon, the Miner's Home Saloon, the Senate Saloon, the Marble Hall Saloon and Concert House. At first an Irish settlement, full of Irish miners and rail-road workmen, Hurley soon became a polyglot town with saloons for every nationality. There were Alex Rossi's Italian House, P. J. Shea's Canadian House, and such diverse saloonkeepers as LeClair, Kaepeke, P. Molignoni, John Aodio, O. Sical, and a partnership of Tuscany and Lalond. On Second Avenue around the corner from Silver Street were two Chinese laundrymen, Hop Wah and Sing Kee.

The landmark of Hurley, famous throughout the North, was the Burton House, "the hotel with a thousand windows." Built in 1886 by John E. Burton, who discovered the Aurora Mine and took 50,000 tons of ore from its open pit, the hotel had a block-long veranda, scrollwork cornices and twin cupolas high above the clump of hobnail boots on the plank sidewalks. In its dining room, where buxom Swedish waitresses served imported sea food and champagne, men could look out to the sawmills on the river and shaft houses jutting up from the gashed hills. For years the Burton House was a meeting place of railroad men, mineowners, and lumbermen. In 1897 John Burton traded it to Myron Ross of Chicago for three million canceled postage stamps, a collection Ross had made during twenty years as a mail carrier. Burton had always wanted to be a philatelist.

In the last week of June 1887 a fire raged through Hurley, burning out half the town. Two weeks later, with men and teams clearing away charred timbers, a second fire took half of what remained. In a few months the town was rebuilt, gayer and gaudier than before. By 1890 it had fifty-eight saloons, twenty hotels, four oyster houses, three groceries, two druggists, and a Presbyterian minister. The minister soon left Hurley for a more promising parish. Fifteen years later another minister arrived. One day at the edge of town he sat on a log with A. D. Chisholm, a young chemist, wondering whether he could ever build a church in that ungodly place. This young dominie had a vein of iron. He stayed. Years later, in 1955, he wrote to his friend Chisholm in the Pickands Mather office at Duluth, recalling that conversation in the woods. For two years, he stated, he had held a weekly service in an empty hall, but at last the people came. Now, having devoted his entire ministry to the one parish, he was happy to report that he had a beautiful new church and a loyal congregation.

In the twentieth century Hurley dwindled from 7,000 to half that number. The logging camps were abandoned in the ruined woods and sawmills were rusting on the rivers. But the mines were still producing. Pickands Mather had the Odanah Iron Company, C. H. Munger in charge, with the Cary Mine pouring out a steady flow of blue-red hematite. The Burton House still stood, having survived the fires of 1887. It remained a landmark, though it slowly faded to the drab of the false-front saloons and amusement halls. It saw the mines going deeper, a new generation of loggers trucking pulpwood from second-growth timber, and men still crowding into the honky-tonks on Silver Street. At last on a bitter February morning in 1947 it burned to the ground.

Ironwood, built in the woods under the Norrie location, was deep in mud. It went up in a season, saloons, boardinghouses, and amusement halls lining Ayer Street, men clumping over the high duckboards in loggers' and miners' boots. The most popular saloon was run by George Kerbitz, with a flophouse room in back. The biggest amusement hall was the ornate Alhambra, with a horseshoe bar, tables on the floor and the balcony, and a bawdy stage show. It was run by bald Paddy O'Neill who boasted that with his bare head he could butt the panel out of any bar in town. Another famous saloonkeeper was a French Canadian who had fought with the Rebels in the Civil War. Frenchy had a running quarrel with his wife; every week he carried her sewing machine down Suffolk Street to the express office, ordering it sent back to her old home in Peshtigo. Before the train came she retrieved it, every time.

In September 1887 fire broke out in a shed behind the Alhambra Theater. It swept the business district. They rebuilt it, more solidly, on higher ground out of the mud. The new Ironwood had 55 saloons, 16 hotels, 15 boardinghouses, one Chinese laundryman, and an A. Lieberthal, seller of ocean tickets. It was common for Old Range miners to send steamship passage and railroad fare to relatives in the Old Country.

On Suffolk Street, between the two miners' boardinghouses, lived J. D. H. Stevens, the county's first probate judge. Judge Stevens had won election by a majority of five over an Ironwood saloonkeeper. Soon after the election a narrow-eyed man arrived from Chicago and took the defeated candidate back to Illinois on a charge of highway robbery. Had three of Stevens' votes gone to the other man, the first judge of Gogebic County would have spent his term in the Illinois penitentiary.

The hills beyond the Norrie mines were dense with timber. All winter wolves howled in the swamp below the East Norrie and deer came to the hay barns at the edge of town. Within a few years the Norrie tunnels reached under the town and blasting shook the bottles off barroom shelves. Subsidence, which eventually required abandoning some of the Norrie drifts, began early. At the head of Suffolk Street stood the No. 3 shaft house. One day its old log barn slid into a cave with the barn boss and ten horses in it.

Two miles out of Ironwood on the historic Newport hillside grew up the settlement of Jessieville. It was like a town in Wales, steep streets climbing up to the mine rigs and looking over the far wild valley to the hills of Ontonagon. In 1890 a four-mile streetcar line linked Hurley, Ironwood, and Jessieville. It was a convenience for the miners and a wonder to lumberjacks just in from the woods. Some of them rode it all day long.

Six miles east of Ironwood between the humped Gogebic ridges the town of Bessemer grew up in the valley. Besides the historic Colby, with a vein of rich Bessemer ore 250 feet across, it had a solid line of mines along the range, the Anvil, Palms, Valley, Ironton, Puritan, Blue Jacket, and First National. On payday miners streamed in from the locations, and a dozen languages clamored in the Bessemer barrooms. It was a wholly iron town, with red dust painting its plank sidewalks and a newspaper

called *The Pick and Axe*. With a look at notorious Hurley the
editor wrote: "The law-abiding population predominates here,
the place being noted for being quiet and orderly." Still, in its
first years Bessemer supported forty-eight saloons, and the town
officials felt compelled to pass laws against alley rioting, improper
diversions, and smoking on the dynamite wagon.

In 1886 Wakefield, on the shore of Sunday Lake, was a tent
town. Front and Sunday Lake Streets were chopped through the
forest, and amid roots, stumps, and cliffs of building lumber the
first frame buildings rose. At the edge of town were the rich Sunday Lake and Brotherton mines, both eventually operated by
Pickands Mather, with many smaller workings in the woods
around. Some high hopes speak in the names of the old locations:
Miracle, Star, Speedwell, Ironsides, Crown Point, Eureka, Me-
teor, Iron Prince, Iron Queen, Iron Duke, Emperor. In 1887
there came a rumor of gold in the Gogebic. In Wakefield the
South Washburn Mining and Smelting Company sold 50,000
shares at $25 on their promise to mine gold and silver. When
the last shares were purchased the organizers left the country.
There was neither gold nor silver in the district, but for a year
some Wakefield counterfeiters did a profitable business in stamp-
ing out "silver dollars" in a shack above the town.

In the summer of 1887 Mike O'Brien opened his Colliseum
Variety Theater on Front Street. It advertised imported actors
but the popular attraction was dogfights on the stage. Miners
and loggers paid a day's wage to see the fun. Besides his fighting
dogs Mike had a pet monkey that ran over the bar and climbed
the scrollwork, to everyone's delight. On Christmas Eve 1887,
with a full house and a gala show, the monkey overturned a
kerosene lamp. In two hours half of Wakefield was a smoking
ruin. Only deep snow saved the rest of the town. The Perry
House, halfway down Front Street, was saved by hanging icy
blankets in the path of sparks and flame. Soon afterward the Perry
brothers traded their hotel to Matt Van Orden for his Mikado
Mine. It later became a Pickands Mather property, producing a
modest tonnage of soft red hematite.

Logging was a winter business. In deep snow over the frozen
swamps the men swung their axes, rocked their saws, and drove
their teams on the icy skid road. The Gogebic country had a
champion loader and skidder, a big blue-eyed Scotsman with a

piping childlike voice. With two yoke of oxen, Squeaky Tom McDonald loaded and skidded to the rollway 1,900 pine logs in a single day. The Ontonagon River was a great driving stream. On the spring crest of snow water millions of logs surged down to sawmills at the river mouth. Eastward over the bright blue rim of Lake Superior the Gogebic lumber went to make everything from telephone poles to toothpicks.

Behind the spring drive on the rivers lay whole counties of cutover land. The timber was quickly gone. When the last logs went through the mills the engineer tied the whistle cord and let steam die in the boiler. The long whistle wavering over the ruined forest marked the end of the empire of logs. When it died away loneliness came down. Raspberry vines spread over the rusted rails of the logging line, the tote roads grew up in deer brush and aspen, the trampled rollways became a burrow for muskrats. Logging left a trail of empty camps and ghost towns.

But the mines went on producing. The old Iron King, later called the Newport Mine, on the hill where Raphael Pumpelly had seen a stain of yellow in the rock, was opened in 1886. In the late nineties it appeared exhausted. Ferdinand Schlesinger bought it for $50,000 and everyone thought he had lost his mind. (Schlesinger had dreamed of forming a great iron and steel corporation, but got caught in the Panic of 1893; eight years later United States Steel did it.) He had been mining in Mexico; when he came back to Lake Superior he got the financial backing of Mark Hanna and took over the played-out Newport Mine. He employed as manager a persistent geologist, J. R. Thompson, who had studied with the great team of Leith and Van Hise at the University of Wisconsin. All of his energy was devoted to mining out the known remaining tonnage and spending the profits from that mining in seeking new ore bodies. The consensus of geological opinion at the time indicated that as the ore-carrying dikes were impervious it was useless to look for concentration beneath them. This thinking was shared by all the Cornishmen heads of the larger operating companies in the district, and they ridiculed Thompson's ideas. What they did not know was that the persevering Thompson had discovered a great underground longitudinal fault in the district which not only severed and separated the dikes but shattered their theory as well. As long as profits permitted, Thompson persisted in deepening the then deepest shaft in the iron formation. Ultimately,

and as funds ran short, he prevailed on Mr. Schlesinger to permit
him to continue the exploration by using a diamond drill in the
shaft bottom and spending on the work only his salary. A. D.
Chisholm, then a chemist in the analytical laboratory, recalls that
for weeks the results on the drill samples were not at all encouraging. Then one morning the drill foreman came in, shaking his head ruefully. Last night, he explained, they had struck
a terrific water pressure that took the drill and thrust it up the
shaft till the rods gave way. Now, he added, they had got the rods
out and a lot of reddish stuff was welling up through the
drill hole. They had reached rich soft ore at 1,400 feet. That
was more than half a century ago. Now the Newport shaft is down
to 3,200 feet. It has yielded thirty-five million tons since it was
presumed to be exhausted.

But even Schlesinger gave up before the ore was gone. He
sold the famous Newport and Anvil mines, along with other
mining properties, to Harrison Williams, who in turn sold out
to The Steel and Tube Company of America. In 1923 The
Youngstown Sheet and Tube Company acquired the property
from Steel and Tube and the next year Pickands Mather took
over its operation. They have carried the Newport steadily deeper,
into successive concentrations of ore.

In the early years before every miner had an automobile,
a mine was also a community. It had a mine office, a superintendent's residence, a house for the mining captain, boardinghouses
for the men. At a big mine in the nineties each nationality group
had its own boardinghouse—Cornish, Finnish, Swedish, Slovenian, Italian, Austrian, Croatian—with native food as well as language, and with all others sharing a common resentment of the
Cornish miners who because they spoke the manager's language
quickly became shift bosses and mine captains. The muckers
and trammers puzzled over that: they were all from the Old
Country, yet somehow the Cornishmen spoke the New World
language. In town on Saturday night they stepped off the duckboards into the mud, muttering "Evening, Captain," as the great
man passed.

For warmth in winter the boardinghouses were banked with
snow halfway up the windows. The night and day shifts met at
the long lamplit table, one group eating breakfast, the other supper; then the off shift turned into the bunks just vacated by the
men going to work. None of them saw daylight in the winter
months. The night shift slept through the short winter day, the

day men tramped over the squeaking snow before sunrise and came back from the dryhouse under the evening stars.

A mine was a melting pot. A good captain knew tags of a dozen languages, and the Finns, Slavs, and Croatians soon began mixing some English with their own tongue. After a decade the boardinghouses were mixed, with Italians shouldering Finns and Croatians and all of them reaching for the same dishes. Polisausage, lutfisk, ravioli, and salami, once exclusively the dishes of the Poles, the Swedes, and the Italians, were now relished by all, and every mouth watered at the smell of a Cornish pasty.

The larger mines employed a doctor, the men paying a dollar a month for medical and surgical services. The healthy men grumbled at this expense, but they soon learned how to get something for their dollar. At the end of the month they went to the doctor for a bottle of castor oil. They used it to grease their boots.

The Panic of 1893 cut production by half on the Gogebic, but within a few years the mines were expanding. A recruiting agent—in the mine offices they called him "the man-catcher"— made regular trips to Chicago. Across Canal Street from the smoky old Union Station stood a solid wall of employment agencies, each window chalked with lists of jobs in the Kansas wheat fields, the Minnesota lumber camps, railroad section gangs, and construction crews. Here the Gogebic man-catcher, speaking six languages and waving a roll of money, soon picked up a carload of men. He bought them shoes, shirts, and overalls, and a bagful of bread, cheese, and salami, and herded them onto the train. On the range he marched them from one mine office to the next until the last man was hired. Then he collected his commission—he was paid by the head—and went back for another carload.

It took millions of years to leach and fold and gather the iron in the hills, and that solemnity lies over the country still. Everyone feels it, the geologist, the company man from Cleveland or Youngstown, and the old pumpman smoking his pipe in the sunset. There is the hum of the mine rig; the skip comes up out of the deep heart of the earth; it unloads high in the head frame and dumps ten or more tons on its way to the consumer. A whispered rush of ore, and then the silence.

Iron has shaped the restless, ever-changing world, and yet the land that produced it still is wilderness. It created the assembly lines, the skyscrapers, the never-ending traffic on multilane highways. It has changed the face and the character of America, while it remains unchanged. At evening on the Colby hillside above the village of Bessemer, there is sunset and the first white star and a thrush singing in the cedar swamp—as though millions of tons of hematite had not come out of the ground to glare in the night skies of Youngstown and South Chicago. In the dusk the crumbling old mine works looks like a ruined chapel.

Iron has crowded people into huge and strident cities, but the range country is empty, brooding, and elemental. The towns of Ironwood, Bessemer, and Wakefield could all be lost in a single district of Detroit or Pittsburgh, the cities they created. In all of northern Michigan, a region half as big as Ohio, there are not as many people as in the city of Toledo. Chase Osborn, an early iron hunter, camping on Lake Superior, exulted in the knowledge that he was breathing air never breathed by any human being. It still feels that way. On a winter night, with snow falling around the silent shaft house and on the ghostly stockpile, the range towns lie in a deep stillness, as though they were on another planet from Gary, River Rouge, or Pittsburgh.

By 1910 the mine shafts were deep underground, the mules cutting their paths in the wet red rock between the tramming tracks. Then the Gogebic was a settled district and the old explorers and landlookers were gone. Hermit Langford died at the poor farm in Ontonagon and was buried in potter's field. A. Lanfear Norrie was a cosmopolitan, sometimes recalling in New York and London his seasons in the wilderness. One of his investors, Theodore M. Davis, was living in a houseboat on the Nile and excavating the tombs of the Pharaohs. George M. Wakefield, who brought supplies to the range by dog sled before the first mines were opened, was prospecting for copper in Alaska. George A. Fay and Joe Sellwood had gone on to another iron bonanza north of Lake Superior.

In 1906 Raphael Pumpelly, whose numerous family lived in a huge gingerbread mansion at Newport, Rhode Island, came back to visit the Newport Mine. He had just ended a long expedition in Turkestan; on the way home he had stopped in Egypt to visit his friend Theodore Davis and to see the newly opened tombs of the kings. But what he talked about was old times on the Gogebic, when he decided to take a chance on two sections where an outcrop showed a stain of iron.

CHAPTER 6

The Long Ladder

ON AN APRIL DAY in 1884 a rangy youth of nineteen with a sea bag on his shoulder was striding along the New York Central tracks from Buffalo to Cleveland. While a long freight roared by he put down his bag and looked over the wind-stirred waters of Lake Erie. Out on the horizon stood the white sails of schooners and a tall-stacked freighter trailed a feather of smoke. His eyes went west, toward the waterways that led through straits and rivers, past cities and farms and forests, to the iron ports of the North. The Great Lakes—there was a luring in the name and in the light that lay on the restless water. When the caboose flashed by, the roaring faded from the rails. There came the lap of water on the shore and a blackbird singing in a willow tree. As he walked on west it was like striding into the future. He had dreamed of this in his boyhood, four thousand miles away.

In the village of Claypole, where the River Trent marks the border between Lincolnshire and Nottinghamshire, young Harry Coulby worked on his father's farm. He had left school at eleven but his mind was hungry; he wondered about the world beyond the hedgerows and the stone-walled lanes of Lincolnshire. He had already devoured all the books in the school library.

Over the English fields came a whistle, high and thin with distance. The boy's eyes came up, following the train across the distant meadows. While his hoe hacked again he still followed it in his mind—through green Sherwood Forest and over the gray moors of Yorkshire, or down through the fens and copses to the vast web of London.

In the summer of 1879 Harry Coulby put away his hoe. He walked the lanes to Newark, in Nottinghamshire, a station on the London, Midland and Scottish Railway. There he became a learner, without pay, of telegraphy. He called himself fifteen, though he was six months short of that. He was a big strong lad and a rapid and thorough learner. Quickly his mind fastened onto the dit-da-dit of the receiver; he could read telegraph code all his life.

In three months he was ready for a job. He was sent to Ilkeston village, at a salary of twelve shillings a week, then to Marple at fourteen shillings. A year later he was in the big railroad office at Derby junction, with a salary of eighteen shillings. Trains clanged through Derby night and day, and the eighteen-year-old clerk was not content to watch them. On a spring day in 1883 there came a telegram addressed to Harry Coulby, Esq., instructing him to board a ship in Liverpool. He had applied for foreign service with the British Cable Company.

From the rail of the steamer *Leonora* the boy from Claypole counted the ships in the Mersey, the lofty masts, the raked spars and funnels, ships from all the gulfs and oceans of the world. In the long evening light he watched the shores of England fade and the gas buoys winking in the channel. Twenty-six days later he walked ashore at Santiago under the green Cuban mountains and reported at the office of the West Indies & Panama Telegraph Company, Ltd.

After two months he began to burn and shiver. His head swayed and his hand trembled at the transmitter. He went to bed with malaria. His salary of $800 a year had not begun; it was being credited to his account for passage overseas. To pay for medicine and doctor's services, he had to borrow thirty dollars. When he asked the company for money there was no response. That, and a disagreement with an officious fellow clerk, led Harry Coulby to turn his back on Cuba. In March 1884 he stowed away on the steamship *Cienfuegos*, bound for New York. Twenty years later, when he managed two fleets of steamships on the Great Lakes, Harry Coulby said: "In business there are short ladders and long ones. On some of them the top rung isn't much higher than the bottom. If I found myself on one of these short ladders, I stepped off and tried to find one that reached higher."

When he slipped ashore in New York the stowaway was weak from hunger and shaking with fever. A Catholic hospital took him in—in later years no Sisters of Charity ever came out of his office empty-handed. He was young and quick to recover. In two weeks he was on his way—north to Albany and west to Buffalo, working at odd jobs for his meals and a little money. His goal was the docks of Cleveland. From boyhood reading he had dreams of the Great Lakes. "The name itself, 'Great Lakes,' fascinated me," he said years later. "I wanted to see those lakes. If possible I was going to sail them."

When he reached Cleveland the season was well along and the fleet was manned. Only the big *Onoko* was hiring, and when the youth climbed aboard the mate shook his head—he had no berth for a greenhorn. So the historic *Onoko,* first iron bulk freighter on the Lakes, lost a chance to hire the man who in twenty years would be the commanding figure in the trade.

Cleveland in 1884 was bustling and building. Harry Coulby joined a construction crew, building an addition onto the old Court House at the northwest corner of the Public Square. All summer he pushed a wheelbarrow up the wooden ramps. In the evenings at a commercial school he studied the operation of the newly developed typewriter, and on Sundays in his little room at the Central Friendly Inn he practiced shorthand. That fall he became a stenographer, at $40 a month, in the office of the Lake Shore and Michigan Southern Railroad which Amasa Stone had built.

There were two daughters of Amasa Stone, one the wife of Samuel Mather and the other the wife of John Hay. In 1884 the Hays were living in an East Boulevard mansion ("the barn I built for my Hay," said Amasa Stone) which until recently was the home of the Western Reserve Historical Society. John Hay was at work with his colleague John Nicolay on the final manuscript of their ten-volume *Abraham Lincoln.* Nicolay was in Washington, and to collaborate at that distance the two men carried on a prodigious correspondence. Hay needed a secretary, and he found one at the railroad office. So young Harry Coulby became acquainted with a gifted man and through him with some of the currents of American history.

In 1858 John Hay, who grew up at Spunky Point, later Warsaw, Illinois, had entered his uncle's law office in Springfield, next door to the office of Lincoln and Herndon. In 1861 Lincoln took Hay, twenty-three years old, to Washington as a personal secretary. In the stress of the war years Hay saw Lincoln at the closest range: he saw his humor and his melancholy, his kindness and his firmness. Often he was awakened at midnight by the gaunt president in his nightshirt, wanting Hay to laugh with him at some jibe in the book he was reading while waiting for sleep. "The Ancient" Hay called him, and "the Backwoods Jupiter." After Lincoln's death Hay served in diplomatic posts in Paris and Vienna, and then became an editor, under Whitelaw Reid, of the New York *Tribune*. In 1875, having married Clara Stone, John Hay settled in Cleveland (which he did not like) and began work on the great biography of Lincoln.

By 1884 there were mountains of manuscript on Hay's desk. Day after day, month after month, he dictated the final text to Harry Coulby. While the pages grew, Coulby checked hundreds of details in files of White House correspondence. It made the boy from Claypole a lifelong admirer of Lincoln and it left an impress on his mind and character. The work was finished early in 1886. It ran serially in the *Century Magazine* from 1886 to 1890, and in those years Harry Coulby read it all again.

Amasa Stone had died in 1883, ending his long suffering and illness, and in 1886 the Hays left Cleveland for Washington. Coulby might have gone with them, but he had not forgotten the Great Lakes and chose to stay in Cleveland. Hay recommended him to his brother-in-law Samuel Mather, and on April 10, 1886, he went into the employ of Pickands Mather. His salary was $50 a month, but he had put his foot on a long ladder. Said he twenty years later, "A chance is enough for anybody, especially in the United States in the twentieth century, when opportunities for young men are better than at any time since Christopher Columbus set foot on America."

Now the boy from Claypole was surrounded by the business of the Lakes. His window in the Western Reserve Building looked down at the ship-filled docks, at steamers rounding the breakwater, and tugboats easing barges through the twisting river channel. In the office were all the facts and figures of the traffic, and from it went the orders that kept vessels moving through far-off Whitefish Bay, into the docks of Allouez and Ashland, past the windy reach of Thunder Bay and the dark cape of Keweenaw, through the flashing Straits of Mackinac, past the starlit wilderness of Drummond Island and the glaring skies of Detroit. Harry Coulby learned about navigation, fuel consumption, and the hazards of Great Lakes weather. His stretching mind had room for the endless details of the trade—capacity of scores of different vessels, dock facilities from Duluth to Buffalo, co-ordinated schedules, loading and unloading mechanisms.

He learned the U's and V's in the company code book so that he could use them without thinking. *Ugliness*—Load . . . with . . . ; *Ulterior*—Load with . . . instead of . . . ; *Ultimate*—Load with . . . if possible; *Umbrage*—In order to hasten dispatch can we load with . . . instead of . . . ; *Umbrella*—Yes, you may give . . . instead of . . . ; *University*—Must be loaded as per original instructions; *Uproar*—If it will help dispatch you may load with . . . ; *Vacation*—. . . now on her way up light, will be ready for ore . . . Load her with . . . ; *Vaccinate*—. . . now on her way up with coal for . . . in tow of . . . Will be ready for ore . . . Have cargo ready; *Vagabond*—Orders for . . . were mailed you . . . ; *Vapor*—We can load the . . . promptly on arrival; *Varnished*—You must not quit work until the . . . is loaded; *Vernacular*—. . . is unloaded and cleared; *Visible*—. . . cleared but returned, owing to bad weather; *Vulgarism*—Have everything in readiness to commence fueling . . . immediately on her arrival.

This movement of ships and cargoes was to be Harry Coulby's career. Within a few years he had climbed from stenographer to director of the Pickands Mather fleet. As manager the terms he habitually used were the restless, urging words: *Volcano*—Give her good dispatch; *Voracity*—See that there is no delay; *Volubilate*—Get her out as quickly as you can; *Voyage*—Get the . . . fueled as quickly as you possibly can; *Volleyed*—Try and make a record on this boat.

The 1890's were up-and-down years in the iron-ore industry. Production grew at the beginning of the decade, sagged after the Panic of 1893, and surged to new volume at the turn of the century. But in these years the Pickands Mather shipping interests steadily enlarged. In 1888 the company had invested in the historic N.Y.P. & O. dock at Cleveland and improved its facilities. Other dock interests were acquired in Fairport and Erie, and in 1893 the company built a fueling dock at Detour on the St. Marys River. The fuel dock became an important link in Lake transportation.

With Harry Coulby's energy and acumen Pickands Mather reached out to new vessel interests. The company had dock facilities, an unmatched communications system, and an organization reaching from the head of the Lakes to the Niagara River. It had the experience, efficiency, and judgment to provide smoothly co-ordinated marine operations. In the 1890's the firm formed the Huron Barge Company and acquired for it the whaleback steamer *Pathfinder* and the barge *Sagamore*—the names were taken from Cooper's *Leatherstocking Tales* at the suggestion of Samuel Mather's wife, a descendant of James Fenimore Cooper. In 1894 they built the steamer *Kearsarge*. In 1895 they became operators for the American Steel Barge Company and built the big steamer *Victory*. Two years later they built the barge *Constitution* as the *Victory*'s tow.

At the beginning of the navigation season in 1901, a combination of interests formed the colossal United States Steel Corporation. It consolidated many mining properties on Lake Superior and at the same time gathered in extensive shipping interests, including the fleet of forty whaleback vessels—pigboats to the Lakemen—built by Alex McDougall at Superior, Wisconsin. Overnight, the Pittsburgh Steamship Company, its marine division with more than a hundred vessels, overshadowed all the independent fleets on the Lakes. With that merger Pickands Mather lost the operation of the Minnesota Steamship Company fleet. But Harry Coulby, who had become a Pickands Mather partner in 1900, meant to keep the company in an important position on the Lakes. He formed the Mesaba Steamship Company, building the steamers *Amasa Stone* and *Samuel Mather*. He took up management of the "Wolvin fleet," the vessels of the Acme, Peavey, and Provident Steamship companies. In 1906 he formed the Lackawanna Steamship Company, which a few years later developed into the Interlake fleet.

Meanwhile the giant fleet of United States Steel was plagued by delays, collisions, and mismanagement. The huge marine merger had been engineered by A. B. Wolvin of Duluth. Wolvin had interests in railroads, copper, iron ore, timber, ships. A man with the energy of ten, he could never stay with an undertaking. Having brought together the United States Steel fleet, he left its management to subordinates, and it was soon in trouble. In 1904 Judge Gary called Harry Coulby, asking him to manage the Pittsburgh Steamship Company. Coulby agreed, on the condition that he would also retain his Pickands Mather partnership and the operation of its vessels. So the boy from Claypole headed the two leading fleets on the Lakes.

A big bulky man with a large head and a determined jaw,

Harry Coulby was both commanding and simple. In the meeting room he sat in beautiful English-tailored clothes, chewing a long cigar and telling homespun stories. With a glint of humor in his eyes he teased the serious Henry Dalton. To his associates he was the Bulldog, strong, determined, tenacious, though sometimes surprisingly gentle and always fair. They called him, when he was still in his forties, "the Old Man." Sometimes removed from them by the brooding in his eyes, he still kept a countryman's simplicity. Once Frank Armstrong, a partner in the firm, met Harry Coulby in New York on Coulby's return from a visit to England. They dined together so that Armstrong might bring Coulby up to date on company business. But there was no time for business, with Coulby telling all about the people at Claypole —neighbor Bingham and his new Shropshire ram, Mrs. Plumtree, widow of the old parish vicar, and the old telegraph operator at Ilkeston station.

Both practical and reflective, Harry Coulby admired Lincoln above all men, and he adopted Lincoln's method of making a point with a story. In a discussion of cutting costs he described his mother telling the children at teatime to spread the butter thin—it tastes as good and there will be some left for supper. In urging economy he recalled the telegraph operator on the Midland Railway who snorted at messages that wasted words. Around the table in the meeting room he snapped his question: "What have you got? You? You? You?" Then, sinking back into his big chair, the crow's-feet crinkling at his temples: "The horse didn't leave much in the stable this morning."

Like a man driving a span of horses, he held the reins of the Pittsburgh and Interlake fleets, co-ordinating their power and movement. At annual joint meetings of captains and engineers of the two fleets he could throw out a new idea, get the men to talking, and soon have them thinking it was their own. He settled strikes by walking the gaslit waterfront, finding the sullen workmen and talking to them about the companies, the fleets, and the Lakes trade. When a mates' strike idled the ships he called the men into his office to discuss every moot question. Next day steam was up in the boilers, whistles roaring, and the fleet began to move.

As fleet manager Harry Coulby traveled the long Lake lanes he had dreamed of in his boyhood. He knew all the channels, every dock and harbor, and every detail of a hundred different ships that carried coal to the North and iron ore to the nation's steel mills. At last, four months before his death, he stood with his partner Samuel Mather on the bridge of the steamer *Harry Coulby*, bringing to Cleveland 14,098 gross tons of ore, the largest cargo ever to enter the port. In his mind flashed the old code word *Volleyed*—Try and make a record on this boat. When he died in London in January 1929, following a Christmas visit to his native village, the newspapers of England and America described him as "Master of the Lakes."

CHAPTER 7

The Giant Range

THE original Duluth and Iron Range Railroad did not touch Duluth but came down to Lake Superior at Two Harbors, twenty-seven miles up the north shore. In the spring of 1884 it had not yet reached the Vermilion Range, then Minnesota's only iron district. The road was completed to Mesaba Station, thirty miles south of Vermilion Lake and near the present town of Hoyt Lakes; to that point it carried men and materials for railroad construction and for the mines just opening up in the Vermilion district. The first locomotive, the sturdy, high-stacked "Three Spot," had been brought up by scow and hauled by horses onto the track at Two Harbors. With cordwood crammed in its firebox and Lake Superior water sloshing in its boiler, the Three Spot got up steam, tooted its whistle, and hauled the first string of cars into the Minnesota wilderness.

One of its passengers in the last week of May 1884 was William P. Chinn, an eighteen-year-old iron miner from Michigan. At track's end Billy Chinn climbed off the train and looked at a shack with MESABA lettered over the door. Around it tents and shanties huddled in the half-cut woods, with teams dragging pine logs toward the whine of a sawmill. Not knowing that he stood on the edge of the greatest iron deposit in the world, he heaved his pack onto his shoulders and started north to Vermilion. He had the brushed-out railroad path to follow.

In this same spring season Harry Coulby was walking the New York Central tracks to Cleveland. The two men would be associated with the same company in years to come.

Billy Chinn, who as general manager of Pickands Mather &

Co.'s iron mines would leave his name on the Minnesota ranges, came from a line of miners. His father was one of the Cornishmen who left the depleted tin mines on the Channel coast and came to southern Wisconsin to work the lead and zinc deposits around Mineral Point. It was a Cornish community, and Billy Chinn grew up among Trevarthons, Polglases, and Pengillys—

> If names begin with Tre, Pol or Pen,
> You may know that all are Cornishmen.

They built solid limestone houses, like the white cottages of Cornwall, in a neat row on one side of the valley and worked their mine pits on the hillside opposite. At mealtime the women stood in their doorways and waved a cloth to show that food was on the table. The town was first called Shake Rag, though it later became Mineral Point.

From Shake Rag the Chinn family moved north, with the copper boom, to the Keweenaw wilderness on Lake Superior. Billy Chinn completed schooling at Calumet; then, at fifteen, he went to the Menominee district and started iron mining. His first job was picking ore out of rock dumps. Then he became a timekeeper and underground pump boy. In the long shifts while the pumps were pulsing like a great heart underground, he devoted much time to books. He didn't mean to be a pumpman all his life.

It was a good time to be young in the north country. Big new mines were opening above the ancient cliffs of the Menominee River, a land fever was raging in the Gogebic hills, and over the bright waters of Lake Superior came rumors of rich beds of iron and a rush of men to the wilderness near the Canadian border. When the ice was out of the harbors Billy Chinn packed his duffle and started for the Vermilion country.

From Mesaba Station he tramped north through a wild emptiness of black spruce and tamarack. He slept at night in a railroad camp, among Irish, Finnish, and Italian laborers. A broad-shouldered, self-contained youth, he shook his head when the foreman wanted to put him to work laying crossties. He was a miner, and at daylight he was on his way. At the town of Tower he found three partly built houses among a scatter of tents, shacks, and makeshift machine shops. There was a big log boom on Vermilion Lake, with a mill turning out pine planks and mine timbers. He walked on to the Soudan location and went to work for the

Minnesota Iron Company. The next month the first load of ore left a Minnesota mine.

His job was blacksmith's helper, at a dollar a day. On Saturday nights he went to the boiler house to help the firemen scrape flues. He came out black as a chimney sweep, but with fifty cents extra in his hard square hand. From the blacksmith's forge he went underground, working in candlelight with pick and shovel, learning to drill the blasting holes and charge the powder, timbering up a new working place in the ore body. When he came up in 1898 he knew every job in the drifts, stopes, and slices. Then he went to the great new iron range, the Mesabi.

There are said to be sixteen different ways of spelling the name Me-sa-bi, but they all mean something fabulous. To the Chippewas the word meant "Giant" or "Grandmother of All." Before men knew of iron in the earth it applied to the long granite ridge, the ancient height of land between Lake Superior and Lake Winnipeg. In the 1890's it became the name for the greatest reservoir of iron ore then known, a bed of iron formation a hundred miles long and up to two miles wide with many pockets of deep, rich hematite ore. Thousands of miners, like young Billy Chinn and veteran Joe Sellwood, had passed over the Mesabi on the rough way to the Vermilion district. Under their trails, like a huge layer cake, lay the banded ore formation. Beneath ten to a hundred feet or more of glacial drift began the ore and paint rock, then a layer of rich blue ore, then yellow ore, then, after an intermediate band of paint rock, the yellow ore again, and beneath that the high-grade blue ore—all part of a vast bed of iron formation on the Mesabi, later called cherty taconite. When the diamond drills bored in and the drill cores were brought up, there was a luring profile of the giant range. But the first men groped and fumbled like a miner with a burned-out lamp.

Among the stubborn men of history are the seven Merritt brothers of Duluth. They believed there was ore, a vast body of iron ore, in the Mesabi, and they would not give up searching. Over the ice-locked winter land and the sinking ground of summer they explored the wilderness. They bought up land from homesteaders, woodsmen, and lumber companies. They packed in supplies and dug test pits. Other men toiled and dreamed for a season, and put their gear away. The Merritts kept on. At last, in November 1890, one of their cruisers found good ore at Mountain Iron, and a few months later John McCaskill led them to a mass of iron ore tangled in the roots of an upturned tree near Embarrass Lake. These discoveries, fourteen miles apart, became the Mountain Iron and the Biwabik mines, and a new iron rush began.

In 1871 when Duluth was a wilderness village Congressman Proctor Knott of Kentucky in a debate over a railroad land grant derisively described the glories of Duluth and the "untold treasures of its commerce," listing gold, silver, and coal mines and vast gardens of wheat and cattle. He failed to include iron, which would make his ironic prophecy come true. Twenty-one years later hundreds of vessels hurried over Lake Superior, crowded with explorers and speculators, railroad and lumber men, merchants, miners, and missionaries. They saw the raw woods town of Duluth spreading along the lake's edge with cross streets rising steeply up the wild hillside. Their eyes went to the long ridge against the northern sky and they pictured the fabled range beyond, a hundred miles deep in the bush and muskeg. Up there were big logging camps mowing the huge stands of pine, sending the logs on the spring crest of water to the head of Lake Superior and to the Mississippi. Lumber was a fortune which stood in the way of bigger fortunes. In the logged-off land men would soon be gouging out the canyons of the Mesabi.

Duluth in 1892 was the most excited city in America. Men milled through the lobby of the Spalding Hotel, buying and selling mining stocks, spreading reports and rumors, crowding around bearded explorers just in from the range, their boots splashed with the red and purple of the test pits. Another jam filled the land office, entering quarter sections on homestead claims or buying whole tracts with bundles of Sioux and Chippewa half-breed scrip.

A hundred miles away in the woods and swamps men were hacking into thickets and throwing up shanties to make the required "improvements." Canadians, declaring intended citizenship, were locating "farms" of rock and pine lands, to be sold to the lumber and mining companies. Timber cruisers were even claiming settler's rights in tracts of muskeg. In many a desolate quarter section a man knee-deep in water lettered with a charred stick on a blazed cedar tree HOMESTEAD.

There were hundreds of tales of men and fortune in the Mesabi wilderness. Some have been told and retold; others lie forgotten in the dusty land-office records of Duluth and Washington. Some men made fortunes and more men missed them, by a turn of chance or guesswork. A few stumbled into wealth and more stumbled out of it.

In 1891 the Mahoning location was stumpland, with a gang of men under R. B. Dear stripping overburden with shovels and wheelbarrows; this was the beginning of the famous Winston-Dear Company, contract strippers. The Dear children played over the future Mahoning Mine and hiked through virgin timber to fish and swim at Carson Lake. For a year they went to a one-room school; then its site was carried off to Ohio steel mills.

James E. Jopling, the young Englishman who learned about iron mining in Marquette, strode through the commotion of Duluth with his friends Charles H. Munger of Pickands Mather & Co. and Joe Sellwood who had become a Duluth banker as well as a mining man. Then he went up to the range with his old friend C. R. Van Hise of the United States Geological Survey. To reach an exploration camp twenty miles west of Hibbing he had to ride over a muddy forest trail. Five miles out of Hibbing he came to a team of drowned horses in a mudhole. When the mud reached his saddle skirts and it began to rain, he turned back. At Hibbing's sprawling camp two cruisers offered to show him a wonderful deposit of ore. For a week they toiled through dense country in an early snowfall, and found no iron. Forest fires had destroyed the cruisers' landmarks.

Morris Thomas of Duluth bought for pine timber the lands which now comprise the Fayal, Spruce, and Adams mines. He sold the timber rights to Murphy, Dorr, and Flynn of Michigan, insisting that they take the land also. The lumbermen objected; like Thomas, they were averse to taxes. The deal hung fire while Thomas looked for other buyers. Finally the Michigan men took the timber and the land—which would have made Thomas one of the most wealthy men in America.

The Pillsbury family, from New Hampshire by way of Minneapolis, bought up land scrip and acquired thousands of acres of pine. When the timber was cut H. M. Bennett proposed to search the land for iron ore. If he could find 100,000 tons he was to have half interest in mineral rights. Bennett went to John M. Longyear, offering half of his half for any ore the experienced Longyear could uncover. Longyear had already bought 24,000 acres—all the government land subject to cash entry in a three-mile belt along what promised to be the Mesabi ore formation.

But the maps were inaccurate, throwing his locations three miles off the main course of the range. Now came Bennett with interests in the heart of the ore formation. Longyear teamed up with him. They found not a hundred thousand but a hundred million tons. For years the mines near Nashwauk village paid huge royalties to both the Pillsbury estate and the Longyear-Bennett partnership.

Wright and Davis, lumbermen from Lower Michigan, bought 25,000 acres well situated on the Mesabi iron formation. But they had overextended themselves with other timberlands. In the depression of 1894 they tried to sell their Mesabi tract for seventy-five thousand dollars. There was no market, and Wright and Davis reluctantly held on. Ten years later James J. Hill bought the tract for four million dollars.

In the summer of 1891 prospector John McCaskill found an uprooted tree with red-brown earth at its roots. He dug a test hole there, a pit which a few years later yawned into the Biwabik Mine. In 1893 the first ore was shipped from the Biwabik. This historic mine fully exposed the make-up of the range, so that its name was given to the entire Mesabi iron formation, extending for a hundred miles from Babbitt on the east to Grand Rapids on the Mississippi. Biwabik, an Indian word meaning "reddish rock," was a fitting name.

The Biwabik formation is flat-lying, with a slight slope to the south. The horizontal ore body varies, ten feet thick in shallow places, five hundred feet in the deep deposits, and several hundred feet across. It may occur just under the surface, exposed by a blown-down tree or the ruts of a wagon road, or it may be buried by two hundred feet of overburden; the overburden averages seventy feet. The soft ore could be scooped up with shovels. Cornish mining captains opened the early mines through shafts, and underground mining predominated for a few years. With more information about the size of the ore bodies many Mesabi mines were transformed into yawning, varicolored canyons, with railroad haulage, and later trucks, bringing ore to the surface.

In the early years a sturdy, slope-shouldered man with granite eyes and a black mustache walked over the range from old Mesaba Station to Frank Hibbing's camp in the pinery. Slight but rugged, he could walk all day and all night through the roughest country. On early explorations he had set the pace for a file of Indians, with a double pack on his shoulders. In "three-shirt weather," when the thermometer dropped far below zero, he wore one wool shirt and an unbuttoned mackinaw. He was Robert Murray, who became superintendent of Pickands Mather mines in the Hibbing district.

In his Hibbing office was W. G. Brown, chief clerk, who had come up from Michigan in 1903. First assigned to the office of the Corsica and Elba mines, which Pickands Mather had acquired in 1901, he worked for a dollar a day, soon raised to a dollar ten, spending Saturday nights scraping flues in the boiler house for a fifty-cent bonus. His superintendent was a former flue scraper, W. P. Chinn, now working twelve hours a day over a strewn desk under a hanging kerosene lamp. There was work enough to share with his new assistant.

When C. H. Munger opened the Pickands Mather supervisory office in Duluth, Billy Chinn became district manager of the company mines on the Mesabi. On Monday morning at six o'clock he was in the office ready to begin the week's work. Before attacking the papers on his own desk he made the office rounds, seeing that everyone was on the job.

This is the background for a stubborn story that has been tagged on one man or another in Chinn's office, and hotly denied by each. There was a payday once a month, on Saturday night, and on Monday morning when Billy Chinn checked his staff, a man was missing. He came in at noon, looking haggard and complaining of a pain in the stomach—perhaps a touch of appendicitis. Chinn went silently back to work and the latecomer slid behind his desk. There was no recurrence of the ailment until the next payday, and then the next. On the fourth Monday morning an ambulance was waiting outside the office. When the latecomer arrived, Chinn sympathetically inquired what had detained him—that stomach-ache again? The victim nodded. Chinn opened the door and the ambulance drivers came in. "Take him to the hospital." The patient, protesting that he felt fine now, no pain anywhere, none at all, was picked up bodily and carried off. When they reached the hospital Chinn was there with the surgeon.

"What was your complaint?" the surgeon asked.

"I had a little pain in my belly. But it's gone now. It won't—"

"Four times," said Chinn grimly. "A bad case. Take his appendix out."

So a Pickands Mather man lost his appendix and never again was late on Monday morning.

The Mesabi developed with giant strides: one mine in 1892, nine in 1893, eleven in 1894. In 1895, with production approaching three million tons, it surpassed the older ranges in Michigan. By 1905 it was outshipping all the other ranges combined. In 1910 more than a hundred mines produced nearly thirty million tons of ore, and the Mesabi was a world's wonder. Railroads fanned up to the range from Duluth, with ore trains night and day carrying the red, brown, and yellow hematite to half-mile-long loading docks in Duluth-Superior Harbor. In these years men streamed into the new Mesabi towns and cities. Pickands Mather with its properties on the older ranges moved office men, mine captains, shift bosses, and foremen from the Michigan mines. Laborers came by boatloads and trainloads. Cleveland with a large Slovenian population sent thousands of Slovenes to the Mesabi. Pittsburgh sent thousands of Croatians. Bloomer-trousered Serbs and earringed Montenegrins arrived straight from the Old World, with the soil of their native land still on their boots. They marched into the pits singing their folk songs and loaded hematite for the furnaces of the Lower Lakes. Scandinavians trooped in from the logging camps; they quickly became expert with diamond and churn drills. Every location had excitable Italians and impassive Finns. Some had a few fezzed Turks and turbaned Syrians. The humanity in the mines was as varicolored as the pit walls; it was a strong bright life-stream of many characters and temperaments. A dozen languages could be heard in a single open pit. By 1910 there was a full score of nationalities on the Mesabi.

Along with the rush of fortune hunters to the Mesabi, the State of Minnesota acquired some valuable locations. In all States west of the Alleghenies Federal law reserved one section in every township for the support of public schools. When the Territory of Minnesota was established, farsighted officials proposed setting aside two sections—one sixteenth of the territory—as township school lands. Congress consented, and, when the State was later created, also deeded lands for the support of the university, an agricultural college, the building of roads, and other internal improvements. Later it deeded large tracts of swampland which had no agricultural value. Through the various classes of land grant the State of Minnesota held title to thousands of acres on the Iron Range. Still other tracts were acquired as indemnity lands: where sections granted to the State had been previously homesteaded or purchased, the State was allowed to select other public lands in their place. Since little farmland was left by the time these selections had to be made, the State chose land in the forest areas. When the Mesabi iron formation was discovered, much of this land was found to be squarely upon it. In 1922 the State Auditor wrote: "The Minnesota School Fund will receive more money from one section of school land, the Hill Iron Mine, than the States of Michigan, Wisconsin and Iowa combined have received or ever will receive from all the lands granted to them by Congress."

The Scranton Mine at Hibbing was opened up by Pickands Mather under a State of Minnesota lease in 1904. For almost twenty years it was an underground working, later an open pit. In this half century it has produced nearly twenty-five million tons of soft red hematite and has yielded the State millions of dollars in royalties. The huge Scranton Mine is about depleted; less than two million tons of ore are left, and the Pickands Mather lease expires in 1960. But many other State leases cover producing mines or reserve properties, including vast tracts of taconite that will bring an income to the State for generations to come.

In addition to these revenues, the State of Minnesota and its municipal subdivisions since 1914 have collected more than a billion dollars in taxes on iron ore. Minnesota has a vast stake in the riches of its wilderness terrain.

In 1918 Billy Chinn left the clank of steam shovels and the throb of sump pumps for an office overlooking Duluth harbor. For four years he was assistant manager, under C. H. Munger, of Pickands Mather's iron-ore properties. In 1922, on Munger's transfer to the Cleveland office, William Philip Chinn became general manager of the company's mines. Since the spring day when he tramped out of Mesaba Station with the uproar fading behind him, he had seen Pickands Mather grow to the second largest producer of iron ore in America. He had a memory of Michigan in 1881, a shallow working where an uncle and two sons with picks, shovels, and wheelbarrow labored all day to mine one tone of ore. Now, in the huge mines of Minnesota one man might produce a hundred tons a day. One man, plus the blasting patterns, the electric drills and pumps and shovels, the co-ordinated mechanical haulage—all the skills and machinery that had developed in the span of one man's memory.

PART II

The New Century

By skill with fires and fluxes is made
that kind of iron from which comes steel.
—GEORGIUS AGRICOLA, 1556

CHAPTER 8

Arrived and Cleared

O^{N A} restless spring day in 1892 the new Pickands Mather-operated freighter *Maritana* loaded 4,800 tons of Menominee ore at Escanaba. It was the largest cargo yet caried on the Lakes, and the *Maritana* was the biggest carrier afloat. Three hundred and fifty feet from stem to rudderpost, she was powered with a triple-expansion engine, three 3-door Scotch boilers, and a 15-foot propeller. When her whistle roared, clearing Escanaba Harbor, she was the pride of the Lakes.

But the pride was soon humbled. Beyond the harbor mouth Captain Root rang "Full Speed Ahead," and the engines responded. The *Maritana* began to heave and shudder. In the galley a pot of soup slopped over on the stove and down below a fireman missed the fire door with his shovel of coal. Thinking they were still in shallow water the engineer slowed down. Ten minutes later he brought her up again. Again the ship began to spring and jitter. Slacking off, Engineer Waterbury went on deck and found Captain Root lurching aft, "meeting the high spots on the deck." They exchanged some strong words about the builders and went on to Chicago at half speed.

Captain Frank Root, son of an army captain who served posts at the Soo, Mackinaw, and Green Bay, was a strong-minded and plain-spoken man, a veteran of both fresh and salt water. At fifteen he had shipped out of New York as an apprentice sailor; he learned seamanship in square-riggers on the stormy run to Liverpool. Returning to the Lakes as a youth of eighteen, he sailed barks and schooners in the grain and lumber trade. In 1872 he was the only survivor of the schooner *White Squall* when it sank after a collision in foggy Saginaw Bay. As the iron-ore trade outgrew the grain and lumber business, Captain Root carried the "red cargo" down the Lakes. In 1889 when the Minnesota Steamship Company was organized, Frank Root was engaged as master of the steamer *Manola*—for which he named his newborn daughter. In 1891 he brought out the *Marina*, the first steel steamer built at South Chicago, and the next year he was given the proud new *Maritana*—which he brought down to Chicago, with her first cargo, running at half speed.

At the end of that run, steaming into the long, empty slip of the Illinois Steel Company, Captain Root saw the manager of the Chicago Shipbuilding Company waiting to meet his newest vessel with its record cargo. Muttering, the captain reached for the telegraph lever. Down in the engine room the bell clanged and Chief Engineer Waterbury saw the indicator go to full speed ahead. Half a minute later, with another jangle, it went to full astern. Said the chief years afterward: "I never, in all my sailing, saw a ship spring as she did. I thought the poor *Maritana* would go to the bottom of the slip in two pieces."

But she stayed afloat, stopping abreast of the astonished shipbuilder on the dock. There were some hot words—the builder charging the captain and engineer with trying to break the best ship on the Lakes, the *Maritana*'s men asking if it would be better to have her break in two in the middle of Lake Superior. The builder stalked off without asking about the record cargo.

A few days later, after some small adjustments in the engine room, the *Maritana* took guests aboard—friends of the shipbuilding company—for a trip to Two Harbors. The lake was smooth, the weather fine, and they jogged along at reduced speed. The second day Captain Root rang the engines up, wanting to reach the Soo before dark—in those years ships did not run the unlighted St. Marys' channels after sundown but anchored off Sailor's Encampment at the head of Mud Lake. Through the smooth Straits of Mackinac the *Maritana* came jumping. In the forward cabin the guests gave up their poker game; chips wouldn't stay on the table. They rounded Point Detour and jiggled past Lime Island. The old channel followed the long way around, through Big Lake George; there the *Maritana* jerked through glassy water in the sunset. At supper Captain Root told the engineer: "I'll have some of the guests on top of the pilothouse. When I ring for full speed, give her all you've got."

Rounding the upper end of Sugar Island with the first lights of the Soo glimmering in the distance, he pulled the lever. The ship sprang like a bronco and two guests tumbled over onto the deck below. When they tied up at the Soo the first men down the ladder were the *Maritana*'s guests. They couldn't leave fast enough.

The "pride of the Lakes" jerked on to Two Harbors and loaded another record cargo for Lake Erie. On the way down Captain Root found a telegram at the Soo, ordering him to stop at Port Huron and wait for inspection by a team of marine designers. They looked over the *Maritana*, concluding that the engine was too large for her light construction. Some corrections were made and the *Maritana*, soon dwarfed by larger vessels, carried her cargoes between the iron harbors and the smoking cities on the Lower Lakes. But she was jittery all her days.

In Lanigan's at Duluth, where Lakemen met around the big table strewn with coffee cups and newspapers, Captain Root never tired of telling how he got rid of his passengers on the *Maritana*'s first run to Lake Superior.

New capacity in the ore fleet was not as simple as a set of blueprints on a drawing board. It was won by trial and error, by restless experiment, and unrelenting effort. It was accompanied by the thunder of cargo into cavernous holds, by the creak of bulkheads, and the strain of keel plates. Behind a modern fleet are years of strenuous evolution.

Change was the word for the 1890's on the Lakes. A thousand sailing vessels whitened the shipping lanes and made a leafless forest in the harbors. They were wooden ships, many of them built for the ore trade, but the trade had outgrown them. At the end of the century, the graceful barkentines and schooners were carrying lumber, posts, pulpwood, tanbark, potatoes, apples, barrels of whisky, pork, and flour. Sliding down the ways came the new steel freighters, powered with steam engines, running a steady schedule between the lonely ports of Lake Superior and the spreading cities down below. This was part of the evolution of the age of steel. Iron ore produced steel ships to carry more ore to the undying fires of the blast furnaces.

With the new speed and efficiency of the trade, the old Lakes lore was fading. In their watch and watch—six hours on deck and six below—seamen from salt water still talked of Liverpool and Hamburg, of Marseilles, Singapore, and Buenos Aires. But they forgot the old Lake legends—of giant whales in Lake Huron and mysterious wrecks off Thunder Bay and caverns in the floor of Lake Superior where deep currents carried the bodies of lost sailors. Stories of floating islands and inverted, shifting capes— the effect of mirages and drifting fog banks on Lake Superior— had no place in vessels that steamed on schedule, independent of wind and weather. There was no more use for capstan and halyard chanteys, except when a couple of sailors hoisting stores aboard by block and tackle broke briefly into

> A-way, you Rio,
> Heave way for Rio!

The old sailing-ship races, with a broom lashed to the winner's masthead, were forgotten when the steamers churned steadily toward the Soo.

Change from sail to steam was a change from personal owner- ship to company operation. Often a schooner's captain was part owner, and his friends owned the rest of the vessel. Steamships meant investment on a new scale, and the larger investment required skilled management and co-ordinated operation. There was a significant change in vessel names—from the poetic *Wanderer, Polaris,* and *Hesperides* to the workaday *Charles W. Wetmore, Joseph L. Colby,* and *Colgate Hoyt,* the names of the corporation men.

Consolidation came to the carriers as it had come to the mines. No ship captain could command the capital to build new dock facilities and to launch a fleet of steel freighters. To keep the mountains of ore moving down the Lakes required the resources of strong organizations, such as the Minnesota Steamship Com- pany which was organized in 1889 and put under Pickands Mather management.

In 1892 the firm sold the *V. H. Ketchum,* which ten years earlier had been the wonder of the Lakes. With its heavy rigging and cluttered decks, the famous four-master was unsuited to the changing ore trade. The *Ketchum,* her engines removed, eventu- ally became a tow barge, and was wrecked in a sudden storm on Whitefish Bay. Also in 1892 the wooden *Samuel Mather* with her three masts and twin funnels was lost in Lake Superior, and two big new Minnesota Steamship Company vessels went into service—the *Mariposa* and the palsied *Maritana.*

In this year Pickands Mather formed the Huron Barge Company and soon had the tricolor house flag flying over the steamer *Pathfinder* and her tow, the *Sagamore*. For years Captain Peter A. Petersen, a short, blond, sturdy man with singsong Scandinavian speech, sailed the *Pathfinder*, towing the *Sagamore* up and down the Lakes with an enviable record. After an eight-day run he dropped the barge at the harbor mouth, where it lay at anchor till a tug took it into the dock. Then, out on the open lake again, the steamer picked it up. This was simple enough in fine weather but it became a touchy business when both steamer and consort were pitching and rolling in a gale. The first problem was to get a line aboard. Approaching from windward, they threw a weighted heaving line. Attached to the heaving line was a one-inch line, strong enough to haul the towing cable. In a head wind the four-inch cable was heaved up with a winch and the barge weighed anchor. Captain Petersen handled his tandem craft with skill and judgment; in the wildest weather he never banged his barge or broke a towline.

Despite a deep depression in the steel business Pickands Mather organized the Interlake Company in 1894, with the new steamer *Kearsarge* as its first vessel. In the following year Interlake built the *Victory* and two years later the barge *Constitution*. The *Victory* was a handsome freighter, 387 feet long, with a clear, up-sloping deck, a nicely tapered bow, raked masts and funnel, and bridge wings extending from her pilothouse. A big ship for her time, she seemed to shrink when new channels were dredged and the 800-foot Poe Lock was opened at the Soo in 1898. She was lengthened to 459 feet in 1905. After nearly half a century under the P. M. flag she was sold in 1940 to Canadian owners who renamed her the *Victorious*.

At the turn of the century the *Victory* and the *Constitution* were a famous pair, but they had a close call in November 1905 when an early blizzard lashed Lake Superior. The *Victory* and her consort, laden deep with ore, were making their last run of the season. Some ships put back to Duluth when the storm struck, but the *Victory*, laboring with her heavy tow, was too far out. The full fury met them off Keweenaw Point. In mountainous seas the towline parted; the *Constitution* was adrift and quickly lost in the blizzard. After half a day's search, groping through a fury of snow and sea and in constant danger of ramming the barge and sinking them both, the *Victory* struggled on to the Soo. Days later the helpless barge was sighted off the north shore of Keweenaw Point. She was safely towed to port before the winter ice locked in. After this storm of 1905, fore-and-aft lines were required on all Lake vessels so that men could cross the wave-swept decks.

In a later and easier season on the *Victory*, Captain Sig Matson ran a steady ship on a punctual schedule. Captain Matson, born in Copenhagen, was a big broad man, blunt and stolid-looking until you saw the humorous blue eyes behind his steel-rimmed glasses. One day on a visit to the engine room he found the clock five minutes slow, and that bothered him. The clock lost five minutes a day, the engineer said, setting it ahead. Captain Matson told the engineer to take the clock out of the galley and use it in the engine room and to send the engine-room clock ashore for repair. The engineer didn't think that was necessary; the clock was just dirty, and he could clean it. He took it apart, laying out all the wheels and springs and sprockets. While he was at work Captain Matson came in. He bent over the desk, said an encouraging word, and left. The engineer assembled the clock, which ran perfectly. But there was a small brass wheel left on his desk. Frowning, he took the clock apart again, and reassembled it. Still there was the extra piece. Once more he laid out the mechanism, muttering and shaking his head. When he had put it back together, with a wheel left over, the supper bell rang.

After supper, where he kept shaking his head over his plate, he went straight back to his cabin. The captain appeared and inquired about the clock which was now half torn down.

"It runs fine," said the baffled engineer, "but I can't find where to put this damned extra sprocket."

"Better try it again," said the captain.

The clock never lost a minute all the rest of the season, and it never ceased to worry the engineer. Night after night he took it apart and put it together, and he always had a wheel left over. When they laid up at the end of November, Captain Matson sent a deck hand aft to get a part of the captain's clock—a sprocket wheel that he had added, months before, to the parts on the engineer's desk.

In Cleveland on February 21, 1890, hundreds of people lining the Cuyahoga and the hills below Detroit Street, watched the new *Mariska*, pioneer vessel of the Minnesota Steamship Company, slide down the ways. When she splashed, sideways, in the narrow river, every bell and whistle in the basin clamored. No such excitement accompanied the shipbuilding in Duluth-Superior in the record year 1892. In that season there was a launching every Saturday night for eight weeks, and on the ninth Saturday two ships and a tug went down the ways. Launchings had grown commonplace at the head of the Lakes.

The Duluth shipbuilding boom came from the invention of Alex McDougall, a veteran Lake captain who never saw a chart but whose commands included the famous old liner *Japan,* with a life-sized Japanese carved in wood atop her pilothouse. He saw great changes on the Lakes, and one of the changes was of his own making.

According to legend Captain McDougall woke one morning excited by a dream in which he had seen a cigar-shaped freighter nosing steadily through choppy seas. Whether or not it began with a dream, his design evolved from years of planning. In 1888 he completed his drawings of a ship with rounded sides and a spoon-shaped bow, and with forward and after cabins perched on heavy stanchions above the tubular hull. He called it a whaleback—a name so arresting that it will never be forgotten, though Lakemen called his vessels "pigs." With financial help from Charles W. Wetmore of New York the two ends of the first whaleback barge, named *101,* were built at Brooklyn. Shipped to Duluth, they were joined to a center section which McDougall had built there. This first whaleback was loaded with ore at Two Harbors in June of 1888. Twenty years later the historic vessel foundered on the coast of Maine with a cargo of barreled coal tar.

With a flat bottom giving stability, a rounded upper structure offering little resistance to wind and waves, and a pig nose that made steering easy, the first whaleback attracted attention up and down the Lakes. In the next eight years forty of these distinctive craft were launched at Duluth-Superior. Many of them were barges: it was common to see a whaleback steamer towing two or three whaleback barges, like a ponderous procession of whales nosing into the seas of Lake Superior. Most of the pig-boats were built for the American Steel Barge Company formed by Charles W. Wetmore, Colgate Hoyt, and Charles L. Colby of New York. Hoyt, a brother of James Humphrey Hoyt who was legal counsel for Pickands Mather in Cleveland, became president of the company. He had interests extending to the

Pacific Northwest and he believed in whaleback steamers for ocean service as well as on the Lakes. At Everett, Washington, which they expected to be the terminus of the Great Northern Railway, Hoyt and his partner Colby built a shipyard to turn out whaleback freighters. The Panic of 1893 crushed that venture, after they had built a single vessel, the *City of Everett*. It sailed successfully on salt water until it was lost in a tropical storm in the Gulf of Mexico in 1923.

On the Lakes the new whaleback fleet was ready for increasing cargoes. In 1892 Wetmore agreed to help the hard-pressed Merritt brothers to complete their Mesabi railroad in exchange for the contract to haul their ore down the Lakes. But the Panic of 1893 squeezed Wetmore, and the Merritts turned to Rockefeller. He finally bailed them out and in the process came into possession of their richest ore lands. The new American Steel Barge Company needed efficient operation; in 1895 its management was given to Pickands Mather. Now, with thirty whaleback steamers and barges added to the vessels of the Minnesota Steamship Company and their own Huron Barge Company, Pickands Mather was the dominant marine agency on the Lakes.

Control of so much shipping led Pickands Mather into the fueling business. In 1893 Colonel Pickands sent W. L. Sherwood, a half brother of Henry Dalton, to the head of Lake Huron to locate a dock site. At Detour he rented a dock from the Haynes Lumber Company of Chicago; it was soon loaded with coal and began operation before the end of the season. In 1907, needing more capacity, the company built a new dock at Spring Bay, a couple of miles above Detour. They moved from the Haynes dock and began fueling steamers at Spring Bay in 1908.

To supply fuel to the big fleet of the Pittsburgh Steamship Company, the Pittsburgh Coal Company in 1908 built a dock at Point Aux Frenes, Michigan, two miles above Lime Island. Their dock was rested on flat rock, with nothing to secure the piling. In the spring of 1909 it was loaded with a mountain of coal. When the first freighter coming alongside bumped it, the dock shook, swayed, jackknifed, and sank out of sight. The Pittsburgh Steamship fleet then fueled at the P. M. dock. Until 1912 when the Pittsburgh Coal Company built a fueling dock at Lime Island, a property later acquired by The M. A. Hanna Company, the Detour dock had all the northern fueling business.

Eventually the Detour Dock Company became a joint operation, owned half by Pittsburgh Steamship Company and half by Mather Iron Company, a P. M. subsidiary, and managed by Pickands Mather.

After four years of depression, beginning in 1893, confidence came like a spring wind and the iron and steel business began a spectacular boom. During the lean years weak companies had gone under, but the strong companies increased their holdings. In 1897 control of the huge Mesabi ore lands were in three hands —Rockefeller's Consolidated Iron Mines, the Oliver Iron Mining Company, and the Minnesota Iron Company in which Pickands Mather had a substantial interest. With a new surge of business Rockefeller needed ships to carry his Mesabi ore, and he turned to his old Cleveland friend Samuel Mather—asking Mather to procure twelve new ships, the biggest in the trade. Here was a striking example of confidence and good faith. Pickands Mather was a leading competitor, but Rockefeller, knowing Samuel Mather to be honest and straightforward, made his proposal. In ten minutes he gave Pickands Mather an order for three million dollars' worth of vessels.

At this time there were nine or ten shipbuilding companies on the Lakes, scattered from Buffalo to Chicago, all hungry for orders after the lean years. Instead of announcing a plan to build twelve ships, Samuel Mather sent specifications to the various builders, whom he then called to his office in the Western Reserve Building. These men, who had built virtually all the steamships in the cargo fleets, supposed they were competing for a contract for one or two vessels. At the last hour Mather sent word to each of them, awarding contracts for their entire capacity. Each shipbuilder, thinking he had the entire contract, went down to the Weddell House to buy the competition a consoling drink, not knowing that his rivals were bound for the same place with the same idea; the bar was busy that evening. Within a few days life came to all the idle shipyards. Soon rivets were racketing into twelve great carriers, up to 475 feet long, a new step in shipbuilding and in transportation on the Lakes.

These were not whalebacks—no pigboats were built after 1898. McDougall's ships ran smoothly in rough seas and through drifting ice fields. But they were unhandy at the docks and their narrow hatches hampered cargo handling. The twentieth-century freighters were all straight-sided with broad hatch openings. They steadily increased in both length and breadth as the Lakes trade grew.

When the vessels were delivered Rockefeller had his Bessemer Steamship Company, the newest fleet on the Lakes, and in Cleveland he erected the Rockefeller Building on Superior Avenue as headquarters for iron and shipping interests. He asked Pickands Mather to manage the fleet, but they declined because of conflicting obligations.

In 1899 Henry W. Oliver tried to buy ten whaleback steamers to carry his growing production of Mesabi ore, but Rockefeller blocked him. The next year Rockefeller agents bought the entire American Steel Barge fleet of thirty whaleback vessels. Oliver then ordered construction of five big freighters and organized the Pittsburgh Steamship Company. As the century ended huge interests were jousting with each other and big new shipping lines were taking shape.

At this time a consolidation of shipbuilding was coming, like the consolidations in mining and transportation. It materialized in 1899, with the forming of the American Ship Building Company, a combination of nine different companies in Cleveland, Detroit, Chicago, Milwaukee, and Duluth-Superior. This was the accomplishment of a remarkable steel and shipping lawyer, James Humphrey Hoyt. From his windows in the Western Reserve Building between two floors of Pickands Mather offices, J. H. Hoyt looked out at the traffic in Cleveland harbor. His mind went farther, seeing the duplication of plant and effort and the inefficiency of scattered shipyards. A magnetic and dynamic man, Hoyt was in a powerful and strategic position: he was legal representative of the Rockefeller fleet, he was the marine lawyer for Pickands Mather, and he was at this time organizing for Carnegie and Oliver the Pittsburgh Steamship Company. Shrewd, hearty, adroit, and farseeing, he guided into existence the American Ship Building Company, merging scattered and rival interests. Its first president was William Liston Brown of Chicago, the partner of Henry Pickands in Pickands, Brown & Company. In the old P. M. code book his name was "Hatchet." He could cut through all kinds of obstructions.

J. H. Hoyt watched the American Ship Building Company grow strong, resourceful, and efficient. In 1903 his own name was given to the steamer *James H. Hoyt,* the first vessel with hatches spaced on twelve-foot centers. He saw the restless evolution of bigger and more efficient vessels. In 1906 when thirty-four freighters with capacities up to 12,000 tons and lengths to 550 feet were sliding down the ways, the *Marine Review* observed: "The average carrying capacity of the modern freighter has grown so fast that it is now almost double what it was just three years ago." During the next ten years Hoyt saw the Lakes trade grow to a magnitude that would determine the outcome of a world war. He was talking about that on a sunny day in March 1917 on a golf course at St. Augustine, Florida, when his life abruptly ended. He had driven into a sand trap. There he swung his niblick, looked up, and was struck between the eyes by another golf ball. It crushed the frontal skull. He died in St. Augustine two days later. By that time his son, Elton Hoyt 2nd, had begun a notable career in the iron and shipping business of Pickands Mather.

At the end of the century the older iron ranges on Lake Superior were in full production and the immense value of the Mesabi mines was becoming evident. With the growing flow of iron ore came a demand for better dock facilities. In the 1870's it took a week to discharge a thousand tons of ore—by shovel, wheelbarrow, and horse-drawn hoist. In those years scores of small vessels, with tugs and tenders fuming around them, crowded the harbors. The docks swarmed with men and mules; buckets dangled from overhead rigs and flatcars jerked past. With the twentieth century, clamor diminished in the harbors and tonnage multiplied. In a quiet slip, with a grind of power on a summer afternoon, thousands of tons of cargo were unloaded, ore cars moving methodically under the huge clamshells and the stockpile growing against the sky.

In South Chicago, where Jay Morse organized the Illinois Steel Company, an academic-looking man named Robert Aspin developed the first unloading rig that wholly dispensed with hand labor. A far-wandering youth, Bob Aspin, born at St. Johns, Newfoundland, had voyaged around the world before he was twenty. He sailed the Lakes during the Civil War and settled in Chicago in the 1870's. There he designed the docks of the Illinois Steel Company, equipping them with a long battery of Champion ore hoists which remained in service for more than twenty years. The next step was the giant Hulett unloaders, first powered by steam, then by electricity, which like a giant arm and hand reached into a freighter's hold, closed on tons of ore and lifted it to the dock. In 1899 the first Huletts were installed on the docks at Conneaut, Ohio. Then the biggest ships could be unloaded in a few hours.

In 1898 Judge E. H. Gary, backed by J. P. Morgan, had organized the Federal Steel Company around the nucleus of Illinois Steel, the company Jay Morse had founded. Federal Steel took over all the ore lands of the Minnesota Iron Company, the Duluth and Iron Range Railroad, and the fleet of the Minnesota Steamship Company. In 1901 white-haired Andrew Carnegie was ready to retire. He sold his vast steel business to J. P. Morgan and associates for bonds and stock worth nearly half a billion dollars, and the United States Steel Corporation was formed. United States Steel needed Rockefeller's ore fields and his Bessemer Steamship Company; Rockefeller sold them for $88,500,000. Into its Pittsburgh Steamship Company the Corporation gathered more than a hundred vessels, including all the whalebacks except the P. M. *Pathfinder* and *Sagamore*. When the *Sagamore* sank in 1901 in Lake Superior after collision with a package freighter, the *Pathfinder* was the only independent "pig" on the Lakes. Though the original *Sagamore* was lost, the name was revived on the Lakes a few years later with the launching of the freighter-style barge *Sagamore*.

Pickands Mather was left with its own small fleet—the half-dozen vessels in the Huron Barge Company and the Interlake Company. But the partners looked ahead, to the forming of new combinations and the gathering of other fleets under the P. M. house flag. By that time Colonel Pickands was dead, Jay Morse had retired from business and was hunting quail on his Georgia estate at Thomasville, and Samuel Mather, a director in the new steel corporation, was preoccupied with long-range plans in heavy industry. But at their desks in the Western Reserve Building seasoned Henry Dalton and restless Harry Coulby were intent on building up another shipping domain.

In 1904 Pickands Mather had four steamers and two barges, and the company was managing another pair—the *Appomattox* and her tow, the *Santiago*—for the Boston Coal, Dock and Wharf Company of Duluth. It was a small operation compared to the big P. M. marine agency of a few years earlier, and restless Harry Coulby must have been tempted when Judge Gary offered him control of the Pittsburgh Steamship Company. The "Steel Trust

For a hundred years ships built in Great Lakes yards have gone into the water sideways, with spectacular speed and splash. (*Courtesy of E. R. Dowdell.*)

The tug *Jay C. Morse*, built in Buffalo in 1867, survived shipwreck on her first run to Lake Superior.

In the 1890's the overburden was scraped away and the first iron ore was scooped out of the Mesabi pits.

Primitive methods brought up the first shipments from the Mahoning Mine, which has yielded more than 100,000,000 tons of iron ore.

The experimental washing plant at Coleraine, Minnesota, in 1907 was the first attempt at beneficiation of low-grade ores.

Crushing plant under construction at the Volunteer Mine, Marquette Range, in 1926.

The harbor at Erie, Pennsylvania, when schooners still carried coal and iron ore.

In 1894 the Pickands Mather docks at Ashtabula had the newest facility—
a McMyler Car Dumping Machine.

Congestion at the Soo, spring of 1900, when whalebacks were a new design.
(*Courtesy of E. R. Dowdell.*)

THE SOO LOCKS IN 1950

Once Indians carried their canoes around the falls of the St. Marys River. Now the locks lift and lower more than 100,000,000 tons of commerce during the eight-month season.

When snow blanketed the Menominee Range, stableman Tom Johnson at the Baltic location exchanged the ambulance wheels for sled runners.

EARLY SAFETY MEASURES

Safety drills were lifelike and efficient.

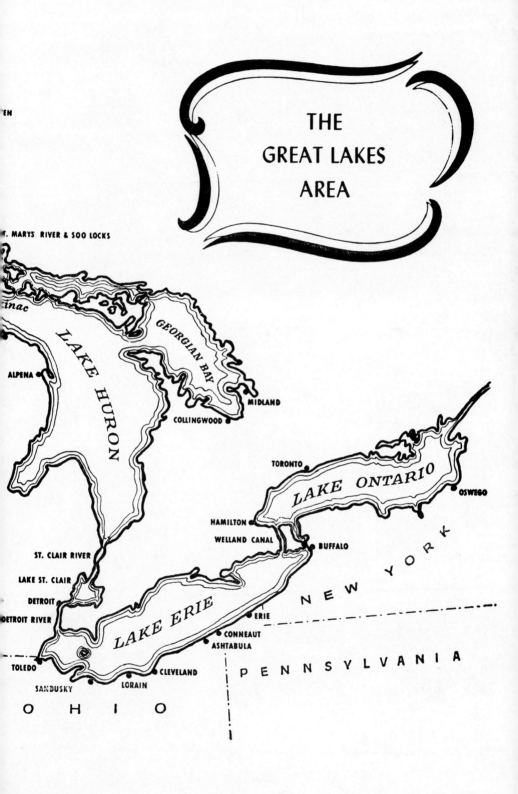

THE
GREAT LAKES
AREA

There has been a steamer *Samuel Mather* on the Lakes since 1887.

The four successive steamers *Samuel Mather* illustrate the evolution of Great Lakes freighters.

Electric lights and electric trains increased production.

UNDERGROUND IN THE VULCAN MINE

Lunchtime on the eleventh level.

Season 1926. Moving the Cyclone Drill into the northwest corner of the Volunteer Mine.

Pickands Mather company picnic, summer of 1926, at

Season 1957. Beneficiation Plant at Tioga No. 2, the mine farthest west on the Mesabi Range. All the ore must undergo washing, and the larger share of it must be given heavy-media treatment, using either the float-sink or cyclone process.

ome of William McLauchlan, North Royalton, Ohio

A one-horse load of ore samples was the total production of the Scranton Mine in the Depression year 1932.

The Embarrass Mine, once a lake bed.

In the Scranton pit—crusher and conveyer loading.

The Toledo Lakefront Dock.

On the Calumet Flats of South Chicago, the Federal Furnace plant of the Interlake Iron Corporation spreads over almost a hundred acres.

In the 1920's ties of business and friendship linked (*left to right*) E. G. Grace, Samuel Mather, J. A. Campbell, Charles M. Schwab, and Henry G. Dalton.

In bracing weather came the fall inspection trip to the mines. *Left to right:* Elton Hoyt, 2nd, E. G. Grace, and Samuel Mather.

INSPECTION, LAKE SUPERIOR MINES

October 1926

Fourth Row: H. G. Heedy, J. P. Weddigen, W. H. Gallagher, Jr., L. C. David, J. M. Shields. *Third Row:* W. A. Rose, P. R. Mather, C. K. Leith, C. E. Robinson, C. H. Munger. *Second Row:* W. P. Chinn, R. H. McMaster, C. A. Buck, Elton Hoyt, 2nd. *First Row:* H. G. Dalton, E. G. Grace, Samuel Mather, J. A. Campbell, C. D. Caldwell.

The 25,000-ton steamer *John Sherwin*, latest addition to the Interlake fleet, went into service in the spring of 1958.

FIRST LOAD AND LAST LOAD

(*top*) The young tree symbolizes the growth of a new mine; (*below*) the broom stands for a "clean sweep" in a mine at the end of production.

Ore fleet in the ice in Whitefish Bay at the opening of navigation.

Ships tied up at Muskegon, Michigan, idled by a steel strike.

On Lake Superior November means
ice-sheathed bows and frozen decks.

In 1883, as its first vessel property, Pickands Mather & Co. acquired part ownership of the wooden steamer *V. H. Ketchum*. Seventy-five years later a painting
of the *Ketchum*, by the late Carl Gaertner, hangs in the observation room of
the steamer *Elton Hoyt 2nd*. The painting shows the P. M. house flag fluttering
from the third (mizzen) mast.

In 1952 the steamer *Elton Hoyt 2nd* was launched at Sparrows Point, Maryland. That summer, with superstructure knocked down for low clearance on the Mississippi and the Illinois Waterway, it passed through the Chicago River.

The town of Hoyt Lakes, Minnesota, was built in the wilderness.

Plant of Erie Mining Company, near the end of construction, 1957.

The wilderness shore at the mouth of Two Islands River, Lake Superior, November 1953.

The mouth of Two Islands River, July 1955. Taconite Harbor under construction.

Taconite Harbor, with a ship loading a cargo of iron-ore pellets at the dock.

Fleet," as sailors knew it, was in need of a strong hand, and Harry Coulby, at thirty-nine, was ready for a long step up the ladder. But he was loyal to his own firm and he believed in its future; he would not leave Pickands Mather. So, in a striking instance of co-operation within the competitive steel industry, he was made president of the Pittsburgh Steamship Company while retaining his Pickands Mather partnership. His charts showed the position of more than a hundred ships, columned manifests listed the cargoes—coal, limestone, and the many grades of iron ore— dock reports traced the movement of vessels into the long, dim, lofty ore docks and under the huge hunched Huletts. The Lakes trade was taking giant strides—forty million tons of bulk cargo in 1904, fifty-eight million in 1905, sixty-six million in 1906, seventy-five million in 1907—and the reins were in the big, firm hands of Harry Coulby.

By this time Coulby had lost all trace of English accent, and his mind had stretched to the dimensions of the biggest mines, the longest docks, the largest transportation system in the world. He spoke shortly, he made quick and firm decisions, and he kept the whole inland commerce in his bulldog head. Fortunate in his associations, he was himself an imposing man. In these years he was discovering, as were the colleagues around him, his own capacities. The Lakes would not see another man like him, but the order and dispatch which he developed would mark the trade for years to come.

Harry Coulby set up annual meetings at the beginning of the navigation season. In March, when ice still locked the northern channels, he met with the fleet captains, discussing schedules, loading depths, dock capacities, navigation problems. Under his leadership plans for inside and outside courses were developed; when the system was generally adopted in 1912, captains could go to sleep without the old dread of collision in the crowded navigation lanes. With the engineers he discussed schedules, fuel consumption, and maintenance of equipment. With the chief cooks, he discussed equipment in the galleys and stores in the pantries. In all these meetings the big short-spoken man was ready to hear any complaint, question, or suggestion, and when he had a proposal to make he soon got the men to pushing it as their own idea. After a few seasons he brought together the officers of the two fleets, Pittsburgh Steamship and Pickands Mather, in his annual meetings.

In the early years of the century the independent steel companies, seeing the necessity of a stable ore supply, were beginning to invest in their own reserves. For the Lackawanna Steel Company at Buffalo, Pickands Mather in 1905 purchased two iron-ore properties on the Gogebic Range—the neighboring Sunday Lake and Brotherton mines whose deep shafts would eventually join. The firm immediately began operating these mines for Lackawanna Steel, an operation which would be continued in later years when Lackawanna was absorbed by the Bethlehem Steel Company.

In this same year Pickands Mather organized the Mesaba Steamship Company and began contracting for four big carriers —the *Amasa Stone, Samuel Mather, Jay C. Morse,* and *D. O. Mills.* In 1906 the firm took over management of the Provident and Acme companies. And in this year Pickands Mather organized the Lackawanna Steamship Company, contracting for eight freighters at a total cost of $2,225,000. The steamers *Hemlock, Odanah, Calumet, Cyprus,* and *Verona* all came out in 1907. Three other vessels were added to the Lackawanna fleet in the year following.

Of the six big steamers launched in 1907, one was lost before the season ended. The *Cyprus,* a 420-foot carrier, went into service late in September; a shipyard strike at Lorain, Ohio, had slowed her construction. Under Captain F. B. Huyck she made a run to Lake Superior and brought back a load of iron ore. It was the only cargo she ever delivered. Back up the Lakes in ballast, she loaded 7,103 tons of ore at Superior, clearing the harbor on the morning of October 9. It was heavy autumn weather, with seas breaking over the long cargo deck. Apparently the *Cyprus* had no tarpaulins, or if she had they were still stored away in the forepeak. For two days the vessel wallowed on through heaving seas, her unsealed hatches taking in tons of water. Thirty miles west of Whitefish Point, just after nightfall on October 11, she pitched over in a sickening list. Her cargo had shifted and there was no way to get her back on even keel. Helpless, with her propeller out of water and the seas pouring over, she sank like a stone. Four men of the crew of twenty-three clung to a life raft. All night they drifted in the stormy darkness. The wind carried them to shore—and to the white chaos of surf. Numb and exhausted, three of them were washed off and drowned. Only one survivor, second mate Charles Pitz, was left to report the loss of a big freighter that saw just three weeks of service.

At the beginning of the navigation season of 1913 came a step which made Pickands Mather the second largest fleet operator on the Lakes, a position it has held ever since. Organizing the Interlake Steamship Company, it brought together all the vessels formerly operated by the firm—the Lackawanna Steamship Company with seven ships, the Mesaba Steamship Company with four ships, the old Interlake Company with two ships, and the Huron Barge Company with two ships. To these fifteen vessels were added the total of seven ships of the Provident, Standard, and Acme companies. Finally the new Interlake Steamship Company bought seventeen vessels from the Gilchrist Transportation Company. There were then thirty-nine ships under the P. M. house flag, and for the first time appeared the now-familiar white lettering on the dark red bow:

SAMUEL MATHER

THE

INTERLAKE

STEAMSHIP CO.

In this memorable year the Lakes trade for the first time moved a hundred million tons of bulk cargo; it also suffered its worst natural disaster. The terrific storm of November 8-11, 1913, totally destroyed thirteen big carriers and took the lives of 235 seamen. The new Interlake Steamship Company lost two ships, the *Argus* and the *Hydrus,* both formerly of the Gilchrist Transportation Company; and it suffered serious damage to the *Victory* and the *D. O. Mills.* No other storm in Great Lakes history was so extensive, so long continued, and so fearful in its force. (The narrative of its destruction will appear in a later chapter.) Nearly half a century has passed since the November hurricane of 1913, but it is still the Big Storm.

The trenches and shell holes of World War I were four thousand miles away from the Great Lakes, but the urgency of war production stained the skies of Lake ports and shipping lanes. In 1916 the Interlake Steamship Company bought thirteen vessels from the Cleveland Steamship Company, and in a further addition to its fleet built its first 600-foot ship, the *Henry G. Dalton.* The movement of bulk cargo swelled to 117,000,000 tons in 1916. At the same time 508 rivet gangs were working day and night in Great Lakes shipyards, building freighters for ocean service. At the end of Lake navigation in 1917 sailors watched scores of new ships hurrying toward the Welland Canal and the salt water of the St. Lawrence before winter ice should lock them in. They were a new kind of Lakes-built vessel, stubby, high-riding, with a raised fo'c's'le and a raised poop and a tall stack jutting from the midship superstructure. This was a design foreign to the Lakes and the Lakes trade; these wartime ships were built for service on salt water. Two hundred sixty-one feet long, they could barely squeeze through the old Welland Canal locks. Because they were built on inland waters they were all named as Lakers—*Lake Crystal, Lake Hemlock, Lake Harris, Lake Folcraft, Lake Licoco.* More than two hundred of them were sent out to merchant duty in the time of war. Some were sunk by submarines, some tossed in the cold gray seas of the North Atlantic, some plowed the blue waters of the Caribbean and the Gulf of Mexico. After the war was over scores of them, with white letters $_{SB}^{US}$ (United States Shipping Board) on their abrupt black funnels, plodded from Canada to Cuba, and a dozen ports in between, in the coastal trade.

With the end of the war the United States Congress passed the Volstead Act, and the smuggling of a few bottles of contraband was a sporting and profitable sideline in coastal ships and in Lake vessels carrying Canadian wheat down the Lakes. In the 1920's the Interlake fleet carried large tonnages of wheat, oats, rye, and barley, loading American grain in Duluth-Superior and South Chicago and a bigger volume of Canadian grain at Fort William-Port Arthur. At Buffalo the Federal inspectors came aboard. They walked past coal passers bent over pails of suds, washing sweat rags on the fantail, and looked into coal bunkers, flashing their lights over dusty I beams and into dark corners. They came up, went forward, and walked past deck hands bent over pails of suds, washing socks on the foredeck. They went down into the forepeak, poked around the paint room, looked through the chain locker and into big coils of mooring line. Then they gave the vessel clearance and went ashore. Aft and forward the men wrung out their laundry, removed sudsy bottles of Johnny Walker or Canadian Club, and poured the soapy water into the harbor. Sailors were never so zealous at their laundry as during the Prohibition years.

The Lakes trade averaged more than a hundred million tons annually during the 1920's. In 1923 the Bethlehem Steel Company took a long step, acquiring the Lackawanna Steel Company along with other steel companies and their mining properties; Pickands Mather was made the Lakes dispatcher and Lake Superior district mine operator of the Bethlehem Steel Company. In this same year The Youngstown Sheet and Tube Company acquired the properties of The Steel and Tube Company of America and of the Brier Hill Steel Company. In the following year Youngstown Sheet and Tube, in which Samuel Mather had acquired large interests, assigned to Pickands Mather the management of its iron-ore properties on the Marquette, Gogebic, Mesabi, and Cuyuna ranges. These were the beginnings of a long alliance between Pickands Mather and the Bethlehem and Youngstown companies—an alliance which would be put to a critical test in the decade to come.

To move an increasing production of ore, the Interlake Steamship Company built in the middle twenties six new freighters of the 600-foot class. One of them was the *Samuel Mather,* the fourth vessel to bear that name. Though earlier *Samuel Mather*s had experienced the hazards of the Lakes—one going down in fog in Lake Superior, one lost with all hands in an autumn storm on Lake Huron—the name was the most persistent in the Lake fleets; there had been a *Samuel Mather* carrying cargo since 1887.

The first master of the *Mather* was blustery Peter M. Cartwright, who later brought out the new *Colonel James Pickands.* Captain Cartwright was a huge, hearty man who did everything on a big scale—eating, drinking, working, laughing, praising, blaming. When George Callahan, later manager of the P. M. Marine Department, was a young vessel agent at Duluth, he was wakened by the telephone before daylight one Sunday morning.

"George!" boomed Captain Cartwright, who had just docked the *Mather* at Superior. "I've got a toothache. Had it for two days. A toothache as big as a house. It's driving me crazy."

George Callahan promised to get a dentist. He called back to Captain Cartwright, arranging to take him to the dentist's office at 6:00 A.M. When they got there the dentist, still puffy-eyed with sleep, peered into the captain's mouth.

"I think I can save this tooth—"

"No!" roared the captain. "I want it out!"

"All right," the dentist said. "It's your tooth."

He hooked up the tank of nitrous oxide and gave him a full dose. Still Captain Cartwright thrashed around in the chair.

With a faint grim smile the dentist gave him another dose, and finally a third. The captain was more restless than ever.

At last the puzzled dentist said, "Captain, I can't get this gas to take effect on you. Have you been drinking anything?"

"Drinking—" boomed the captain, "I've been trying to kill this toothache. I drank two quarts since we left the Soo."

"If I could deaden this—"

"What are you waiting for?" the captain cried. "Just take your pliers and yank it out."

Another of the new ships in the later twenties was the famous *Harry Coulby*, which on her maiden trip delivered a record cargo of 14,098 gross tons of ore to Cleveland and then proceeded to break her own record by loading 14,471 tons of Gogebic ore at Ashland. For seven years, 1928-35, the *Coulby* loaded the largest cargoes on the Lakes. Again in 1937 and in 1940 and 1941 she held the record. In her final record cargo in 1941 she carried 16,333 gross tons of iron ore.

In 1929 the Interlake Steamship Company bought the five vessels of the Youngstown Steamship Company. This transaction made Youngstown Sheet and Tube a substantial Interlake stockholder, and it marked a new step in the enduring business relationship between Pickands Mather and The Youngstown Sheet and Tube Company. Interlake then had a fleet of forty-nine ships. There was pride in the achievement behind him when Harry Coulby went to England to spend the Christmas holidays. His sudden death in London and his burial at Claypole village kept him from seeing his fleet idled by the Depression years that were about to come.

CHAPTER 9

Men of the Menominee

THE LEGAL FEE for marriage was two dollars, but the minister who married the heir to the Chapin Mine got two hundred thousand. After the Civil War the Chapin brothers went north from Lower Michigan and entered a forty-acre tract in rough woods between the Menominee River and Lake Antoine; it was the site of the future town of Iron Mountain. In the land office they claimed it for $1.25 an acre. But back in Lower Michigan they wondered why they had sunk fifty dollars in a tangle of cedar and scrub oak. After his wedding one of the brothers handed the clergyman their deed for the forty acres. The preacher, considering himself swindled, packed the deed with his old sermons and forgot it. A few years later, in 1880, the big Chapin Mine was found. It produced a quarter of a million tons in 1882, and the Chapins were claiming royalties, though they had no certificate of title. A young lawyer traced the clergyman to a town in California, and the preacher found the unrecorded deed in his barrel of sermons. After a prolonged and strenuous lawsuit, while the mine was yielding millions of dollars' worth of iron ore, the Chapins settled with the minister for $200,000.

It was not scientists but woodsmen who discovered the riches of the Menominee. The geologists Credner, Pumpelly, and Brooks tramped over millions of tons of ore, vainly searching for formations like those of the Marquette district. Dr. Credner found outcrops of silicious ore which he judged unprofitable; Pumpelly and Brooks, selecting 50,000 acres for the Lake Superior Ship Canal Company, considered saw logs the only wealth of the Menominee. So the geologists looked for timber and left the woodsmen to find fortunes underground.

Shortly after the Civil War Thomas and Bartley Breen, pushing up from Menominee in search of profitable timber, found rich blue hematite between the Menominee and Sturgeon rivers. There in 1872 Dr. N. P. Hulst began exploration for the Milwaukee Iron Company and developed the famous Vulcan Mine. In the smoke-hazed fall of 1871, when the forests of Oconto County were burning, John L. Buell and wandering Jack Armstrong were camped at a spring on the site of the future town of Quinnesec. While Armstrong was cooking supper Buell scrambled up the western bluff and found an iron outcrop; his test pit was the beginning of the Quinnesec Mine. In the winter of 1874 Buell hauled the first Quinnesec ore—fifty-five tons—by sled and wagon through blackened woods to the Lake port of Menominee. In the furnace there they provided the high quality of Quinnesec ore.

In 1877 the first train arrived at Quinnesec from Escanaba, over the Chicago and Northwestern line, and in 1880 the railroad was extended to Iron Mountain. Late in the spring of 1878 an Irish station agent named Kilgallen splashed through a cedar swamp and discovered an outcrop of iron ore. It was the site of the Norway Mine. A corduroy road laid through the swamp became the main street of the town, with its buildings stilted upon cedar poles. In summer the water was covered with a green scum and the bullfrogs bellowed all night long. The Norway Mine— later a part of the Penn group, along with the Vulcan, Cyclops, and Curry, operated by Pickands Mather—was a rich deposit. The underground workings spread and the town grew—until it caved into the green-scummed swamp. Then a new town was built on dry land, and under the old townsite, at the richest point on the hematite formation, the great Aragon ore bed was found.

By 1878 there were five producing properties in the new district: the Breen, Cyclops, Norway, Vulcan, and Quinnesec. The railroad company had doubted whether it would be profitable to go into the district, but construction was paid for in the first full year of operation. Since then the stretch of track from Escanaba to Iron Mountain has paid for many hundreds of miles of railroad on the western prairies.

The next year the great Chapin Mine was discovered. It shipped 35,000 tons in 1880 and nearly 300,000 four years later. A notoriously wet mine, its continued workings were made possible by a big Cornish pump with a capacity of 3,000 gallons a minute. Dr. Hulst, who developed the mine, believed that there was more ore east of the Chapin; either the Chapin deposit extended eastward or another rich deposit lay beyond it. In 1887 the Pewabic Mining Company was formed and exploration began. The company had extensive land but little money, and diamond drilling ate rapidly into their capital. After three months the Carnegie Brothers and Company of Pittsburgh came into the venture; for $100,000 they bought a half interest in the exploration. This was the Carnegies' first investment in the Lake Superior iron fields, and its success led them into the other ranges. Their extensive interests were later assembled in the Oliver Iron Mining Company.

The Pewabic exploration was limited to two years. After twenty-two months the prospect looked dark, but Dr. Hulst remained confident. In the beginning of the twenty-third month the drill cores brought up what he had been waiting for. The Pewabic Mine was found, a deposit of soft red and blue hematite of remarkably high quality. Wrote the Michigan Mines statistician in 1897 of the Pewabic: "Shipments for an entire season have given iron averaging 66 per cent and phosphorous .007 per cent. This has probably never been equalled by any other mine in America."

The Pewabic was opened in 1887, with Pickands Mather as its sales agent. The firm later took over its operation and the mine produced nearly ten million tons before it was exhausted in 1918. In 1889 the firm acquired an interest in the Hemlock River Mining Company and began exploration up the Paint River and the dim and winding Hemlock. A property discovered by leathery old Matthew Gibson and his son Thoburn on the banks of the Hemlock was acquired in 1890, and the versatile Jack Armstrong, whom the P. M. partners had known in Marquette, was placed in charge of operations. To assist him came two men from Republic, Michigan—Charles E. Lawrence and William H. Jobe. They hired a crew, gathered equipment, and built a settlement just west of the workings; at first called Hemlock, it was soon renamed Amasa in honor of Samuel Mather's son. The Hemlock Mine shipped 35,000 tons in 1891. This was the beginning of operations which in thirty years carried Pickands Mather to an important position on the range.

In 1892 restless Jack Armstrong joined the rush to the Mesabi, and methodic young C. E. Lawrence was left in charge. Like the original P. M. men, Charles Edwin Lawrence had begun his career in the iron business in Cleveland. As a boy of fifteen he became a messenger in the office of the Republic Iron Company, and from there he went north to the big Republic Mine on the Marquette Range. A stocky, serious young man of twenty-two, he arrived in the Upper Peninsula in May 1888; there was ice in the Michigamme River when he came and snow stayed in the woods till the second week of June. After two years keeping books at the Republic Mine, he went to work in the office of the Fitch Iron Company, in which Pickands Mather was interested, at Ishpeming. The Fitch Mine was opened in 1890 on the site of an old exploration. It soon closed down, after shipping a modest 40,000 tons, and Lawrence was ready for a new assignment. He was sent to Amasa as bookkeeper for the Hemlock Mine. When the Hemlock was idled by the Panic of 1893, Lawrence went to Duluth and took a clerical job in the office of A. B. Wolvin. A year later he was keeping books for the Consolidated Mines that had come into Rockefeller's control, and then for the Minnesota Iron Company whose mines would soon pass into the hands of United States Steel. All this time Lawrence was learning about mines and men. When business revived on the Menominee in the late nineties he returned to the Pickands Mather properties there.

In 1900 the newly formed United States Steel Corporation absorbed the Minnesota Iron Company, in which Pickands Mather had important interests. Pickands Mather then began to expand its own ore properties. In 1901 the firm organized the Corsica and the Hobart iron companies on the Mesabi and bought a substantial interest in the Odanah Iron Company on the Gogebic. In the same year it formed The Verona Mining Company, under the direction of Charles E. Lawrence, to develop prospects in the Menominee. In the next decade Lawrence became a familiar figure in the scattered locations, driving his buckboard or cutter from Amasa to Quinnesec, from Crystal Falls to Iron River, clattering over the plank bridge and disappearing up the long hill to his home in Caspian, Michigan. He was elected president of the Lake Superior Mining Institute in 1915, and for years he served as president of the Caspian Village Council.

Development of the Menominee Range moved from east to west. On the west side of Iron County iron lands were tied up through the 1890's in railroad litigation. When settlement was made at the beginning of the century, Lawrence gathered in options on many properties and The Verona Mining Company proceeded to explore them. That long, arduous, and costly task resulted in the opening up of the Baltic, Caspian, Fogarty, and Bengal mines.

The railroads had title to some of these iron lands; other titles were held by speculators, lumbermen, and homesteaders. One of the homesteaders was a penniless Irish immigrant, William Young, who had come to America in 1866. After three years in Detroit he worked his way on a schooner to Marquette, where he took a job tending a charcoal furnace in the woods. When the furnace closed down in 1873 Young crossed Lake Superior and chopped timber for the Canadian Pacific Railway. Hearing of discoveries of iron ore along the Menominee, he came to the new range, riding muleback over the tote roads of the logging companies. He arrived on the site of the town of Stambaugh, Michigan, in 1882 and took a job constructing buildings at the old Riverton Mine. He cleared the first street in Iron River and filed on a homestead where the Bengal Mine was eventually developed. As the largest fee owner of the mine he received a steady flow of royalties in his declining years.

In the 1880's a political rivalry divided the eastern and western districts of Iron County. County meetings had been held in Iron River, but Crystal Falls, a great lumbering center and the supplier of thirty logging camps and a dozen iron mines, was determined to be the county seat. According to a persistent legend some men from Crystal Falls came to Iron River and engaged the local officials in a poker game. While the game was in progress another delegation from Crystal Falls packed up the county records, loaded them in a boxcar, and shipped them to the Mastodon Mine. From there, with an escort of jubilant citizens, they hauled them in a wagon to Crystal Falls, which has remained the seat of Iron County.

The Mastodon Mine was older than the county rivalry. In 1879 the far-wandering Jack Armstrong discovered iron ore on lands selected by Raphael Pumpelly for the Canal Company. Two years later John M. Longyear, trudging through the swamp south of Crystal Falls, found an outcrop of "clean hard hematite" rising five feet above the surface and a hundred feet long. Rooted in the outcrop of ore was a big dead cedar trunk, with red chalk written on a weathered blaze, *Bojoo Nitche*—Chippewa for "Good morning, my friend." This beckoning discovery attracted Ed-

ward Breitung of Marquette, who organized the Mastodon Iron
Company and shipped the first ore in 1882. After the Panic of
1893 the mine was idle for twenty years. In 1913 the Balkan
Mining Company, organized by Pickands Mather, acquired the
Mastodon property and later developed it along with the neighboring Balkan and Judson mines. The Balkan-Judson yielded a
steady production for twenty years.

The old Hemlock Mine, the foundation stone of Pickands
Mather interests in the Menominee, closed up in 1919, and a
broom rode down to Escanaba on its last carloads of ore. Under
C. E. Lawrence exploration had begun on the Warner property,
a mile south of the Hemlock; in two years this property was developed from homestead land to a producing mine. A few years
earlier Pickands Mather had bought the Wilkinson lands west
of Crystal Falls; on one of its forties their explorers found an
extensive body of ore. A mine was projected and partially developed. After World War II it was thought that there would be a
need for its particular grade of ore, but the demand did not
develop and the property is being held in reserve. The mine is the
Lawrence, named for the superintendent of P. M. properties in
the Menominee.

Charles E. Lawrence was concerned with men as well as with
mines. By 1908 he had supervision of twelve hundred employees
on the ranges. At the Baltic location he built the first clubhouse
for miners in the Upper Peninsula. A roomy frame building, it
had baths, barbershop, bowling alleys, billiard tables, card room,
reading room, and music room with Gramaphone and Pianola.
Open seven days a week to miners and their families, it was so
successful that Pickands Mather built a second clubhouse at the
Caspian location in 1912. The rooms buzzed with a babel of
voices—English, German, Italian, Polish, Croatian—and red-stained
boots tapped time to the music of the electric piano. For single
miners the clubhouse offered a place of relaxation and enjoy-
ment, a kind of home that was not provided by the boardinghouses where tiers of bunks lined the walls and meals were served
in three sittings. Even the friendly boardinghouse of one-armed
George Teller, with a bottle of wine at each place on the long
table, did not invite conversation. The miners ate earnestly and
in silence, like the loggers in the woods camps. By Saturday night
they were restless to get into town for a few hours in the saloons
and amusement halls. On Sunday there was Mass in the native-

language church, and then back to the crowded boardinghouse. The clubhouse gave a new dimension to their lives, and it made them American. Cornishmen, Croatians, Italians, Finns, and Poles all met in the clubrooms and shared their leisure together.

Still there were national rivalries that smoldered like peat fire in the woods, ready to flare up when the wind came. On a Saturday afternoon in Caspian there was a Slav wedding at the Polish church, followed by a boisterous Old Country dance at the company clubhouse. Beer flowed like a river there and accordions filled the room with music. The girls wore bright native costumes and flowers in their hair. The couples danced to lively Polish airs, singing together on the choruses. There was a dinner plate on the table; each man threw a silver dollar on it for the bride—if the plate broke he had a free dance with her. At ten o'clock the hilarity attracted a gang of Croatian miners on their way home from town. At midnight, when the wedding feast was ready, the visitors refused to leave. The dance turned into a free-for-all, Poles and Croatians slugging it out around the disputed table. In that turmoil the bride and groom slipped away without a taste of their wedding supper.

Superintendent Lawrence was an orderly man who was determined to bring order and restraint into the raw iron country. On a Monday morning he told his young assistant, A. J. Scott: "Take the team and go down to those boardinghouses and pick up all those wine bottles and beer kegs. Throw them in a deep place in the river. I want them out of sight." A stiff-collared, big-nosed, strict-minded man, he tirelessly condemned cigarettes and whisky, though he talked around a cigar in his mouth. Moderation, he insisted, was the key to health, happiness, and long life. One evening at a school board meeting in Caspian a fellow member referred to him as an old man. At the words Lawrence jumped to his feet and turned a handspring on the platform. As he sat down his deep voice boomed: "Never call me an old man!"

But he did grow old. He was not impervious to the strain of travel in all weather and the unending problems of getting ore out of the deep, contorted folds of the Menominee. He retired in 1932 and was succeeded as superintendent of Pickands Mather mines in the district by William G. Hanson. Known over the range as "Wink," Hanson was an intent man always blinking, as though he had just stepped out of a mine mouth. He had the hard experience of superintending idle properties during the Depression years, but he saw the skips come up again when the lean times passed.

For years C. E. Lawrence had a running argument with a colleague who will be long remembered in the North. Stephen Royce, Pickands Mather geologist, knew the deep folds of earth almost as though he had formed them, but Lawrence was not impressed; he remembered the blindness of early scientists on the Menominee. "You know, Steve," he would say in his humorless, gravelly voice, "the bushwhackers, bartenders, and river rats around here have found ten times as much iron ore as you geologists." And then he would walk away, leaving Royce to argue with someone else.

Stephen Royce had strong opinions—about politics, economics, religion, medicine, tobacco, food, firearms, automobiles, and air travel. He loved argument, and he was probably the most articulate man in the whole north country. The son of a famed Harvard philosopher, Josiah Royce, he had come to the iron country as a young mining engineer; in later years he served as a roving geologist for mining companies. As a child he had suffered from asthma, but he developed a huge chest and powerful shoulders. He was a tireless swimmer, an ardent collector of rifles, shotguns, and revolvers, a prodigious eater, a furious driver of automobiles, a lover of the northern woods and waters. He kept a racing shell on Fortune Lake. After a session in his office at Crystal Falls he would get into that craft, almost swamping it with his bulky frame, and pull over the water in an arduous race with himself. Or he would drive to a lonely lake and go swimming all afternoon— covering miles with his trudgeon stroke, then floating on his back while he smoked cigarettes and gobbled candy. Once at Gogebic Lake some men found his empty car at the end of the road and footprints ending in the water, but the big wide lake was empty. They sent for the sheriff to report a drowning. When the sheriff arrived, hours later, something was moving far out on the lake. It came nearer, a big dark head and a pair of powerful shoulders. Out of the water walked dripping Stephen Royce, ready to eat, smoke, and argue.

In 1936 Steve Royce and Andy Leith, son of the geologist who had followed the iron-bearing series throughout the Lake Superior region, were sent to Labrador to make a preliminary survey of iron-ore lands for Pickands Mather. They had to fly in—there was no other way—though Royce had positive opinions, with statistics to support them, about the hazards of air travel. When he learned that they were to be provided with $100 parachutes he looked into that subject, finding that there were better parachutes at $200. He demanded the best. The two men got there safely, landing at Knob Lake far up in the northern wilds, and they spent two months in that vast and lonely country. With gasoline hand drills probing into the surface drift they got a glimpse of part of the immense Labrador Trough of iron ore. Back in civilization, his parachute still untested, Royce remarked that he had stood on a range of iron ore that might become a new Mesabi. His excitement was tempered, however, by a belief that the major tonnage was underground and that its production would be hampered by the sub-Arctic permafrost.

Although the report from Royce and Leith offered luring possibilities, this was not a time for a bold venture in mineral exploration. From across the Atlantic came rumblings of the approaching World War II. Uncertain world conditions argued against a large financial risk; at the same time low-cost iron ore was in plentiful supply on Lake Superior. With ore available for any foreseeable demand, the industry was not drawn to a remote and difficult new source of supply. Consequently Pickands Mather, already well along in its research for extracting iron ore from Minnesota taconite, withdrew from the Labrador area. After World War II The M. A. Hanna Company took up a concession there, in collaboration with the Hollinger gold interests.

Stephen Royce went on geologizing in the Menominee, until his death in 1954. But he had seen iron lands which in time would rival the ranges of Lake Superior.

CHAPTER 10

The Strewn Shore

THE YEAR 1913, which saw the forming of The Interlake Steamship Co., was a somber season on the Lakes. In February thousands of Christmas trees washed up on the shore of Door Peninsula in Lake Michigan. Those trees, never strung with colored lights and tinsel, were all that was found of the schooner *Rouse Simmons,* which three months earlier had sailed from Manistique, Michigan, with a deck load of evergreens for Chicago. The three-master had scudded into Lake Michigan in a rising gale on December 3. Next morning the Coast Guard at Sturgeon Bay saw a schooner with tattered sails and a distress signal at her masthead. The Sturgeon Bay Station had only a small boat, too small to live in a heavy sea, but they telephoned to Kewaunee. In their big surfboat the Kewaunee crew put out. Once they glimpsed a schooner with bare masts and decks swept clear. Then she vanished in the blizzard. That was the last of the *Rouse Simmons,* until the Christmas trees washed up in February.

When navigation began in April 1913 veteran shipmasters found more ice than they had ever seen in Lake Superior—for miles beyond Whitefish Bay they crunched through ice fields. On the eighteenth of April the steamer *Uganda* foundered in the Straits of Mackinac, her hull cut through by drift ice. In the same week the *Kearsarge* put in to Mackinac with a crushed bow; her grain cargo was lightered and she underwent repair. On May 1, acres of ice drifted in Whitefish Bay. No regular schedule was begun on Lake Superior until the third week of May, and then vast chill banks of fog hung over the Upper Lakes. Meanwhile torrential rains washed out railroad tracks in the lower harbors.

This was the beginning of a season which ended in the Big Storm, the greatest disaster in the history of the Lakes. It took a somber toll of ships and men. Yet 1913 was also a record season, the first year in which the fleets carried a hundred million tons of bulk cargo.

On Saturday, November 8, 1913, an Interlake freighter was upbound in Lake Erie, laden deep with iron ore. It was a still, mild morning, a long plume of smoke trailing from the funnel and the lake lying lead-colored under a gray sky. "When you see sky under Pelee Island," said the leathery old watchman, "there's hard weather coming."

There it was, a mirage across the leaden lake, the dark long line of Pelee, with a line of sky between it and the water.

The watchman held a match to his pipe and began talking about the summer past. "I never saw so many 'Canadian Soldiers.' We came up the Maumee River on a warm night, not a stir of wind anywhere, and they were around us like a snowstorm. The decks were slippery with those wind-blown insects. Under the bulkhead lights they were piled up three feet deep. We shoveled them over the side, and they kept on piling up, faster than we could shovel." His eyes went back to the cold gray water and the line of light under Pelee Island. "Seems like that island is hanging in the sky."

At Buffalo that Saturday the Interlake steamer *Argus* (formerly the *L. Woodruff* of the Gilchrist company) was loading coal for South Chicago. It was warm for November, the oily harbor water sloshing slowly under an overcast sky. At dusk, with the port lights winking in a rising wind, they cleared the harbor.

Daylight came through heavy clouds and the *Argus,* deep-laden, was rolling in long gray seas. By noon a gale had lifted Lake Erie into torn white ridges. The *Argus* groaned and wallowed through. Snow came; there was no glimpse of Pelee Island. It was dark before they got to Livingstone Channel in the Detroit River. With the engines cut to half speed, Captain Paul Gutch peered through the blizzard for the channel lights. The wind blew all night, with snow swirling at the pilothouse windows. Captain Gutch stayed on the bridge while the mates relieved each other. He would sleep when they got through the St. Clair River; the wind should spend itself by morning.

Two hours before daylight the *Argus* cleared Port Huron, its

lights quickly lost in the storm. Lake Huron was heaving. The
Argus dipped and lifted, pitched and rolled. Briefly they picked
up the lightship, tossing in the dark; then there was only the
whine of wind in the rigging and the smash of seas across the
main deck. A dirty daylight came, and it showed nothing but
blown snow and smoking seas. No one went aft for breakfast.
They made some coffee in the pilothouse and looked down at
the seas breaking white across the deck. Keeping off the unseen
shore, Captain Gutch tried to head into the wind. But the wind
was shifting. It blasted in from the northeast, then with a fury of
snow it came at them from northwest. Thudding into solid water,
the *Argus* lost headway and swung into the trough of the sea.
The wind came louder. Like an avalanche a wave buried the
stern and raged across the deck. The ship rose sluggishly and
Captain Gutch saw the tattered tarpaulins on the forward
hatches. Beside him the wheelsman was spinning a dead wheel
while the ship lurched and wallowed. Outside a new sea rose up,
up. With a thud like a collision it landed. As he was hurled across
the pilothouse the captain heard the crash of glass and the roar
of water. He knew his ship was doomed.

On the evening of that same Saturday, November 8, in a
stinging snowstorm, the Interlake steamer *Hydrus* (formerly the
Gilchrist freighter *R. E. Shuck*) locked through the Soo with a
cargo of iron ore. The captain was glad to leave Lake Superior
behind as he had been in snow for twenty-four hours; the weather
should improve on the Lower Lakes. But at the Soo storm signals were up, two red lanterns with a white lantern between—
a whole gale warning—and in the Coast Guard Station the wire-
less was stuttering about a hurricane. But cargoes had to be
moved, in hard as well as easy weather.

It was not so bad in the river channel, though a northeast
wind snatched the whistle-sound away and Captain Lowe kept
a double lookout peering through the snow. Ahead of the *Hydrus*
was the *J. H. Sheadle,* and ahead of her was the big Canadian
freighter *J. H. Carruthers,* new that season and now on her third
trip, laden with wheat from Fort William, Ontario. At Detour
the *Carruthers* stopped to take on fuel. She would not need it;
the ship would be on the bottom of Lake Huron in a few hours.

Out on Lake Huron the *Hydrus* lost the lights of the *Sheadle,*
and daybreak showed only the torn crests of angry seas. Off

Thunder Bay the wind howled in from north-northeast and the *Hydrus* shifted course to run before it. She ran hard, groaning and creaking, and the seas smoked over her long deck. Off Saginaw Bay, at the widest part of Lake Huron, the wind brought a raging blizzard. In that blindness Captain Lowe took deep sea soundings: they showed him three miles outside the limits of the downbound course. Now the wind was dead north, but the seas swept in from the northeast. Two storms were meeting, with the laboring *Hydrus* caught between them. The daylight waned and from the pilothouse the after lights were a distant glimmer. Back there a sea crashed over, bursting the galley door. It swept the supper off the messroom table. Solid water poured through the passageway. Another sea broke over. It smashed the engine-room skylight, tore off the mushroom stems of the ventilators, and flooded the boiler room. Sloshing through black water, the stokers heaved wet coal onto the fires.

Rolling wildly, her pumps and siphons sobbing, the *Hydrus* was turned around and headed into the wind. For hours she struggled on a northeast course, barely holding her own. Cross seas kept smashing over and the ship grew sluggish. She fell into the trough and could not rise. When the lights went out the great seas pounded her down into darkness.

In the Pickands Mather dock office at Ashtabula, Superintendent E. O. Whitney peered out at the blizzard. He knew about November weather; once master of the whaleback *John Ericson,* he had been on the Lakes for years. He knew that ships would be in trouble before this storm was over.

It was Sunday, November 9, and they were unloading in the slips, the big Huletts dipping and rising in the swirl of snow. By evening the gale had become a hurricane. Snow raged across the harbor, and when Captain Whitney tried to telegraph his dock report to Cleveland, the wires were down. He tried the telephone. It was dead. He gathered up his dock reports and took the train to Cleveland.

On Monday morning in the Pickands Mather office the Vessel Department men looked out at the storm-tossed lake. Their ships were in trouble, and they were powerless to help. They could only wait for word while repair crews labored with hundreds of miles of broken communication lines. All day they waited, and all the next day. On Wednesday the long storm was over, the ragged storm signals came down, the sun shafted through tattered clouds onto the heaving lake. But no ships arrived. All over the Lakes shipping was stunned by the big storm; it was a week before cargoes moved again. Meanwhile came the somber news: nine big ships lost or wrecked on Lake Huron, other vessels lost on Lake Michigan and Lake Superior. Of the Interlake fleet, the historic *Victory* was aground in Livingstone Channel in the Detroit River. The big *D. O. Mills* was on the sand at Harbor Beach, Michigan, below Saginaw Bay. The *Argus* and the *Hydrus* were sunk in Lake Huron with no survivors. Wreckage from the two vessels had washed up on the Canadian shore near Goderich, Ontario.

Captain Whitney was sent by the P. M. office to search for bodies from the *Argus* and *Hydrus*. With crew lists and identifications he went to Detroit, consulted with William Livingstone of the Lake Carriers Association, and proceeded to Goderich. With some Lake Carriers men he boarded the Canadian government steamer *Lampton* to begin a search from Kettle Point to Cove Island. Though the lost vessels had foundered on courses near the American shore, the west-running seas washed bodies and wreckage all the way to Canada. On the beach near the villages of Kincardine and Southampton, Captain Whitney identified hatch covers from the *Argus* and the *Hydrus*. There were bodies nearby. Four oars and a life raft from the *Argus* came ashore just south of Kincardine. In ten somber days they picked up a hundred bodies and took them to Goderich for identification.

There the searching party heard grim stories of the storm. The *H. M. Hanna*, upbound on Lake Huron, was cast on a reef near Port Austin Light. Seas smashed her after cabin, carrying away the starboard lifeboat, and tore off her pilothouse. When the captain saw Port Austin Light he dropped his port anchor to bring her head into the wind, but she slammed on the reef and broke in two. For thirty hours the crew huddled in the flooded engine room. When the wind and sea subsided they lowered the port lifeboat and pulled through the surf, leaving the shattered ship behind them.

Soon after the *Hanna* had passed Port Huron another freighter of the Hanna fleet, the *Charles S. Price,* loaded with coal, steamed out of the St. Clair River and into Lake Huron. She was found two days later, floating upside down a few miles off the Michigan shore. Around the body of her chief engineer was a life jacket from the package freighter *Regina,* which had been reported missing. This mute evidence told of a collision in the raging sea, of men from both crews struggling in the water and grasping at life buoys while their ships went under.

Near St. Martin's Island in northern Lake Michigan a Coast Guard party found the barge *Plymouth,* adrift and lifeless. When the towline parted and the cabins were demolished her crew of seven had lashed themselves to the rigging to keep from being swept into the sea. Their frozen bodies were found with the lashings locked in ice.

On Lake Superior the *George Stephenson,* upbound in ballast, had passed Whitefish Point when the storm struck. By midnight Captain Mosher was fighting a big sea and a blizzard; he kept course by soundings and so gained the shelter of Keweenaw Point.

Next morning the *Stephenson's* crew saw a ship aground on Manitou Island. She showed no lights or smoke, but a distress signal fluttered from her foremast. At noon Captain Mosher sent his mate ashore to notify the Coast Guard. The blizzard raged all day, but at dusk the snow thinned and the wind went down. The *Stephenson* steered through Gull Passage at midnight. "There was moonlight," Captain Mosher reported, "and I saw the steamer lying there with her decks above water and her cabins on her."

This ship was the *L. C. Waldo,* loaded with 7,000 tons of iron ore. Disabled, she had been thrown on the reef running out from Gull Rock. Then the sea battered her after quarters and the crew, clinging to life lines, scrambled forward. For two days they huddled in the cabin while the waves washed over. On the third day they were taken off by the Coast Guard crew from Eagle Harbor.

After forty-eight hours of struggle on Lake Superior the *William Nottingham* ran out of fuel. She had outlived the storm, but steam was dying in her boilers and the seas were carrying her toward the rocks of Coppermine Point. The captain sent his men into the hold. They shoveled wheat up on deck and into the bunker hatch. Down below the stokers threw it onto their dying fires. The drafts whined and the wheat took flame. The *Nottingham* toiled on to Whitefish Bay. There she struck a shoal and the big seas broke her. Three of her men were lost while trying to launch a lifeboat before the Coast Guard came.

The *Argus* and the *Hydrus* of The Interlake Steamship Company were twin vessels, built in the same yards in the same season, 1903. They came to the same end, one upbound with coal, the other downbound with iron ore, at the same hour in the fury and darkness of Lake Huron.

Even amid disaster there were comic episodes. The Interlake freighter *D. O. Mills* was driven ashore on Lake Huron between Pointe Aux Barques and Harbor Beach. Hans C. Hansen, later master of the *Elton Hoyt 2nd* and the *Robert Hobson,* was then second mate of the *Mills,* under the Scottish captain James Jackson. When the *Mills* went aground, Captain "Yim Yackson," as Hansen reported, got the crew forward away from the seas that were pouring over her stern. That is—when they tallied the roster—they were all there except the wife of the Negro steward, who was signed on as second cook. Seasick and terrified, she had refused to cross the wave-swept deck to the forward quarters. The cook was too frightened to go back to get her. The rest drew straws, and Hans Hansen found himself with the short matchstick. He buckled on his oilskins, seized a life line, and went aft. He got the seasick woman onto his back and came forward. On the way she had a fresh spasm of seasickness, and the crew would not let the tainted mate into the shelter of the cabin. This was not Hans Hansen's first shipwreck. As a boy in Norway he had gone to sea in sailing vessels; on Christmas Day in 1900 he was shipwrecked off the coast of Scotland and spent five days in an open boat. But this was the worst. "Yaa, by Yimminy," he declared, he would yust as soon yump overboard as carry a seasick woman over a pitching deck.

For two weeks the searchers patrolled the Canadian shore. In Goderich, in a big cold wharf shed, they made identification of the bodies and arranged for their shipment and burial. Then Captain Whitney went home to Ashtabula in time for a grave Thanksgiving Day with his family.

CHAPTER 11

Last of the Mine Mules

THE MULE schooners, dropping anchor in Iron Bay, carried the Lakes' only self-unloading cargo. Prodded by pitchforks, the animals leaped into Lake Superior and swam ashore. Enlivened by that cold plunge, some of them frisked through the streets of Marquette before the mine men got halters on them and led them to the railroad cars. The next day they were dragging scrapers in the pits at Ishpeming. They quickly learned about mining—quicker, the Cornish captains said, than the stolid shovelers and wheelbarrow men.

When young Samuel Mather watched the work in Landy's Pit, mining was a matter of manpower and mule-power, aided by some dynamite. With pick and shovel, scraper and dump cart, the men and mules worked together, sweating in the summer sun, breath smoking in the bitter air of winter. When the first shafts were sunk and the drifts opened, men and mules went underground. The men came up at the end of a shift, but the mules stayed down. Ventilation lines kept the air changing, hay and oats went down in the man cage, and the mules were at home in that unchanging climate. They soon gave the damp drifts a rich barnyard smell that made the Serb and Austrian miners homesick for the little farms of the Old Country.

By 1890 there were hundreds of mules on the Lake Superior ranges, with new carloads arriving from St. Louis every spring. They were animals of a special breed, broad and strong and close to the ground, built like a table with a leg at each corner. When they arrived at the mine shaft they were all colors—white, brown, gray, sorrel, often coal black except for a mealy nose. Once underground, they all took the color of iron ore.

But first there was the business of getting them into the mine. After seeing the damage a fractious mule could do to men and machinery, the miners made a special harness for the trip underground. Blindfolded, the mule was slung in a harness suspended beneath the man cage; or, strapped in a leather jacket, the mule was worked into the man cage and lowered away. Either method was safe for both the men and the mule. Hundreds of feet down were the mule barns, long dim aisles fragrant with hay. When a newcomer was brought down, the animals lifted their ears, sniffed the air, and greeted him with a chorus of braying.

The first tramming was hand-tramming, men slogging through the dim drift pushing a loaded car to the dump pocket at the hoisting shaft. Later the mules took over, hauling a string of cars, standing while the load was dumped, then hauling the empties back to the ore face and sniffing at a miner's pocket for a bite of tobacco while they waited. Every three days fresh hay and oats came down, once a week came fresh straw for their bedding. Mine mules were well fed and well treated. No whips or clubs were permitted underground, and if an exasperated miner used the flat of his shovel that only made a stubborn mule more stubborn.

The mules liked underground life and quickly learned every bend and turn in the long tunnels. A powder blast, rumbling like thunder through the drifts, lifted their ears with curiosity, but they never balked or bolted. They could find their way in a pitch-black mine, never mistaking distance or direction. The tunnel floor was usually soft and damp; the mules' small hoofs cut into it, making holes six inches deep between the ties and tram rails. Day after day, year after year in the main drifts, they stepped daintily in the same holes without ever stumbling. If the long ears once touched a cap timber the mule remembered; he always ducked at just that spot even in inky darkness.

In the spring the mules were brought up for a month at pasture. It was an event like circus day for the boys of a mining town. The mules came up trussed and blindfolded, sniffing the fresh spring air, lifting their ears, braying with pleasure. Contrary to general belief, mine mules were not blind. But they had grown accustomed to darkness, and only by degrees could they adjust to daylight. Gradually their eyes were exposed and after a couple of days they were ready for full sunlight. With the last blinders removed and a slap on the red-stained rump, the mules were off. They leaped and capered, kicked and cavorted. They raced up and down the pasture and rolled in the sunlight and summer grass. They laid back their ears and brayed to the bright green world. A few weeks later, back underground, they took up their dim life cheerfully, one shift going into the stalls while the other shift left, like the men in the boardinghouses.

On the surface were mine horses, hauling timber in the woods. They were not as knowing as "Little Pete" far underground; he always stopped on the stroke of noon and would not take another step until he had finished the last crumb of oats in his nose bag. After World War I both the mules and horses disappeared from the mines. The mules gave way to electric haulage, and the woods teams were replaced by big steam tractors.

There were many hundreds of mules in the Lake Superior mines at the turn of the century. Most of them were stubborn, but hardly any were mean or ugly. A few of them were pets. In the Chandler Mine, Captain John Pengilly used a saddle mule to travel to the scattered workings in the tunnels. His mount would come at a whistle and would stand like a statue when the stirrups were crossed over the saddle. All the mine mules worked without reins, driven by the trammer's voice. Some of them learned to understand five languages.

In his dim, monotonous life the mule somehow preserved individuality. There were forty mules in a big mine and no two just alike in temperament and character. Molly was mischievous, Mike was stubborn, Madge was ingratiating, Minnie was sly, Mandy didn't like wet feet, Myrt was a mudder, Mable wanted to be scratched between the ears, Maud was touchy. In one of the Hanna mines a self-important mule was called Mark. He thought he was the boss.

For twenty or thirty years in some mines, the mules did the hauling. Intelligent, strong, and patient, they plodded down the dark drifts with their long ears flopping and a bell tinkling from their collars. Their music and their friendliness were missed when the mines progressed to electric haulage.

The last mules came up to daylight in the early 1920's. But for years afterward in the dark deep drifts the rich smell of the mule barns lingered, and men in the dryhouse talked about old Mike and Molly that had shared the shift with them. Every mine had its own stories, probably improved with time. Mose always kicked on Monday morning, after Sunday rest. Molly knew that four cars were her quota and she counted the "tunk" as the slack came out of the chains. At five tunks she stopped, looked over her shoulder and waited till the last car was uncoupled. Powerful old Mike would bite, strike, kick at everyone except his Croatian driver, who could pet him like a kitten. Once he laid back his ears and went after the superintendent. "Good old Mike," they said in the dry—and may his bones have rest.

In the years of mule haulage shafts were relatively shallow and close together. The skips were small and it was a short haul from the working place to the hoist. With electric haulage the scale changed. Shafts went deeper, the "motor" moved a longer string of cars to the big skip that rose up swiftly to the light of day. Hoists achieved new speed and capacity; pumps and ventilators grew more efficient. In the old shallow shafts a natural flow of air provided ventilation. One shaft was cooler than another; the air moved through like the draft in a furnace. When the big electric ventilators were installed, the flick of a switch brought a fresh wind far underground. Still, there could be a lack of fresh air in certain dogholes and slices, and the miners sometimes tapped the air line of the drill crews. A normal blast driven in a section twelve by fifteen feet could be drilled in half an hour by two good miners, two good drills, a good air compressor, and proper air lines. But often a foreman had to check the line to see if someone wasn't blowing air to ventilate a working place.

The new scale of operation worked on men's fancy, producing tall tales underground. One story told of two miners boasting about the deepest mine on the range. Jack Selmy said he once went into the engine house where he found the engineer tilted back, sound asleep, while the hoisting engine was working at top speed. Jack woke him up, pointing excitedly at the winding cable. The engineer blinked, pulled out his watch, and settled back in his chair. "She's only halfway up," he said with a yawn, "and I go off in three hours. She won't land on my shift." Unimpressed by this tale, Joe Savroni told of going to a mine to get a job. When he asked for the captain the shift boss said he had just stepped on the cage at the bottom level. "Come back tomorrow night," he added, "and you can catch him when he lands."

There are one hundred and sixty ways of metal mining, said one engineer; but all those methods fall under a few general practices. An open-cut mine could be developed by benches, the "Glory Hole," and placer mining. An underground mine could be worked by breast stoping, underhand stoping, overhand stoping, top slicing, caving, and by various combinations of these methods. From early years the Lake Superior mining industry has been aided by ready co-operation and exchange of experience and technique. The Lake Superior Mining Institute held its first meeting at Iron Mountain, Michigan, in 1893. It spread the gospel of co-operation. For thirty years at its annual meetings mining men from all the ranges traded stories, exchanged experiences, and heard papers on geological formations, methods of mining, analysis of ores, improvements of machinery and mine equipment, methods of accounting, and measures of welfare and safety.

On the wall in the Sunday Lake mine office on the Gogebic is a framed exhibit of underground lights: the "sunshine" paraffin oil and wick, the candle lamp which came in 1900, the carbide lamp carried by miners from 1912 to 1935, and the modern electric lamp with its belt-hung battery. Portable electric lamps were a vast improvement over the smoky "sunshine" wick, and when electric power lines ran deep underground the darkness was banished. Over the foremen's desk hung a perpetual light, the pumpman had a lighted engine room, and the long drifts were lighted like a city street. Electric drills bored into the rock, electric fans brought air, and electric pumps sucked water. The electric locomotive put an end to mule haulage; now ten-car trains or long conveyer belts carry the ore from the working face to the loading chutes. The electric hoist can lift thousands of tons a day from a depth of 4,000 feet.

During the years of World War I a shortage of labor spurred mechanization in the mines. With the muckers and trammers "Somewhere in France" and with the war demanding huge tonnages of iron ore, machines went underground. They proved more efficient and profitable than hand labor, and the change had come to stay.

George Rule arrived in Minnesota from Cornwall in the

1880's. In the old Chandler Mine on the Vermilion he took a job loading railroad cars, by wheelbarrow, from the stockpile. He had the art of shoveling, his feet planted and his shoulders rocking; they said he could load a hundred cars a day. Then he went underground, working with pick and shovel, ax and crowbar. In a ten-hour shift the old-time miner might work at a dozen different jobs. But with mechanization miners became specialists. There were muckers and trackmen, drillers and powdermen, pumpmen and plumbers, timbermen and skip-tenders— all underground. On the surface were engineers, machinists, electricians, carpenters, timber-framers. To a visitor it is astonishing to see the endless timberwork that goes on in a mine. Ore comes up, timber goes down. Miles of lagging frame the drifts, cribbing encloses the raises, bulkheads guard against gas, fire, and water, and brattices regulate the flow of air. Natural wood has a short life underground; curious proliferating molds attack it in patterns of beauty and decay. But in recent years the chemists have changed that. Now mine timbers are treated with Osmose salts to resist the destructive fungi.

For thirty years the hissing old steam shovels had snorted in the pits, loading ore into trains hauled up the long benches by "dinky" locomotives. In Pickands Mather mines the first electric shovel was used in 1924—an eight-ton shovel with a crude hoist. Bill Gallagher, chief engineer for P. M. in the Northwest, improved it, developing a herringbone gear that worked as smoothly as old George Rule's shoulders and lifted eight tons at a bite. Quickly it came into general use. Now seven-yard electric shovels fill Diesel trucks of thirty-ton capacity. With a grind of power the big trucks climb the grade. The trucks cost $50,000 each, but they earn their way.

Mahnomen is the Chippewa word for wild rice. Where rice once grew on the Cuyuna near the Mississippi River, the trucks now bring up soft brown hematite. In the Mahnomen Mine in 1937 Pickands Mather first used truck haulage out of the pit. It proved successful; trucks could haul ore faster than a locomotive on a steeper grade than the old benches required by the railroad. Truck haul spread, slowly at first but more rapidly as deep pits small in area were mined. In 1937 2 per cent of the ore produced in open pits was moved by truck. In 1945 the percentage had climbed to 58. Now most of the ore in open-pit mines is brought to the surface by truck, or by the still newer conveyer belts. The old pit locomotive, puffing up the red and purple benches, has followed the mine mules into history.

The first automobiles on the ranges were company cars, soon stained as red as the ore trains on the railroad. They plowed through mud, dust, and snow, making the circuit of the mines. In the early 1920's Philip Mather, making an inspection trip through the Upper Peninsula, saw one of the early cars. At the end of the day he stood on the porch of a mine office talking with L. M. Hardenburgh, P. M. mine superintendent in the Gogebic district, and veteran C. H. Munger who was then head of the Mining Department in Cleveland. Behind them the door flew open and out came a clerk, the last man to leave the office. He ran to a Model T Ford at the roadside and began to crank. Nothing happened. He went around, readjusted the spark and the throttle, and cranked again. After five minutes he was alternately mopping his brow with a handkerchief and bending at the crank handle.

Then seldom-speaking Superintendent Munger observed: "Hardenburgh, that looks like the old company car we used to have here."

"Yes, sir," said Hardenburgh, "that's the car."

"You sold it to him?"

"No, sir. It was thirteen, fourteen years old. About played out. We gave it to him."

Mr. Munger looked startled. "Gave it to him? Company property? That's bad. Would it be too late to arrange to sell it to him for a small sum?"

Hardenburgh looked down at the clerk still toiling at the crank. "Perhaps not too late, Mr. Munger. But I don't believe this is the time to open negotiations."

The old system of mine signals was a yanking of ropes sometimes accompanied by yelling up the shaft. Electric bells came with electric lighting, and the big mines installed telephone systems. In open-pit mines as the cut grew deeper the vast gulf swallowed up a man's voice; even the huff and grind of the big machines was lost in that yawning silence. Portable radios put men back into communication. In 1956 Pickands Mather organized on the Mesabi Range the Mesabi Radio Corporation, to manage radio facilities in its mines. Now there is radio-telephone communication between the taconite plant at Hoyt Lakes and the dock at Taconite Harbor.

The process of mechanization meant fewer men in the mine and greater production. With new methods and equipment, despite the deepening pits and levels and the steady shortening of the work week, a general average shows men four times as productive as they were in 1915. When Pickands Mather took over the Penn mines on the Menominee in 1923, Captain William Kelley was asked how many tons were produced per man. He gave a wry, ironic answer: "We figure how many men per ton." The time was past when a superintendent could pluck off a man's cap to see if he was sweating, but by skill and mechanization the production could be multiplied. In 1919 the Bennett Mine produced eight tons per day per man, a good figure at that time. In 1952, with its efficient mechanization, the same mine produced forty tons per day for each of its miners. During recent years, however, there has been little increase in the workers' productivity.

After World War I steel became increasingly specialized and its manufacture required special grades of ore and uniformity from cargo to cargo throughout the season. In recent years the producers have grown more painstaking and exact. Ore samples, collected daily from each mine, are delivered to the district laboratory where they are ground, dried, weighed on precision balances, and analyzed for their content of iron, phosphorous, silica, manganese, and alumina. While a ship is on its way up the Lakes its cargo is being assembled from various mines, according to the Grading Department's instruction and the consumer's requirement. The ores get mixed as the cars dump into bins on the loading docks. They are mixed again as the material pours into the steamer's hold and still again as it is gathered up by the Huletts at the end of the run. When it arrives at the furnace it is a special ore for a special purpose.

Research is the new word on the old iron ranges. In the Pickands Mather laboratory at Hibbing, on the edge of the yawning Scranton pit, a staff of twenty-five chemists, metallurgists, and mechanical engineers collaborate in various projects. Opened in 1942, the laboratory's first problem was to develop a process of extracting the iron particles from taconite rock, and the next problem was to put the particles together in a form fit for blast-furnace consumption. This research program had the full support of the four companies associated in the Erie taconite project. The owner companies, especially Bethlehem Steel, conducted separate research in the pelletizing of fine-ground iron ore. Certain aspects of the problem were worked out jointly. This co-operative research resulted in a pelletizing technique and furnace operation for the Erie Preliminary Plant which sent the first taconite pellets to the steelmakers. In 1946 the staff began investigating the possibility of beneficiating lean material in ore dumps and open-pit mines. They have examined fine grinding, the uses of heavy media, screening, and other methods of concentrating ores. They have tested drill samples from many locations; in 1957 they analyzed a twenty-ton sample of ore from Wabush Lake on the western edge of Labrador. The results of that analysis pointed to large undertakings in the Canadian wilderness in years to come.

Behind this research is the realization that the iron ores of the future will not be what nature has deposited in folds of subterranean rock but a material which men have crushed, concentrated, sintered, or pelletized. Steel mills now require an ore more precise in size and quality than nature provides, and in the laboratories men work on problems unknown a few years ago. For a company that for seven decades has rendered skilled and technical services to the industry, it is natural to realize that the future demands improved methods leading to a better and cheaper product.

The old boardinghouses are gone from the mine, and only the veterans remember the men in red-stained clothing tramping to the mine collar, given a candle for the long shift, lowered in ore buckets or climbing down hundreds of feet into the shaft. Ten hours later they came up, freshly stained and muddy, eyes blinking in the light, and tramped back to the boardinghouse. Now the men arrive in cars at the parking lot. In the dry room they lower work clothes from a hook overhead and change to the standard underground dress—long woolen underwear, soft wool socks, wool shirt, overalls, hard-toed rubber boots, and a hard helmet. At the lamp room they get a freshly charged battery to clamp on the belt and a light that clips onto the helmet. They signal for the man cage, descend to an illuminated level, pass through a lighted drift, and find their working place. At the end of the shift they come up, turn in their lamps, wash their boots in a boot room, pull their clothes back up on the drying racks, bathe in a hot shower, and don street clothes for the drive home.

Even a motorist speeding past a mine head frame sees the difference. The old steam-powered mine, between a huge ash heap and a stockpile of coal, belched smoke over a sooty landscape; from the engine room came the clanking of valve gear and a hissing of exhaust. The modern mine, powered by electricity, shows a green lawn bordered by flower beds. The place has a Sunday look, composed and quiet. But at the top of the head frame the sheaves are noiselessly revolving and heaped tramcars glide out over the stockpile. Up into sunlight comes the iron ore that has waited underground for a million years.

CHAPTER 12

Smoking on the
Dynamite Wagon

IN THE Gogebic woods between Wakefield and Bessemer Ed Ericson drove a team for a lumber camp. On a stormy night at the beginning of the spring drive he made a hurried trip to town, with lightning all around him and thunder crashing down. In the wagon he had a drowned lumberjack, six men who had run pike poles and peaveys into their feet, and six hundred pounds of dynamite. At the station Ed drew a long breath and grumbled: "By the sawed-off, blue-eyed, holy old mackinaw, the worst damn job (vorst tam yob) I ever hauled—one corpse, six cripples, and six boxes dynamite. And I could light my pipe with the lightning any minute."

The next season he went to work for a mining company, driving the supply wagon. After some unexplained explosions the town of Wakefield passed a law that prohibited smoking on the dynamite wagon. Then Ed turned to chewing tobacco, and his team reached over when they saw him take the plug from his pocket. "Those damn horses," he complained, "keep me broke buying tobacco."

Besides the dynamite wagon there were other hazards in a mining and logging district. With trees crashing in the woods, powder blasts rumbling in the test pits, and tons of rock dangling from the hoists, men lived in daily risk of life and limb. Even the elevated sidewalks were a peril. In 1895 Frank Lewis Bond, the son of an iron pioneer and the husband of Carrie Jacobs Bond, who would become the best-known song writer in America,

was killed by falling from a high plank sidewalk in the town of
Iron River.

On her first day in a forest-hemmed house at the Vulcan location, Mrs. N. P. Hulst, wife of the superintendent, saw a file of
men coming down the hill from Pit Two. They moved slowly
through the woods and as they drew near she saw that they were
carrying a burden. That evening she learned that a mass of rock
had fallen on a workman just after her husband and her small son
had left his side. In his seasons at the Vulcan Mine N. P. Hulst
always hurried to the site of the accident; he was the first to take
up a pick and use it. After a casualty the superstitious miners
feared the dead man's tool and his working place.

As the shafts drove underground, danger increased. Every
district had its somber memories. In Upper Michigan the year
1893, which brought a financial panic, was darkened by two
disasters in successive weeks. On September 27 a cave-in in
Number 8 Shaft of the Norrie killed eleven men. That word
had just reached Mansfield, on the Michigamme River beyond
Crystal Falls, when the river broke into the Mansfield Mine,
trapping twenty-eight men. The mine was closed for two years,
until a new river channel had been dug. Meanwhile, in 1896,
the village of Mansfield was destroyed by fire. The old range towns
lived violently, and some of them died violently. Two decades
later, in 1918, disaster struck the Amasa-Porter Mine on the
Menominee. A cave-in of sand, gravel, and water at the mouth
of the shaft took the lives of sixteen men.

Accidents were a common part of mine reports half a century
ago. In the old Pickands Mather code book *Military* was a grave
word; it meant: "Did not ship much today because of accident
in mine." *Milkiness* was somber: "Serious accident in mine
which has stopped shipment."

In those years shafts and stope openings were unguarded,
gears and cables were exposed, and there was little communication between the surface and underground. But the worst hazard
was the men themselves. Powerful, primitive, ignorant, and rash,
they took every hair-raising risk that offered. They jumped on
and off passing skips, they clung to the outside of moving cages,
they handled a stick of dynamite as casually as a piece of bologna.

Fifty years ago explosives were more sensitive than they are
now, yet it was a common thing for a miner to carry three sticks
of dynamite in each bootleg and several in his shirt. If they were

not thawed out by body warmth the miner heated a shovelful of sticks over some pieces of candle, squatting in the drift and turning the softened explosive on the hot metal. Teeth were the accepted instrument for crimping a cap on a fuse. Many men carried bluish-green powder burns on hands and arms; some were maimed. If a man lost a finger, hand, or foot, he was less concerned about the loss than about preserving the severed part in alcohol. Otherwise, according to the folklore, it would itch forever. When a man lost his life his mates knocked off for the day and passed the hat for his burial. They were a rugged race, and caution was alien to their code.

The wonder is not that there were fatalities in the early years, but that most miners survived. Along with stories of disaster the north country has remembered tales of miraculous escape. In the Bengal Mine Bob Olson was trucking timber on a handcar to a working face where Joe Bianco wanted to "brace up the back" of the drift. Bob called for a heavy timber which Joe needed in Drift Number 10. Up above, Rini Maki, the powerful Finnish timberman, lowered a crossbeam down the shaft, suspending it on a chain attached to the eyebolt on the bottom of the cage. When it arrived Bob freed the log from the chain, dragging the beam onto the floor of the drift. Then he gave three quick jerks on the bell rope and the cage went up. But the chain caught his foot, picking him up in place of the dangling timber. Hanging head down, he traveled a thousand feet to the surface, where the startled hoistman set him free. Without a word Bob Olson stepped into the cage and went back for his cap and lamp. In the early years at Iron River a Finnish miner late for work one morning stumbled into his clothes in the dry and jumped into the empty ore skip to join his shift underground. When the skip reached the lower level two tons of ore poured in, knocking big Kaarlo flat. The skip shot up and Kaarlo was dumped through the chute onto the stockpile. Clambering down the red slope, Kaarlo muttered at "tose tam miners" who wouldn't let a man get to work. The hardy Finns survived hazards that would carry off lesser men. "To kill a Finn," an old range saying went, "you have to cut off his head and hide it."

At the turn of the century, before there was any general insuring of risk in the mines, volunteer Miners' Club funds provided money for hospital and burial expense and for needy families; the funds were supported by both the company and the workmen. In these years Pickands Mather began to formulate a safety program. In 1910 C. H. Munger, general manager at Duluth, organized safety committees and called for detailed reports and recommendations. In November 1911 he made a company-wide study, classifying all accidents reported during the year. In a total employment of 2,968 men in mines, furnaces, and docks there occurred during the year 884 reported accidents, which cost a total of 9,221 days' disability. At the average wage of $2.61 the lost-time cost was $24,067. The report showed that one third of the injured had an inadequate understanding of English and that half the accidents were due to the workers' negligence. It indicated that safety was a matter of education as well as of improvement of conditions.

This report became the basis of a book of rules, published in the various languages required on the Lake Superior ranges and distributed to all employees. In 1913 a range safety inspector was appointed for each district. Gus Bawden, pioneer safety man on the Gogebic, driving a sleigh or a buckboard over his territory, worked fourteen and a half hours three days a week and ten hours the other days. In later years the automobile cut down his time on the road and made him more efficient.

The safety man was an unpopular visitor in the early years. Mine bosses regarded safety measures as an unnecessary frill which the company would soon forget. They liked nothing better than to report an injury that occurred when men were installing railings, guards, and other safety devices. Workers were reluctant to try out helmets and safety goggles, which made them conspicuous and self-conscious. There was no substitute for education, both for the bosses and the men. Later, when the Safety Department supplied protective equipment to all at the same time, the articles soon won favor.

Early recommendations from the local safety committee included some rudimentary measures: shaft openings to be fenced in, hoisting drums to be enclosed, belts to be boxed, gears and cables guarded, explosives to be stored in rock-wall magazines, a printed bell signal code to be posted on each shaft-house landing. From the Cary Mine at Hurley came a recommendation that the dryhouse be fumigated every three months. Already safety was involving cleanliness and sanitation. In 1913 the Workmen's Compensation Act defined employers' responsibility for the safety of their workers. But the company was ahead of legislation. By this time safety programs were permanently established in the mines. Standards adopted by the Pickands Mather Safety Department in 1918 included the guarding of all machinery, installation of ladderways, maintenance of exits, and an approved procedure in the storing, distributing, and handling of explosives.

First aid was all but unknown in the mines of fifty years ago. Now the company carries on regular training in first aid and mine rescue work. First-aid teams from the mines have won State and national contests. Equipment includes fire extinguishers, stretchers, inhalators, and gas masks for rescue teams; a "stench alarm" injected into the air lines can quickly carry to men in every part of an extensive mine the alarm of fire.

In the early years of the safety movement some of the mines were provided with ambulances for the transport of injured men. At the Baltic location, barn boss Bill Johnson kept the mine ambulance shined up, its windows gleaming, and a polished lantern hanging at the driver's side. Mounted on wheels in summer and on four sets of sled runners in winter, it was powered by Bill's best team of blacks. With black cab and black horses some of the miners thought it looked more like a hearse than a rescue wagon.

The Fourth of July was celebrated in many languages on the iron ranges. In the close-lying Gogebic, hundreds of miners streamed into Hurley for the big day. The saloons filled up early, but a larger crowd was at the race track where there was a program of baseball, wrestling matches, and drilling contests, with firecrackers popping all day long and a burst of fireworks at nightfall. A baseball team from the Newport Mine played the Oliver team, the Cary played the Montreal. Big barefoot Cousin Jack wrestlers in rope-and-canvas jackets grappled for holds and hitches around the ring in the Cornish "flying mare." Drilling teams from the iron mines competed with hard-rock drillers from the Keweenaw. One twister and three hammermen worked together. The brawny sledge-men swung in perfect rhythm; the twister would snatch a drill out of the hole and put in another with hardly a break in their cadence. Though power drills had replaced hand drilling in the mines the drill teams kept the rugged art alive. In ten minutes the winning team drilled a ten-inch hole in a porphyry boulder. Their prize was a keg of beer.

After 1911 a new event was added to the Fourth of July celebration. Safety teams competed as strenuously as the mine baseball teams. Their contest was as eventful as a track meet: teams of one, two, three, and four men, each with a laid-out "victim," were judged for speed and skill as they treated wounds, cuts, burns, and every kind of injury from a crushed finger to a broken back.

Fifty years ago the Lake Superior mines had an annual casualty rate of six men per thousand, which was three times the rate in the mines of Great Britain and six times that in the mines of Germany. Safety measures soon made a difference. By the end of World War I both accidents and fatalities had declined to half the former total. Still the companies increased their efforts and the Lake Superior Mine Safety Conference kept up a continual study of problems and solutions. At a meeting of the Conference in 1923 George Martinson, Safety Director for Pickands Mather, took a look at industrial history: "John Ruskin predicted that railroads, by driving stages out of business, would end the demand for horses, and so would ruin the farmer and bring the downfall of England." Since that prediction, he observed, the United Kingdom had grown to be the greatest industrial nation in the world, until the United States surpassed her in the twentieth century. Then he spoke of iron ore, the base of heavy industry, and he linked its production with the safety of mine workers. He talked about mine ventilation, mine lighting, water supplies in the mine, fire hazards and fire extinguishing equipment, mine hoists, shaft stations, alarms, cage safety catches, mine rescue, and first-aid training. Concerns like these, he declared, make an industry sound, humane, and productive. He was speaking not only for his department but for the entire company. The safety program had the full support of the organization, right up to the top. Samuel Mather was never too busy to discuss new measures for the workers' safety and welfare.

In 1935 George Martinson came to the Cleveland office of Pickands Mather in charge of safety in the ships, docks, furnaces, and mines. He began publication of the *Interlake Steamship Log*, constantly stressing safety in the pages of the magazine. He developed a foremanship service, a pictorial bulletin service, and an unflagging educational effort that reached to every employee. At his death in 1948 he left a fully staffed Safety Department backed by the moral and active support of the entire company.

Education has been effective, and the safety record has kept pace with increases in production. Now in a glass exhibit case the Mahoning Mine on the Mesabi displays nine "Sentinels of Safety" trophies. The huge mine has set a world record for safety, having passed three million man-hours without a disabling injury. Ten other P. M.-operated mines, the Buck, Embarrass, Sagamore, Zenith, Danube, Vulcan, Scranton, Cary, Newport, and James, have won top national awards, and still others have Awards of Merit and Honor. In its first year, 1955, one of the Erie Commercial Taconite pits won the Sentinels of Safety trophy.

Now the hazards of the north country are not at work but at leisure; there are more accidents in the woods in the short hunting season than during the whole year's work. With this kind of progress no one has been more gratified than A. D. Chisholm, the general manager who followed W. P. Chinn, who has a tireless concern for the welfare and safety of the men in the mines.

When operation of The Youngstown Sheet and Tube Company's mines was given to Pickands Mather in 1924, the company took over the Isabella Mine at Palmer, Michigan. The new mine captain brought to the property a zeal for neatness and safety. In September the fall inspection group arrived from Ohio. They stared at two freshly painted boulders in front of the mine office, while the captain waited for commendation. Finally Mr. Munger grunted, "Who's buried there, Cap?" No one knew better than C. H. Munger. Beneath that neatness and order were buried the old hazards of frayed ropes, broken ladders, dusty drifts, and unfenced shaft openings, and of ill-equipped, ignorant, and care-less men.

CHAPTER 13

Second Generation

TALL, long-striding, with direct gray eyes and a personality of visible warmth and purpose, Amasa Stone Mather, Samuel Mather's second son, was graduated from Yale in 1907. In the Mather tradition he followed his schooling with a *Wanderjahr,* setting out on a leisurely trip around the world. Along with more standard travel stops he visited Formosa, Java, Burma, Bangalore, and Kashmir. He spent ten weeks hunting big game in British East Africa; some of his trophies are now displayed in the Cleveland Museum of Natural History. On his return to the United States he found an invitation from President Theodore Roosevelt asking him to visit the White House. The President plied him with questions about African hunting, and Amasa Mather gave him the name of Leslie Tarleton, a British hunter who had guided him from Mombasa up to Nairobi and the foothills of Kenya.

A year later, in 1909, when ex-President Roosevelt was on safari in Africa, Amasa Mather was learning the iron business in the Cleveland office and on extended visits to the mines. He was endlessly curious about mining methods, mine accounting, and mining men. He learned from geologists, mining captains, and men in the pits and the workings underground. During the early months of World War I, before entering the Third Officers' Training Camp at Camp Taylor, Kentucky, he served on the Federal Iron Ore Commission. After the war he became head of the Pickands Mather Iron Ore Department.

No man is better remembered on the ranges than Amasa Mather, even a third of a century after his last visit. He came to learn the business, not to inspect it, and he went into the mines like an employee. When he arrived in the North, tanned from a voyage up the Lakes, he was in city clothes, a well-tailored man except for a battered hat that he would never discard. Immediately he bought a pair of overalls and chopped them off below the knee. After a few hours underground he was as spotted and stained as any miner, and he was delighted when an old Finn timber-trammer mistook him for a new laborer.

On early visits to the Mesabi he lived at Elcor in the club-house of the Elba and Corsica mines. He mixed with the men there, sharing their life at work and at leisure. At that time eleven mines were operated in the Elcor district; before his visit ended his overalls wore the red and purple stains of all the work-ings. Then he moved to the district office in North Hibbing be-side the Scranton pit, where there were four bedrooms above the clank and clatter of the mine yard. On some trips his wife, the sister of Elton Hoyt 2nd, shared that lodging over the old district office, a site now mined away and sent to the blast furnaces. On visits to the Gogebic he put up at the old Curry Hotel in Iron-wood. Long a center of iron men, the friendly hotel was named for Solomon S. Curry, who was president of the Metropolitan Land and Iron Company, owners and operators of the East and West Norrie-Aurora-Pabst workings, which were later to become Oliver Iron Mining Company properties. But Amasa Mather had no time for poker parties in the hotel; he was too much inter-ested in production on the range.

To Ironwood in 1912 Samuel Mather came in a private car with a party from Ohio. In the robust north country that rigid man forgot his shyness and distance. One night in the Curry Hotel in a circle of mining men he talked of a recent trip around the world; the Gogebic men still remember his vivid description of sacred white bulls littering the steps of temples and palaces in Calcutta. The next day, after visiting the Cary Mine, the party pulled out of Ironwood. Half an hour later the train returned. With a clanging bell and a hiss of steam it backed into the station where Samuel Mather, who had been left in an outbuilding on the mine property, stood on the platform. He stepped aboard the private car in silence and went straight to his stateroom. His austerity had come back. (As a result of this incident the first indoor plumbing was installed in P. M. mine offices.)

With his stiffened left arm Samuel Mather bore all his life

a mark of the hazard of the mines, and he gave wholehearted support to the company's safety program. But it was his son who noted the broken ladders, littered working places, rotting timbers, and unguarded belts and gears. Amasa Mather was learning the whole complex iron-ore business, but he never forgot the urgency of increasing safety measures.

Amasa Mather foresaw expansion and development; he wanted to make Pickands Mather the largest iron-mining organization after United States Steel. He saw that the growing steel companies could not remain dependent upon suppliers of iron ore; they would need their own sources of raw material. He took a lead in this kind of integration, bringing various steel companies into ownership of ore properties which Pickands Mather, with extensive experience and organization, could manage and operate for them. Here was the company's growing role as an agent providing skilled and technical services for the steel industry. He was in the midst of one of these projects when he died.

In the last week of January 1920 he made two trips to New York and Philadelphia in the course of negotiations with the Midvale Steel and Ore Company. Returning to Cleveland at the end of the week, he worked all day in his office, trying to complete the Midvale project before sailing with his father for a meeting of the International Red Cross in Geneva. He was using a cane that winter, having sprained his back in a fall from a horse. On that day he kept leaning back in his chair and kneading his forehead with his fingers. His office mate, H. C. Jackson, thought his back was hurting. But when Amasa Mather left the office his face was flushed and his eyes were lighted with fever.

For a week at his home in Cleveland he fought a losing battle with influenza. He died on February 9. When word reached the mining towns around Lake Superior, hundreds of men felt his death as a personal loss. In Cleveland his partners had lost a colleague who had been marked for leadership.

As it developed Amasa Mather had brought his own successor into the firm. H. C. Jackson was sent to college by a Yale Scholarship Committee, a group headed by Elton Hoyt 2nd. As an undergraduate Jackson knew nothing of Pickands Mather & Co., even though in his senior year he roomed with Philip Mather, Samuel Mather's youngest son. At the end of his college course Jackson was offered three jobs: one with the National City Bank in Buenos Aires, one with Standard Oil in Hong Kong, and one teaching Latin at University School in Cleveland. He told his roommate that he had a desire to return to Cleveland but doubted his gifts as a Latin teacher. Philip Mather spoke of a brother in a business firm in Cleveland and added that he was coming to New Haven shortly for a baseball game. At the end of the week Jackson met Amasa Mather and learned about Pickands Mather & Co. Starting as an office boy in 1916, he was soon at work in the company's Marine Department and then in the Mining Accounting Department. He became head of the Mining, Ore Sales, Tax, Corporate, Insurance, and Safety departments, also vice-president of Interlake Steamship. A partner in the firm since 1942, he was made associate managing partner in 1956. The value of his forty-two years of experience in the business is reflected in some of the positions he holds in 1958: board chairman of the American Iron Ore Association, and directorates in the American Mining Congress and the Lake Carriers Association.

William G. Mather, president of the Cleveland-Cliffs Iron Company, was a bachelor until the age of seventy. He took into that business his nephew Livingston Mather, Samuel Mather's oldest son. As a young man Livingston Mather went north to Lake Superior. He lived in Ishpeming for six years, working as timekeeper, sampler, clerk, and learning the operations of a company in which his uncle retained a strong hand until his death in 1950. He rose rapidly, becoming head of the Iron-Ore Mine Department of Cleveland-Cliffs, a leading competitor of his father's and his brother's firm. Samuel Mather had a financial interest in Cleveland-Cliffs and was one of its directors. Said William G. Mather: "We never discuss anything important at directors' meetings because my brother Sam sits there."

A complex relationship existed between the two half brothers. Astute and strenuous competitors, they were fellow members of civic organizations and social clubs. For years they were half of a foursome that met every week for golf or bridge. They traveled together—once to Panama, repeatedly to Europe—being accompanied by their sister, Miss Katherine L. Mather, who was mistress of William G. Mather's home until he married. On their travels they collected works of art together, buying from the same dealers in London, Paris, and Rome.

Between the two Mather companies there was a rivalry along with mutual respect. In the Pickands Mather office it was said, "We get along fine with Hanna and Oglebay, Norton, but we

have trouble with Cliffs," while men in the other office were saying, "We manage beautifully with Oglebay, Norton and Hanna,
but we have to watch out for P. M." In the business warfare of
1929-31, when Cyrus Eaton was attempting to create a giant Midwest steel combination, the half brothers were pitted against each
other. W. G. Mather had teamed up with Eaton, against Samuel
Mather's interests and alliances. Their effort to gain control of
The Youngstown Sheet and Tube Company was a vital threat to
Samuel Mather and his partners. Yet in the midst of a bitter
financial and legal contest the two Mathers went on a European
trip together.

They were ardent travelers and they shared a liking for rugged
landscapes, at home and abroad. Both men retained a life-long
love of the Lake Superior wilderness. Once, taking his children
on a voyage to the head of the Lakes, Samuel Mather directed
the vessel captain to sail north of Isle Royale to see the Canadian
cliffs at Thunder Bay. Then, with his rigid honesty, he figured
the time lost by the ship in sightseeing and reimbursed the
company.

After Amasa Mather's death it was natural that Samuel Mather
should want his youngest son to enter the business. Philip Mather
had been an honor student at Yale. After a few weeks in the Cleveland office in 1917 he had gone to war. He had begun graduate
study at Harvard, working under the historians Edward Chan-
ning and Frederick Jackson Turner, when his brother died. He
gave up his studies and went into the business where he remained,
with some interruptions, for fifteen years.

Tall, erect, athletic, a horseman and squash player, the youngest Mather son had more bent for scholarship than for business.
When he first went north on inspection trips he found his
brother's photograph in every mine office; he was told with feeling and frankness that no one could ever take Amasa Mather's
place. Rather than his brother's capacities Philip Mather had the
tastes and temperament of earlier generations of Mathers who
had stirred the intellectual life of colonial New England. Eventually he left the business and settled in the Boston of his ancestors.

On a summer place near Chatham, halfway out on Cape Cod
he had a half-acre cranberry bog, tended by a Portuguese neighbor. Philip Mather used the cranberries for Christmas, sending
them to friends in Ohio and the Lake Superior district. They
were better fruit than the northern variety, but some of the min-

ing men wondered—What can you do with a bushel of cranberries? Then poison ivy took over the bog and there were no more berry crops.

Like Samuel Mather, Colonel Pickands had three sons, one of whom died in young manhood. The oldest, H. S. Pickands, became a partner in the firm; the second, Joe Pickands, was too restless to settle down to business. The youngest son died of an illness early in his career. In November 1913, when the Big Storm made a graveyard of the Lakes, Jay Morse Pickands fell suddenly ill while on a business trip to Ishpeming. He was hurried to Cleveland where he died after an operation on a ruptured appendix. His death cut off the career of a gifted gentleman and business leader.

Henry S. Pickands, named for his uncle, came into the business following his graduation from the Sheffield School at Yale in 1897, a year after his father's death. He entered the partnership in 1898. A big, dark-eyed, handsome man, he covered up a native shyness with a bluff and disapproving manner. Despite an annual affliction of hay fever he was an unrelenting worker; he and Jay McLauchlan often argued about which did the most work. Always civic-minded, he was the first mayor of the village of Euclid, Ohio, serving from 1903 to 1908 at a salary of ten dollars a year. In 1926 he headed a building campaign for University School, where his name is memorialized in Pickands Hall. He was generous to good causes though often frugal in personal expenditure. In the early years of motoring he drove a Pierce-Arrow, which he parked beside the Western Reserve Building. On severe winter days he went out every two hours, cranked the engine, and ran it a few minutes before returning to his office. He could not bring himself to pay for indoor parking. But he never stinted on cigars. He always had a long black cigar in his mouth, except when streaming with hay fever.

That affliction led him to make long visits to the Lake Superior country. In early August he went north, leaving his wife and daughters in Marquette where they had relatives and friends, while he made an extended tour of the mines. He carried a good line of cigars, the mine men remember, and he was at home wherever he went. He loved the north country as his father and his uncle had loved it. He did not have his father's imagination but he had a thorough knowledge of the company business. After years in the Ore Shipping Department he shifted to the blast furnaces, having charge of the plants at Erie and Toledo, which a few months after his death were merged into the Interlake Iron Corporation. At noon on the tenth of August, 1929, at the beginning of the hay fever season, he died at his desk in Cleveland of a heart attack.

Years after Henry Dalton's two sons died in childhood two of his nephews came into the Pickands Mather organization. In 1922, between terms at the Harvard School of Business Administration, George S. Kendrick began work at the West Shore Dock on the Blackwell Canal in Buffalo. It was a good place to get acquainted with the handling of ships and cargoes. In addition to the dock the company ran a ship's stores business and a fuel lighter, the *West Shore*. The Blackwell Canal, long an Irish stronghold, had become a Polish neighborhood, but the *West Shore* still had an all-Irish crew, headed by Captain John Green, Engineer Jerry Higgins, and Mate Michael Sullivan; on the Buffalo waterfront the lighter was known as the "Irish Navy." After a summer in Buffalo and another term at Harvard George Kendrick went into the company's Marine Department in Duluth and then in Cleveland. He served as manager of the department from 1937 until 1945 when he withdrew from Pickands Mather to look after his own business affairs. On the wall of his Cleveland office is a scale model of the Interlake freighter *E. G. Grace*.

Harry Dalton Kendrick went into the company's Coal Department in 1918 and immediately fell in love with the wilderness waterways around the fueling station at Detour. A bachelor with a liking for independence and solitude, he left the business and built a lodge on Drummond Island where he spends more than half of every year. He lives amid long memories of the Lakes trade and the sound of steamers' whistles. In his cabin cruiser he circles the big Interlake vessels coasting in to the Detour Dock. They give him the company salute, two long and three short, the deep blasts echoing over the northern woods and waters.

Through decades of increasing growth the family atmosphere and traditions of the company have been preserved. Henry S. Pickands, son and grandson of P. M. partners, is now in the company's Marine Department, having charge of nonlicensed vessel personnel in the Interlake Steamship Company. Elton Hoyt III, who came into the organization soon after his father's death, is a member of the Pig Iron Department, selling ferroalloys to the

trade. Two sons of A. D. Chisholm serve the organization. Donald
M. Chisholm is associate general manager of the company's Lake
Superior Mining Division, with headquarters in Duluth. A. D.
Chisholm, Jr., has charge of coal sales in the Upper Peninsula;
he is general manager of the Portage Coal & Dock Company at
Hancock and general manager of James Pickands & Co. at
Marquette—the parent company, founded in 1867, of Pickands
Mather.

CHAPTER 14

River of Iron

When the Iron is well hot, it worketh the better.

—WILLIAM CAXTON, 1489

IN THE 1880's William McLauchlan knew every town, village, and crossroads between Cleveland and Buffalo. At the end of a day he left his horse in a livery stable and went to a frame hotel, with chairs banked on the sidewalk on summer evenings and around the lobby stove on winter nights. In the morning he called on the local foundryman, took an order, and walked up the railroad track to his next customer. Soon he was in the buggy again, bound for the next town where a forge or foundry chimney stood smoking against the sky. He was a pig-iron salesman, engaged in the fastest growing business in the country.

Bill McLauchlan was a large man with an expansive nature. He had a word for everyone, from the office boy to the owner. His father had emigrated from Scotland in 1848, but young Bill had grown up in Cleveland and he was wholly American. Breezy, buoyant, always on the move, he had a restless mind, a capacious memory, and a huge liking for people. Men looked after him as he drove away, and they waited for his next visit.

Behind the clip-clop of his horse on the road there were other sounds. Pig iron was a product of many activities—the blast of dynamite in the mines, the rumble of ore trains onto the trestled docks, the whistle of steamers at the Soo, the clank and clatter of unloading rigs, and finally the roar of molten metal from the blast furnaces. Four operations were required in an integrated business—iron ore, ships, coal, and furnaces. In the 1880's the firm of Pickands Mather was reaching into all of them.

The first furnace interests were small and scattered. The new firm, with iron ore to furnish and ships to transport it, and with the sales agency for the Essen Coal Company of Pennsylvania, bought an interest in the Wheeler Furnace Co. on the Shenango River ten miles west of Youngstown. The company had two stacks, the Ella and the Fanny furnaces, across the railroad from each other at West Middlesex. Bill McLauchlan sold their production. He was also selling pig iron from the Struthers Furnace near Youngstown and from the Ohio Iron and Steel Company of Lowellville, a town in the midst of limestone quarries a few miles down the Mahoning Valley. In 1889 Pickands Mather leased the River Furnace at Cleveland and acquired a three-quarter interest in the Alice Furnace at Sharpsville, in the Shenango Valley just over the Pennsylvania line. In those years blast-furnace operators lived on the property, within sound of the blowing engines, and they often named the stacks for their wives and daughters. It was a small and scattered business, frequently owned by a family or a community. The bylaws of a company owning the Jefferson Furnace, a predecessor of the Globe Iron Company, in Jackson, Ohio, stated that only Welshmen could own stock in the furnace.

In the twentieth century the scattered furnaces would pass into the hands of integrated steel companies. One such company was formed in Youngstown in November 1900, when a group of fifty-five citizens subscribed $600,000 to form The Youngstown Iron Sheet and Tube Company. They bought land along the Mahoning River at a hundred dollars an acre and built a puddle mill, a sheet mill, and three tube mills. In the next year came the company's first contact with Pickands Mather—a contract for iron ore. From the start Samuel Mather saw the company's possibilities and he helped it grow. In 1902 the company bought from Pickands Mather the Alice Furnace in Sharpsville, paying $300,000 in stock. Thus began a business connection which has grown increasingly close during the past half century.

Consolidation was inevitable in the iron and steel industry. In 1885 Jay Collins Morse, the roving Pickands Mather partner, was in Chicago where H. H. Porter drew him into a reorganization of the languishing Union Iron and Steel Company. Morse was made president of the new Union Steel Company, which soon took a prominent position in the industry. In 1889 he effected a consolidation of the three leading steel companies of

the West: Union Steel Company, the North Chicago Rolling
Mills Company, and the Joliet Steel Company. These enterprises
were combined into the Illinois Steel Company, of which Jay
Morse became president and in which the firm of Pickands
Mather made investments. In assuming this office Morse resigned his presidency of the Minnesota Iron Company. With
plants in North Chicago, South Chicago, Bridgeport, Milwaukee,
and Joliet, the Illinois Steel Company was ready to supply the
rapidly growing Midwest.

In his office on the tenth floor of the Rookery, on LaSalle
Street, Morse had a neighbor in the firm of Pickands, Brown &
Company. Twelve years earlier the elder Henry S. Pickands had
managed a furnace for Morse in the woods of Lake Superior.
Now Pickands, Brown became the sales agents for the merchant
pig iron produced by Illinois Steel.

The new company grew like corn in the prairie fields. In
1891 it increased its coke and blast-furnace capacities and doubled
its production of steel rails. That year Morse and his colleagues
received seven hundred visitors, manufacturers and financiers
from England, France, and Germany, who were making a tour
of heavy industry in America. By 1892 the company had ten
thousand men in its sprawling plant in South Chicago. When
the World's Fair was in progress in 1893 thousands of tourists
went on from the wonders of Jackson Park to see the smoke and
gleam of Illinois Steel spreading over six hundred acres of prairie
shore. It had fifteen blast furnaces gushing white-hot iron and
nine Bessemer converters painting the murky sky. In the Pickands
Mather code book its name was *Hercules*.

Both in his office and outside Jay Morse was a man of few
words. In the conviviality of the Chicago Club, along with
Marshall Field, George M. Pullman, N. K. Fairbank, and John
Crerar, Morse was quiet and self-contained. At a New Year's
Day Stag dinner he was called on for a speech, a request which
he declined by turning to the man at his side and saying, "My
friend Mr. Raymond will speak for me." Mr. Raymond then
rose and made a sparkling speech, in the name of Jay Morse.
At the end, still speaking for Morse, he invited all those present
to dine with him the following Saturday, an invitation which
they applauded. So laconic Jay Morse found himself host at
a club dinner.

Illinois Steel brought Chicago into rivalry with Pittsburgh

as a steel city. As the rail business declined, the company turned
to production of structural steel as well as bars, shapes, and
plates for the building of ships, railroad cars, and farm machinery.
In 1901 it became a part of the United States Steel Corporation.
By that time Jay Morse had retired to his estate at Thomasville,
Georgia, where he treated his guests to the best quail hunting
in the world.

In the growing iron and steel business lay the roots of many
new enterprises. One of them began with a farm boy in New
York State, who wanted a farm of his own. Starting in 1842
with two crude threshing machines, Joseph Glidden worked his
way west to the prairies of Illinois. Threshing services brought
him enough money to buy a large farm fifty miles west of Chicago.
There in 1874 he secured Patent 157,124 for a strand of wire
with a steel barb twisted in it. To a neighbor he offered half
interest in the patent for a hundred dollars, but the man declined.
However, another neighbor, Isaac Elwood, risked $265 for the
same half interest, and a year later Glidden sold the remaining
half to the Washburn & Moen Manufacturing Company for
$60,000 and a large royalty. The boy who had wanted a farm
of his own ended up with 180,000 acres in Texas, stocked with
15,000 cattle and fenced with Elwood wire.

Washburn & Moen, pioneer wire manufacturers, were a
Massachusetts firm with a western plant in Chicago. Early in
the 1870's young Charles T. Boynton went to work in their
office on Lake Street. He worked the first week for nothing,
sweeping out the office and polishing spittoons, to show that he
was better than the pudgy office boy they had hired. He got the
job. With the rush of settlers to homestead lands beyond the
Missouri and millions of acres of prairie to be fenced, Washburn & Moen put up works at Waukegan, Illinois, to make
barbed wire. Boynton became a salesman, traveling the sparsely
settled northern plains. In the Dakotas, Wyoming, and Montana
he kept bumping into another barbed wire man, John W. Gates—
later famous as "Bet-a-Million Gates." Jolting along on prairie
trains they quickly made up their accounts and then looked
out at the wind-swept country waiting to be fenced. The con-
ductor had a side line. "It's four hours to the next town," he
announced. "For twenty-five cents I could hire you a rifle to
occupy your time." So the salesmen sat at open windows, bang-

ing away at prairie dogs, prairie chickens, sage hens, and coyotes. Occasionally they shot an antelope. Then the train stopped, they dressed out the game and took it aboard. That evening all the passengers had an antelope dinner.

In later years the barbed wire salesmen went into offices. Gates became Chairman of the Board of the American Steel and Wire Company, which in 1898 entered into a loose alliance with the Federal Steel Company and in 1901 was absorbed by United States Steel. Then he retired to England where he raced his famous horses. Boynton and Philip Moen went to the elder Morgan and sold the Washburn & Moen Manufacturing Company; it also eventually went into United States Steel. In 1902 Charles T. Boynton joined the firm of Pickands, Brown & Company, sales agents for pig iron, iron ore, and coke in the Chicago area.

Into its huge grasp the United States Steel Corporation gathered mines, ships, furnaces, and mills. This new colossus stood with one foot in the Pennsylvania coal lands and the other in Lake Superior iron ranges a thousand miles away, and in its shadow the independent companies were almost lost from sight. But the twentieth century was at hand, with all its power and promise. Though Samuel Mather had aided United States Steel in obtaining ore lands and vessels, and though he would sit on its board for twenty-three years, he was still an independent. Promptly his firm pushed into new iron-ore properties around Lake Superior and into blast furnaces on the Lower Lakes.

In 1902 Pickands Mather formed the Toledo Furnace Company. On the east bank of the Maumee River the shell of Furnace "A" grew up from its deep foundations. Shaped like a huge lamp chimney, it rose above the docks and railroad yards. Its steel shell was lined with hundreds of thousands of refractory bricks, resistant enough to withstand the heat that would melt the metal out of iron ore. Beside it like twin silos rose the cylindrical stoves with their hot blast flowing through the bustle pipe to the nozzled tuyères ranged around the narrowed base of the furnace. Up the side of the stack climbed the rigid webbing of the skip hoist, and curling away from the lofty charging floor went the big steel downcomers which would carry the smoke and fumes to the dust catchers and lead the cleaned gas back to the stoves. At the base of the furnace were the cinder notch and the tapping hole, through which would pour the molten matter which a few hours earlier was iron ore, coke, and limestone.

This huge and intricate plant was the product of thousands of years of ironmaking. It had developed, step by step, from the crude stone oven where primitive man with goatskin bellows burned the reddish rocks that would later be called iron ore. Now the bellows was a perpetual roaring blast of heated air, the oven was a towering furnace for an undying fire. It would burn continuously, day and night, winter and summer, charged every five minutes with tons of raw material and yielding six times a day a river of molten iron.

The blast furnace was a giant chemical retort, a test tube in which thousands of tons of material, subjected to a heat of 3,000 degrees Fahrenheit, would react so as to free the metal from the dross. But before it could operate a fire had to be kindled on the cold dark hearth; heat must be generated and circulation begun in the connecting tubes and chambers. Tons of cordwood filled the bottom of the stack. The fire roared upward, hungry for more fuel. Then the layers of coke, ore, and limestone went into the receiving hopper, and inside the furnace shell the unseen process began. Heated air, forced in through the tuyères, roared up through the charge. In that hot blast the coke burned furiously. Its gases removed the oxygen from the ore, transforming it into a spongy mass of iron. The porous iron assimilated carbon from the coke, the carbon was driven away, and again the iron absorbed it. That chemical war went on while the charge worked downward, growing hotter as it settled. In that heat the scavenger limestone crumbled, taking up in molten slag the impurities of ore and coke. Still settling toward the inward-sloping boshes, the iron began to melt, trickling through the incandescent coke, taking on carbon from the fuel and silicon from the slag. On the hearth the melted iron formed a pool, with the molten slag floating on top. From the cinder notch poured white running slag. When the iron notch was tapped, out gushed the river of iron in a fiery shower of sparks. Blast Furnace "A" was in production.

For forty minutes the river ran, radiant as the sun, through sand channels into brick-lined ladles, while behind it the blast roared upward and the reaction continued in the stack. The brimming ladles were tilted into an endless belt of molds. Quenched with water, the liquid metal solidified. The bars of new-made iron dropped, smoking, into railroad cars, and Bill McLauchlan had a new production to sell.

In earlier times the molten iron was led through a sandy trough into cooling beds shaped like a litter of nursing pigs. Though the equipment had changed from the crude stone furnace to the towering stack, the same chemical process reduced the iron-bearing rock to bars of metallic iron. The name persisted. It was still pig iron that the furnacemen produced.

In 1907 a second stack was added to the Toledo plant and production was doubled. It was a farsighted decision that had led to the construction of blast-furnace works on the Maumee. Late to grow industrially, Toledo was a trading town until the Civil War. But by 1870 it had become an important railroad terminus with long trains bringing cargoes for Lake shipment. The Maumee Valley gas field offered cheap fuel for industry, and the city's population quadrupled in the thirty years after 1870. By 1900 it had miles of docks and acres of railroad yards. The twentieth century brought new enterprises, the manufacture of glass, machinery, and motorcars. At its peak the Overland automobile factory turned out a motorcar every thirty seconds.

Heavy industry was spreading westward along a line just north of the fortieth parallel. Toledo, with one of the finest harbors on the Great Lakes, lay in the path of its development. The Toledo Furnace Company, at the door of the automotive market and close to the growing industries of northwestern Ohio, northern Indiana, and southeastern Michigan, had a ready market for its output. It became the foremost producer of merchant pig iron in the country.

Meanwhile Pickands Mather had acquired interests in other blast-furnace plants on the Great Lakes. In 1904 they invested in the Zenith Furnace Company at Duluth; two years later they took a substantial interest in the Federal Furnace Company at South Chicago. In 1912 they acquired a majority of the stock of the Perry Iron Company with blast-furnace works at Erie, Pennsylvania. In 1915 at Canton, Ohio, a short rail haul from Lake Erie, they formed the United Furnace Company, half interest in it being taken by the United Steel Company of Canton. In 1921 this company along with the United Furnace property went into the newly formed United Alloy Steel Corporation, which later became a part of Republic Steel. In 1916 the firm acquired part ownership of the Iroquois Iron Company at South Chicago. When Iroquois was taken over by The Youngstown Sheet and Tube Company eight years later, Pickands Mather became sales agents for the Iroquois plant's merchant pig iron.

During these years Pickands Mather disposed of its interests in the smaller furnaces which Bill McLauchlan had represented on his horse-and-buggy travels. The time of the horse and buggy was past, as was the time of the neighborhood blast furnace. Great ironworks were replacing the local units, and corporations were supplanting community enterprise. Behind this change was something more than the efficiency of large operations; there was a revolution in science and technology.

The old blast furnaces burned coke from beehive ovens, rows of rounded kilns seeping their gases into the open sky. But across the Atlantic, while Bill McLauchlan was first driving over the Ohio roads, two scientists made related discoveries. A French chemist named Semet had found a process for obtaining ammonia in the coking of coal, and his brother-in-law, Ernest Solvay, had used ammonia to manufacture soda from salt brine. When the Solvay and Semet processes were brought to America, the old beehive coke ovens were replaced with by-product recovery ovens and the conserved coal tars became the basis of a new chemical industry. The by-product oven, yielding ammonia, coal tar, oils, and gas in addition to the blast-furnace fuel, reduced the cost of pig iron and lowered the price of steel. It made the beehive ovens obsolete.

During their early development of iron-ore properties on Lake Superior, Pickands Mather acquired coal mines in Pennsylvania. In 1891 the firm purchased the Essen Coal Company, a property near Pittsburgh, which was sold eight years later to Henry W. Oliver's Pittsburgh Coal Company. In 1903 the firm formed the Provident Coal Company, which was sold to the Clarkson Coal Mining Company fourteen years later.

Meanwhile the coal trade had grown vastly on the Lakes and a revolution had come to the loading docks. The old wheelbarrow gang had disappeared by 1890, and the bucket system went out when the ports were equipped with car dumpers in 1895. These brawny machines picked up coal cars, dumped them over with a dusty thunder, and set them back on the track. A test of their capacity came in 1897 when a coal-miners' strike halted coal traffic on the Lakes throughout the summer months.

That year 80 per cent of the Lake coal was loaded onto ships between the first of October and the close of navigation two months later. The car dumpers did the job; they made the loading of coal almost as rapid a process as the loading of iron ore from the trestled ore docks. The unloading of coal at the northern ports was a slower business, but the twentieth century brought successively larger hoists to discharge the cargo into railroad cars or onto the stockpile.

In 1909 William G. Mather, president of the Cleveland-Cliffs Iron Company, went down to Green County, Pennsylvania, in the extreme southwestern corner of the State, to look at coal lands there. Three hundred and fifty feet underground lay the extensive Pittsburgh coal seam, averaging seventy-four inches in thickness. Proposing a joint venture, W. G. Mather turned to his half brother. As a result Cleveland-Cliffs and Pickands Mather each took a third interest in the property; the other third was taken by The Steel Company of Canada, Limited. The property was undeveloped until 1917 when Pickands Mather sold its Provident Coal Company. In that year work began on the Mather Collieries a few miles west of the winding Monongahela River.

In the Pickands Mather Coal Department, William P. Murray had retired and was succeeded by George D. Cameron who entered the partnership in 1916. With him in the department was Frank Armstrong, a native of Ireland. Armstrong developed the Mather Collieries. He built the town, the mine, and the railroad spur. He got the long coal trains moving to Lake Erie and the cargoes loaded and delivered. In later years Stelco bought out the other owners, making the Mather Collieries a captive mine with all its production going to the Canadian furnaces. Pickands Mather continues to operate it, as they have done since the property was first developed.

"Coal," wrote Ralph Waldo Emerson a century ago, "is portable climate." It is also, in the twentieth century, the making of many other things, from perfumes to fertilizers. Seventy-five years ago, when Bill McLauchlan was pulling up his horse at the scattered foundries, a man from Rhode Island made a trip to Europe to arrange the organization of an American Solvay Process Company. On his return, Rowland Hazard built recovery coke ovens and a chemical plant on the site of large brine deposits near Syracuse, New York. The chemical products had a ready market, but he was left with the coke. As the company grew, new coke plants were established near blast-furnace works, and the by-product chemicals were shipped to the central plant at Syracuse. In 1905 Hazard's scattered properties were combined in the By-Products Coke Corporation, and in that year a large plant was built on a site of 390 acres along the Calumet River in South Chicago, where the empty marsh and prairie stretched inland from Lake Michigan. The spreading city of Chicago was a hungry market for gas and coke. An even closer customer lay just across the Calumet River where the Federal Furnace Company, soon to be jointly owned by Pickands Mather, Pickands, Brown, and the National Malleable Castings Company, was getting its first big stack into production. Along the dredged and deepened Calumet River Pickands Mather vessels were unloading bulk cargoes. For every two tons of iron ore the furnaces required a ton of coke. Over the Calumet flats rumbled freight cars—now replaced by a conveyer over the river—and the Federal Furnace ate up the flow of coke from the By-Products company's ovens.

Here was a natural combination of interests, the chemists trapping the coal gas and the furnacemen using the residual fuel to reduce iron ore to pig iron. In 1915 the two companies merged, Federal Furnace becoming a part of the By-Products Coke Corporation. Their interest in the By-Products company led Pickands Mather men into the chemical industry with a wide range of coal-tar products, including refrigerants, plastics, creosote, drugs, dyes, and explosives. During the years of World War I the company was besieged with orders for all its products.

After the merger with the Federal Furnace Company, By-Products stock was held by both Eastern and Western organizations, the Pickands Mather partners being more aggressive and more aware of the future than the Eastern chemical men who were linked with them. In the recession of 1920, when the plant was growing obsolete and By-Products stock was selling at a twentieth of its one-time high, the Easterners were ready to liquidate. The Pickands Mather men, however, were thinking of a renovated plant and a new volume of production. In that tension they supported C. D. Caldwell, a Tennessee man with knowledge of both the iron and the coal businesses, who became president of the company. With the backing of Henry Dalton,

Harry Coulby, H. S. Pickands, and an able young iron-ore salesman, Elton Hoyt 2nd, Caldwell rehabilitated the plant and cut the working force in half without reducing production. C. D. Caldwell entered the Pickands Mather partnership in 1930.

With blast furnaces in Duluth, Chicago, Toledo, and Erie, it was evident to the Pickands Mather partners that economies and efficiencies could be achieved by consolidation. The driving force in the reorganization was Elton Hoyt 2nd. He worked through hundreds of details of the separate furnace properties, and at last the reorganization was ready. In 1929 all the blast-furnace properties of Pickands Mather & Co. were combined in the Interlake Iron Corporation. Encompassing the Perry Furnace Company at Erie, the Toledo Furnace Company, the Zenith Furnace Company at Duluth, along with the By-Products Coke Corporation with its Federal Furnace plant, the Interlake Iron Corporation was the largest producer of merchant pig iron in the world. Interlake Iron unified P. M. blast-furnace interests as the Interlake Steamship Company had earlier unified their shipping interests.

In the 1880's the paths of the Pickands brothers had diverged —Colonel James Pickands going to Cleveland to establish a new firm and Henry S. Pickands going to Chicago, where with William Liston Brown he organized Pickands, Brown & Company. Relationships between the Cleveland and Chicago firms were close; the first Pickands, Brown letterhead carried also the name of Pickands Mather. A commission house, without mines or vessels, Pickands, Brown soon became the leading sales agents of pig iron, coke, and gas in the Chicago area. They were in a position to influence the purchase of coal and iron ore from Pickands Mather; at the same time Pickands Mather could refer sales business in the area to Pickands, Brown. After 1904 both companies had financial interests in the Zenith Furnace Company at Duluth; Pickands Mather furnished iron ore and Pickands, Brown handled the sale of its pig iron.

Finally the businesses of the two brothers, who had once dreamed of a business together, were combined. In 1930 the entire stock of Pickands, Brown & Company was acquired by the Cleveland firm, and Pickands Mather obtained the agency in the Chicago area for the sale of coke and pig iron from the production of the Interlake Iron Corporation, The Youngstown

Sheet and Tube Company, the North Shore Coke and Chemical Company, and the Milwaukee Coke and Gas Company.

William McLauchlan had retired in 1918, though he still stood up at the speakers' table to tell stories at the annual fleet dinner for Interlake captains, mates, and engineers. In the Pig Iron Department he was succeeded by his son Jay Chandler McLauchlan, a man of dark, strong features and a magnetic nature. Like his father he was a natural salesman. Following graduation from Yale he began his career in 1903 in Detroit, selling pig iron for Pickands Mather and steel for the Lackawanna Steel Company.

Impulsive, impetuous, generous, and expansive, Jay McLauchlan had hosts of friends who admired both his accomplishments and his misadventures. In Detroit he became acquainted with George Henry, president of the Ontario Jockey Club. Henry invited his friend to the track at Windsor, reserving a box for him and recommending a bet on a dark horse. McLauchlan prepared for the occasion. He bought a silk hat, a checked suit and fancy waistcoat, gray gloves, and an ascot tie. When the day came the skies were overcast and he covered up his new clothes in a bulky raincoat. Rain poured down as he reached the track. In dampened spirits he trudged to the stable, looked at the long-odds horse, and decided not to bet. He passed up the race and went to the hotel bar. When a friend admired his race-track garb McLauchlan said, "I'm through with horse races. I'll sell it to you." He made the transaction then and there and went back to Detroit in his raincoat.

In 1917 he went into the Pickands Mather home office, entering the partnership a year later. During World War I he served as chief of the Pig Iron Section of the War Industries Board. He died in Cleveland in 1929, just before the organization of the Interlake Iron Corporation. His father died soon after.

During Bill McLauchlan's span, America had changed from an agricultural to an industrial nation, and the iron business had changed with it. When he started out in 1883 thousands of tons of pig iron were going into horseshoes. When he died it was going into new alloy steels for the manufacture of airplane engines.

CHAPTER 15

The Tallest Oak

O<small>N HIS</small> daily trip to the Western Reserve Building Samuel Mather passed the old Lennox Building, with three floors of apartments above a row of shops, at the corner of East Ninth Street and Euclid Avenue. Attached to it was an oval structure which housed a Civil War cyclorama. Thousands of visitors climbed to a central balcony and viewed the horror and heroism of the Battle of Shiloh on a huge circle of canvas. After a few years that spectacle was replaced by the Battle of Gettysburg, and Gettysburg was followed by Lookout Mountain. Then, in 1896, the building was rented to a school for bicycle riding.

In 1920 the corner was cleared and a steel skeleton began to rise on deep foundations. Iron ore from Lake Superior was going into a twenty-one-story building in Cleveland's spreading business district. In 1924 the Union Trust (later the Union Commerce) Building was opened, the second largest office building in the world. On the twenty-first of March Pickands Mather & Co. moved in. It was the beginning of a new season, with freighters fitting out in a dozen harbors and ore trains moving onto the docks, when the P. M. staff took up quarters on the twentieth floor.

Now there were eight partners, a dozen departments, and some two hundred personnel. To the new location they brought a sense of the company's tradition and various mementos of the past. The engine plate of the wooden *V. H. Ketchum,* first vessel to be operated by the company, was mounted on the wall of the Vessel Engineering Department. Old photographs of ship-lined Whisky Island and new pictures of the docks at Ashtabula and Buffalo showed the development of dock facilities. In the Marine Department pictures of three successive ships named *Samuel Mather* told a story of bulk freighters and their cargoes. Photographs of the early partners brought reminders of the past into the new library room.

In this room the company officials carried on a practice begun by Henry Dalton in 1912. In the early years the morning mail was not distributed until Mr. Dalton had considered what he could attend to and what he could assign to his associates. When the growing business brought more correspondence than he could supervise, he called a morning meeting of department heads. Its original purpose was to parcel out the mail, but it soon developed into a business meeting, with each department reporting on matters and questions of general concern. Henry Dalton usually presided; in his absence Harry Coulby, H. S. Pickands, or another partner took charge. Under Harry Coulby it was a brisk meeting, promptly assembled and soon adjourned. He instituted a fine for being late—so much a minute; the fund was used to buy a marine clock, framed in the ten spokes of a ship's wheel, for the wall.

In the new meeting room the activities of a far-flung sales and service organization were reported and discussed. From the wall the clock chimed unchanging sea watches while the personnel around the table changed and grew as the years passed. At first it was Henry Dalton, composed, formally courteous, and seemingly all-knowing, in the chair with Lake Erie distant in the window behind him; then it was Elton Hoyt 2nd, comprehensive in grasp and decisive in judgment; then John Sherwin, alert, informed, ready to focus on any facet of the manifold business.

In the mid-1920's the partners were Samuel Mather, Henry Dalton, Harry Coulby, H. S. Pickands, Frank Armstrong, Jay McLauchlan, Elton Hoyt 2nd, and Samuel Bool. They had been together for years; they understood each other and their own responsibilities. But within a few years half of the chairs were vacant. In 1929 three of the partners died; another followed in 1931.

On a Christmas visit to England Harry Coulby had spent the holidays in his native village in Lincolnshire. Then he went down to London, planning to sail for the West Indies before his return to Cleveland. But he did not make that journey. On

January 18, 1929, his valet found him dead of a heart attack in his London hotel suite. When the news reached America, every mariner on the Great Lakes felt the loss of a leader. That summer in the middle of an August day Henry S. Pickands died at his office desk. Two months later Jay McLauchlan, who had taken his father's place in the partnership, died at his home in Cleveland.

Into the partnership in the next year came four men from Pickands, Brown & Company, whose assets Pickands Mather had bought. C. D. Caldwell, widely experienced and resourceful, was president of the Interlake Iron Corporation. C. P. Wheeler had joined Pickands, Brown at the beginning of the twentieth century. Shortly after the merger, illness overtook him; he died in 1932. Seymour Wheeler and Donald S. Boynton, sons of early Pickands, Brown partners, had been with that company for some twenty years. After 1930 these men operated the Chicago business for Pickands Mather, handling the sale of pig iron, coal, and coke from their office on Michigan Avenue.

In the meeting room in Cleveland the clock chimed on and business continued. The Marine Department, long thought of as Harry Coulby's, was taken over by Elton Hoyt 2nd, who in 1929 was elected a managing partner of the firm. In the Depression years ahead he would carry burdens greater than those of any man in the company's past.

Along with business problems there came an unexpected threat to the memory of an eminent man and the reputation of the firm. In a bizarre and brazen law case a mountaineer from the Virginia-Kentucky border brought suit in 1930 in Lake County, Ohio, for the possession of the estate of his alleged father, Harry Coulby.

The claimant was one Heney Adkins of Grundy, Virginia, who first heard of Harry Coulby when he read a newspaper account of his death. "I was setting in the grocery store at Greenup, Kentucky," he stated, "and I saw in the Ashland *Independent* a story that Harry Coulby of Cleveland had died, leaving about $4,500,000 to charity; that he was connected with a steamship company; and I knew my father's name was Colby, or Tolby, or something like that, and had left my mother to go to the Great Lakes and be a sailor, and I says, 'I bet that's my father,' and I put on my hat and started."

After the Cleveland attorneys had traced Harry Coulby's

movements from a telegraph desk in England to his first employment in Cleveland, and had taken some amusing depositions in Kentucky, the Adkins lawyers dropped the action. Closing the suit, the judge declared: "The plaintiff's case was dismissed for want of prosecution. The Court also feels that it should be dismissed on its own merits . . . a sly, cheap, dishonest attempt to blacken the good name of one of our leading and respected citizens."

Homer H. McKeehan, a close friend of Harry Coulby and principal attorney for his estate, made a personal crusade of the Adkins case to dispel any shadow from Coulby's name for his family and the public. As part of this endeavor, McKeehan wrote an absorbing book about the case, attesting to the unswerving integrity in every aspect of Coulby's life.

His humanity was demonstrated by the terms of his will. Certain bequests went to Coulby's native village, to the Claypole school and the parish church. Much of the estate went to the Lakeside Hospital in Cleveland and to the Cleveland Foundation for the help of sick, crippled, and needy children. His associates at Pickands Mather had not been forgotten. The will placed a quarter of the estate in trust and directed that the net income of the fund be paid to deserving employees. The partners were excluded. Each year awards are made from this fund to employees whose efforts are felt to be worthy of special recognition.

His mansion at Wickliffe, where in 1916 he had served as the village's first mayor, was later occupied for a time by the Sisters of the Holy Humility of Mary. It was such an order that had cared for Harry Coulby when, ill and penniless, he had arrived in the United States half a century before.

In the summer of 1931 Samuel Mather observed his eightieth birthday. A month later he visited the Lake Superior mines. On October 18, after two weeks' illness, he died at his home on the lake shore at Bratenahl on the edge of Cleveland. At the memorial service in Severance Hall Newton D. Baker said, "Out of the forest our tallest oak has gone, one under whose shade we have found shelter."

As a businessman Samuel Mather had a grasp of concrete details in a complex industry. He understood the interlocking realities of production in the mines, transportation by rail and steamship, transfer of cargo at terminals, and manufacture in

furnaces and mills. His holdings in United States Steel, Youngstown Sheet and Tube, and Lackawanna Steel which in 1923 was
merged with the Bethlehem Steel Company, assured a market
for his own firm's production and a source of supply for the steel
companies. When he died Pickands Mather was still a partnership as it had begun. But it had become a far-reaching service
organization, managing mines and vessels and serving as an
operating and sales agency for many corporations.

On the day of his death flags were at half-staff on all the
Interlake ships and work was halted at mines on all the Lake
Superior ranges. Editorials and obituaries appeared in newspapers from Buffalo to the northern wilderness. At Crystal Falls,
Michigan, the *Diamond Drill* observed that this man, who in
brief visits scattered over forty years had spent perhaps a total
of sixty days on the Menominee Range, had made judgments
and decisions that shaped the development of Iron County. The
editorial ended: "Pickands Mather has carved out of the Iron
County wilderness since 1890 many fine communities. Valuation
of Iron County has increased from four million dollars in 1890
to thirty-six million in 1931, a large portion of it managed by
Pickands Mather. So has the trail of one man been drawn across
a tract of wilderness."

The man who had changed the wilderness looked like a
scholar. His long lean face, with snowy hair and mustache, was
lighted by blue-gray eyes, direct yet thoughtful. He belonged
to literary groups, the Grolier Club and the Rowfant Club. The
books in his own library ranged from theological treatises to
Americana. In a habitual attitude he held a slender hand to his
head, half-cupping his ear and his old-fashioned sideburns. "The
tallest oak" was a slight man with a many-sided mind.

Newton D. Baker knew of Samuel Mather's industrial stat-
ure, but it was a humanitarian "shelter" he referred to. In
benefaction, as in business, Samuel Mather had a grasp of details
in complex situations. He took the lead in forming the Cleveland Red Cross War Council in 1917 and served as its chairman.
When large sums were needed for war relief, he formed the
plan for a Victory Chest, which the Council sponsored, to raise
ten million dollars at the end of the war in 1918. Samuel Mather
saw the continuing need for support of civic charities and the
wisdom of an annual united appeal for them. He brought this
into being through the formation of The Cleveland Community
Fund, the first of its kind in America. Throughout the 1920's

Samuel Mather was its honorary chairman and its largest con-
tributor. At his death he left a provision for its continuing
support, along with bequests to fifty-five other charitable and
educational institutions. Major gifts went to the Lakeside Hospital, Western Reserve University, Kenyon College, and Trinity
Cathedral.

Another beneficiary was the Cleveland Museum of Art. In
1909 while the Mather house on Euclid Avenue, now the quarters of the Cleveland Automobile Club, was under construction,
Flora Stone Mather died. Samuel Mather then began collecting
objects of beauty to furnish the house she had planned. He assembled Greek, Roman, and Egyptian enamels, Italian ceramics,
Majolica ware, Persian rugs, German medieval sculpture, Oriental bronzes, Italian, French, and English painting. After his
death his collections enriched the Cleveland Museum and other
institutions.

In this year that brought the death of the last of the original
partners, a Pickands Mather emblem was devised. It happened
by chance, in connection with a company dinner at the Cleveland Athletic Club in the spring of 1931. A song sheet was to
be used at the dinner. To dress it up, E. C. Brunner, then
assistant treasurer of the firm, took a coin and circled it on the
cover. Then he drew a curved line through the circle and put
the initials P. M. on either side. (It was later colored red and
black, with white initials.) Though unaware of it E. C. Brunner
had created a company emblem which would soon appear in
ships, offices, and mines, and on brochures, advertisements, and
company journals. The insignia met a need that no one had
been conscious of until it was filled. First used at the suggestion
of Elton Hoyt 2nd, it became a daily reminder of the unity of
a widespread organization.

When the design was copyrighted it was recognized as an
ancient Chinese symbol representing the interaction of two
forces, Yang and Yin. Yang is the male, Yin the female. Yang is
light, Yin darkness. Yang is spirit, Yin matter; together they
make up the universe. For an ordered life they must work har-
moniously, one balancing and complementing the other. Though
no symbolic intention had been attached to the P. M. emblem,
the symbolism was apt. It suggested the two opposite but com-
plementary impulses in the company, caution and venture, tradition and innovation, continuity and change.

PART III

Tradition and Change

"Gold is for the mistress—silver for the maid—
Copper for the craftsman cunning at his trade."
"Good!" cried the Baron, sitting in his hall,
"But Iron—Cold Iron—is master of them all."
—RUDYARD KIPLING, 1910

CHAPTER 16

The Silent Years

THE OPENING of the Sagamore Mine, on the Cuyuna Range, required the draining of a peat bog eight feet deep. In 1921 as hose lines sucked away the muskeg they uncovered some earlier inhabitants of the mine site. Out came a big triangular skull, a long jagged spinal column, and various bones well preserved in that deep bed of peat. These were the remains of prehistoric buffalo that had roamed the Minnesota land before the last of the great glaciers crept over it. Sent to Washington and assembled in a complete skeleton, the bones were put on display in The United States National Museum.

Animals more recent than the prehistoric bison have been found in the open pits. Deer sometimes wander down the truck road vainly looking for browse, and dead fawns have been found at the foot of the cut. Early one morning in the Embarrass Mine a sleepy pumpman tramping down the truck road turned a corner and found himself staring at a big black bear. The pumpman, wide awake, took off up the road, and the bear scrambled up the bank, sending a rain of red rock down the slopes.

The iron men opened their pits and sank their shafts in a wilderness, and despite the roar of Diesels and the blasts of dynamite the wilderness has persisted. A hundred paces from certain mine pits a man can be swallowed up in brush or mired in muskeg. Within gunshot of the workings poplar trees are gnawed by beavers and wild tracks are written in the snow. In the summer of 1954 the surface crew at Fortune Lake found a tiny fawn wandering on the edge of the pit. Taken into the mine office, it was taught to suck milk from a baby bottle. After a few days it was entrusted to the Michigan Conservation Department. In the winter of 1956 a moose was a regular visitor to the parking lot beside the Embarrass Mine office.

In the years of the Depression the old wilderness silence settled over the pits and head frames on all the ranges. "Shipped every year but 1931 and 1932" is a familiar note in the Directory of Mines. At the huge Mahoning pit, which has shipped more than a hundred million tons of ore, stripping of overburden has gone on every winter for sixty years—except during 1931 and 1932. In all the mining communities maintenance crews kept machinery oiled and shining, but the pits were lifeless and the underground drifts were dark. Some of the underground mines were allowed to flood; others had to be kept pumped on account of the tremendous weight on the timbers. The cost of later rehabilitation determined which mines were pumped during the idle years.

In 1932 Pickands Mather had charge of twenty-three mines on the six ranges, with annual productive capacity of about fifteen million tons. The company's production during that year was about 7,500 tons that came from the Menominee Range, a bare two compartments in a vessel, and a few tons of experimental ore from the Scranton and Mahoning pits. Shipment from all the Lake Superior mines dropped from 23,500,000 tons in 1931 to 3,500,000 in 1932. In that year the industry fell back almost to the level of 1882 when 3,000,000 tons of ore came down the Lakes.

Paralysis came quickly to the range towns. With a single industry the communities were prostrate when the mines closed down. While the rest of the country slid gradually into depression the iron towns fell in like a bear blundering into a test pit. All through the north country mines were either closed or curtailed to part-time operation. Since improved methods had cut the labor force to a third of what it had been twenty years earlier, limited production meant still more limited employment.

Iron mining is a business of many sounds—the din of power drills and the boom of blasting, the throb of Diesels and the rhythmic roar of crushing plants. But these were silent years. Mining companies stretched the work, one day or two days a week, among veteran employees, while the seasons dragged by. Men clustered on the street corners or waited in line at the relief office, their eyes looking up to the idle head frame or off toward the empty pit. These years would have demoralized a less sturdy people than the iron miners. While relief rolls mounted they waited stolidly for times to change.

Some things were in their favor. They had gardens, though the growing season was short. They could cut fuel in the woods and perhaps bring home some game for the table. In the range towns there were no piles of household goods on the sidewalk with a dazed family standing beside them. Many miners owned their own houses. Hundreds lived in company homes; there were no evictions. And, as in brighter years, the range children attended some of the finest schools in the world. For decades the mines had been a rich source of public revenue, and the range towns had provided well for their children. School staffs included doctors, dentists, and nurses. The school buildings, dominant physical features of the communities, had auditoriums, gymnasiums, and skating rinks as well as finely equipped classrooms, laboratories, and libraries. Even though the mines were dead the schools were vibrantly alive.

In the depressed towns people watched their savings dwindle and tried to keep their independence. An old Cornish couple asked the relief office not for a monthly check but only for a new kitchen stove. To puzzled relief officers the weathered Cousin Jack explained that they were making a living by selling pasties, and so much baking had burned out their old oven. With a new stove they could go on providing for themselves. In another town where grocery bills had accumulated before the relief office opened, a storekeeper offered a credit of two dollars a cord for stovewood to supply him through the winter. So many hundreds of cords came in that the grocer had to open up a woodyard. Few iron range families stayed willingly on relief.

The hardy racial groups did what they could to help themselves and each other, and they had the constant concern and support of the management in Duluth and Cleveland. With heavy financial commitments in the Youngstown and Bethlehem companies, Pickands Mather was under severe pressure. Yet the firm was determined to take care of its own people and to hold the organization together. The top men from Cleveland went North, not on inspection visits, but to meet and talk with idled and bewildered men. In the range towns the company provided garden seeds, loaned tractors and implements for use in cutting fuel and growing foodstuffs, and gave financial help to needy families.

The hard times must have been hardest for men who knew both the workmen and the management, who understood the helplessness of the company and the bewilderment of idle miners. In these years A. D. Chisholm was general manager of Pickands Mather mines, with headquarters in Duluth. From there the stricken range towns were out of sight but never out of his mind. He had been a mine man all his life.

Originally from Inverness, Scotland, his people had come to Upper Michigan by way of Canada. A native of Ironwood, young Alex Chisholm, on graduation from high school in 1903, began work at seventeen in the analytical laboratory at the historic Newport Mine. He had what the Cousin Jacks called "an eye for ore," and his mind was reaching into the various aspects of the complex industry. From chemistry he moved into underground engineering and then into the Operating Department of the Newport Mining Company. In 1913 he became superintendent of the Anvil-Palms Mine just east of Bessemer: during three years there he introduced new methods and machinery and dramatically increased the mine's production. On his staff in the summer of 1915 was his friend Arthur F. Peterson, an Ironwood youth who thirty years later became a vice-president of the Bethlehem Steel Company. Following a hitch in the army and graduation from the University of Wisconsin in 1918, Peterson returned to the Anvil-Palms as mine captain. In April 1920, A. D. Chisholm was made general manager for the Lake Superior District of The Steel and Tube Company of America, which in 1923 was acquired by The Youngstown Sheet and Tube Company. In 1921 came the one break in his career in the north country; he went to Brazil on a harbor construction project. In 1927 he was made manager of Pickands Mather's Michigan operations, and on the eve of Depression he moved to Duluth in January 1931 as assistant general manager of Pickands Mather mines.

As a miner or a superintendent Chisholm never dodged unpleasant tasks. When in the past he had had to announce cutbacks and wage cuts, he did not begin: "The home office has ordered—" or, "I tried to stop this, but—" He made a blunt statement and was ready to supply reasons if they were asked for.

Soon after taking charge at Duluth he had the unhappy duty of ordering mines closed down and payrolls pared to the bone. Yet in visits on the ranges he represented to the men the concern and support of their company.

At the onset of Depression he accompanied Elton Hoyt 2nd on a tour of the districts where the company was operating mining properties. At meetings of supervisory people on the ranges Hoyt spoke of current problems, with the steel industry at a standstill, and of the company's need to adjust operations to the economic situation. At his side was A. D. Chisholm who had been through other crises; he had seen strikes and layoffs, the I.W.W. agitation in 1917, and the cutback in 1921. He knew tags of a dozen languages, from Swedish to Sicilian, and could talk to any miner in his own tongue. He had been through the good years and the bad years and he did not look dispirited. His presence there was reassuring.

From these district meetings there linger, in better times, memories of the frankness and concern of the management and of the resiliency of the range men themselves. Men in the North still remember how "Mick" Kelley, one of the mine supervisors, could inject a saving humor at painful moments. His booming voice carried a kind of defiance of misfortune. It cleared the air and suggested times to come again, when the big shovels would gouge into the pits, trains would rumble onto the trestled docks, and iron ore would go thumping into cargo holds.

In 1932 there were forty-nine freighters under the Interlake flag. That year thirty of them carried a total of a little more than three million tons of cargo—most of it coal—a tonnage that could have been carried by eleven vessels. Some of the ships were in commission as little as twelve days, just enough to give them a minimum of maintenance after the long lay-up. Throughout the season crews were shifted from one vessel to another.

At the Interlake Steamship Company offices in Cleveland, Chicago, and Duluth men were begging for work, even without pay, asking only for a place to eat and sleep. The vessel agents shook their heads; there were no jobs of that or any other kind. First consideration went to the licensed men and when they were assigned there was little left. That year, with few smoke streamers over the shipping lanes and no chorus of whistles at the Soo, hundreds of captains and engineers went back to the ratings of their youth. In a single crew six masters and chief engineers were serving as mates, wheelsmen, assistant engineers, and oilers. Ashore hundreds of veteran seamen were left without a call, watching the empty water from their homes on the St. Clair River or the ports of Lake Erie.

In past years The Ashtabula and Buffalo Dock Company had employed three hundred men in its bustling Buffalo dock, fuel lighter, and ship's stores company. In 1932 it was a desolate place. The dock foreman, master mechanic, and machine operators were all put on police duty as night watchmen because there was no work to do. Coal was still moving on the Lakes and Buffalo had once been a coal shipping port. But the trade had moved west to the big coal docks at Sandusky and Toledo, and in Buffalo the dead rigs hunched over the lifeless water.

That summer Captain Hans Hansen kept an idle ship at Buffalo. At evening he walked its echoing deck and watched the stars come out over empty Lake Erie. He had weathered storm and stress at sea, in many waters of the world, but this was a new kind of disaster. Ships dumping foodstuffs in the Atlantic for lack of market, while men were waiting in soup lines in America. Fleets laid up in the harbors because there was a surplus of wheat in Great Lakes elevators, a surplus of sugar in Cuba, a surplus of beef in Argentina, a surplus of coffee in Brazil, and men idle, hungry, and helpless in every city in the world. Farmers plowing up crops and destroying livestock because the relief offices were thronged with unemployed. Stockpiles of ore on the docks and coal in the storage yards and the mills closed down and men outside the gates wondering when there would be work again. It was hard to understand.

A ship's captain knew another kind of stress, the somber force of wind and sea and a vessel's power to resist it. He could fall back on things that brought a satisfaction, the stress of all night on the bridge in bad weather, the lean stubborn strength of a ship and the stamina that a man brought to it, and in the morning the wind going down and then the snug refuge of his cabin . . . the din of the anchor chain racing out after a long voyage, the stillness of an anchor in a tropic harbor, the ship swinging like a shadow with the tide, the engine silent and the masts steady in the starlight, the whole ship silent as a cape and across the bay a lighthouse winking all night long . . . He could remember loading cargo in strange cities, movement, action, the day's work to do, and then time to collect oneself when the hatches were battened down and sea routine began.

After his youth on salt water Captain Hansen had sailed the Lakes for thirty years, carrying coal and iron ore between the lower harbors and the head of Lake Superior, where from the water's darkness the lights of Duluth glittered for miles beneath the northern stars. For fifteen years he had been a master, commanding the *Uranus, Saturn, Verona, J. C. Wallace, Youngstown, Samuel Mather.* There had been some danger—that time on the beach at Pointe Aux Barques; some hardship—slamming through ice in Whitefish Bay, navigating Lake Superior in November blizzards. But never a season like this, tied to the dock by something stronger than steel mooring cables. Sometimes that summer, Miss Calkins of the Buffalo dock office took him for an evening drive, over to the Falls or out in the country and back to Buffalo as the lights came on. In past years Captain Hansen had been an endless storyteller. But he was a quiet man that season.

In Cleveland, where two of the largest banks had been ordered into liquidation and relief agencies were thronged with unemployed, the company had somber problems.

During the confident 1920's new giants were rising in the steel industry. A huge steel business was developing in the Mahoning Valley where The Youngstown Sheet and Tube Company had grown to major proportions. Pickands Mather capital had helped to accomplish the Youngstown—Steel and Tube Company—Brier Hill merger that enlarged The Youngstown Sheet and Tube Company. In 1929 Cyrus S. Eaton of Cleveland proposed to consolidate a number of independent concerns into a giant Midwest steel company. With the collaboration of W. G. Mather of Cleveland-Cliffs, Eaton undertook to get control of Youngstown Sheet and Tube and merge it with Republic Steel as a long step in the creation of the giant new corporation. But the managements of Bethlehem and Youngstown had decided to merge. The P. M. partners had ties of business and friendship with these companies; Henry Dalton was board chairman of Youngstown and Samuel Mather was close to both firms. During a bitter proxy fight and prolonged legal battle, the partners stood by their friends. In 1930 they made a large purchase of Youngstown stock at $162 a share, in order to keep the company from falling into alien hands. The Youngstown Sheet and Tube Company was preserved, but at a severe cost to Pickands Mather. Two years later, with the steel industry almost paralyzed, Youngstown operations fell to 13 per cent of capacity and its stock was selling at six dollars a share. With crushing loans and business at a standstill, Pickands Mather was in its darkest period. Their commitments put a heavy strain on the older members and upon the partnership financially. But their integrity was unimpaired; they paid every dollar of their obligation. By 1937 security values were partially restored and the partners were cleared of contingent liability. In 1942, after ten shadowed years, the sun broke through. With normal debt and business climbing, there were bright prospects. At the beginning of that year, with Samuel Bool retiring from the firm, John Sherwin, Alex D. Chisholm, Herbert C. Jackson, and George W. Striebing were admitted to the partnership.

Henry Dalton lived through the years of stress but his health was broken. In 1939, shortly before his death, he took his first trip North after an interval of nearly a decade. He was impressed with the mechanical and technological changes that had come to the mines. After the dark years he saw new skill and energy at work. On this trip W. B. Castle, who had been manager of the company's coal operations at Marquette and Hancock and had become president of the Zenith Furnace Company, gave a dinner for Mr. Dalton at the Kitchi Gammi Club in Duluth. That was one of the happy events in the last year of his life.

It was natural for Billy Castle, brother-in-law of W. P. Murray, to entertain. Short and stout, he had a gift for friendship and hospitality, and he regularly gave a cocktail party for the fall inspection group. He possessed the rare combination of wanting people of all ages for his friends and making his friendship appealing to them, traits that made his contemporaries, their children and grandchildren equally close to him. His martinis were famous. During Prohibition they were mixed with imported gin, he claimed, because of the caloric effect on his weight from the bootleg variety. The door of the Castle home was always open to friends of all ages, with the martini shaker ready, until Billy Castle's death in 1953, his ninety-second year.

The shaker and the silver glasses used with it are now in the home of A. D. Chisholm, where the Castle tradition is carried on.

Back in June of 1933, when American industry was prostrate, Henry Dalton had given a company dinner at the Kirtland Country Club in Cleveland. It was a dark uncertain year, but it was also the fiftieth year of the firm and the fiftieth anniversary of Henry Dalton's original employment as the Pickands Mather office boy.

Standing before his associates, an erect man with dark hair, a frosty mustache, and keen and kindly eyes, he talked of the early years of the company. He described its small beginnings, its difficulties and discouragements, and the opportunities that had followed. He spoke of what had been the company's strength in times past and what would be its strength in the years ahead.

All over America in the period of Depression there was a searching for foundations. In time of difficulty a society instinctively turns to its past, rediscovering its sources. During the growing years the men of this company had taken little account of the past, and Henry Dalton's retrospect came as a revelation. Having described the diverse characters of the company's founders, he stated: "These three men had one thing in common; they were men of sterling character and integrity. They undertook no transactions except those which would stand the test of honesty and fair dealing."

Now, twenty-five years later, that speech is still remembered, and the printed text is preserved in a booklet program of the dinner. But the text does not carry all that was there. Through the words shone the character of a man who for fifty years had given the company his own great talents and his shining integrity.

At that dinner Henry Dalton was surprised by a gift from all his associates. He was presented with a thermometer-barometer which now hangs in the meeting room. When he died, two days after Christmas in 1939, the shadows had lifted and a new era of growth had begun.

CHAPTER 17

Shadow of a Man

BEYOND the Duluth airport U. S. Highway 53 bores into the northern woods. After seventeen miles northwestward it swings straight north, toward Hudson Bay. White birch lines a forest of black spruce and tamarack, with an undergrowth of elder, sweet fern, Labrador tea, and thimbleberry. The twentieth century seems to be left behind.

But after sixty miles the country changes. The land lifts into the Mesabi Range, and woods give way to the busy range cities. Beyond Eveleth and Virginia the road curves through a rolling land where red-brown mine dumps rise above green forest, with a far blue line of hills against the sky. Biwabik is quiet now, with the ore gone from its deep pits. Aurora has the feel of a frontier town. It lies at the eastern end of the range, on the edge of primordial country. A road leads on through five miles of solitude. It crosses an embankment between two gleaming lakes and ends in an unexpected town, bright, neat, ordered, in a ring of wilderness.

Hoyt Lakes is the newest town in the North. Its streets slope slightly and there is a feel of being on high land above the twin blue lakes and the endless forest; it is near the northern divide from which streams flow to Lake Superior and Hudson Bay. A clean, serene town, it lies just out of sight of a huge industrial plant. It was named for a man who led the iron-ore industry into a new land of promise, the concentrating of Minnesota's vast reserves of taconite. Elton Hoyt 2nd lived nearly a thousand miles away but he cast a shadow over the northern woods and waters.

The desk clock in Elton Hoyt's office in Cleveland always read ten minutes past three. He was not a man for whom time stood still, yet he always had time for deliberation. After the death of Henry Dalton in 1939 he was in command of Pickands Mather, but he did not make arbitrary decisions. Sitting in the aromatic haze of his Egyptian cigarettes, a striking man with dark eyes and white hair and mustache, he was both keen-minded and considerate. When there was a difference of opinion he had time to talk a matter out until agreement was reached. Then he would get up with a limp, throwing his left leg out, and walk to the window or the door. When he went back to his desk it was still ten minutes past three. The time never changed in his office until he was surprised by a new clock on his desk in January 1942. Its inscription read: "Presented to Elton Hoyt 2nd as a token of esteem and affection by Masters and Chief Engineers of The Interlake Steamship Company."

The son of a great steel and admiralty lawyer, Elton Hoyt 2nd had entered the employ of Pickands Mather in 1911, following his graduation from Yale, at a salary of thirty dollars a month. Halfway through college he had been stricken with poliomyelitis, which left him permanently crippled. For the rest of his life he wore a steel brace on his left leg. But he had been a crew man before his affliction, and he retained a strong physique and driving energy. Until his final years he was an ardent horseman, the one sport that was left to him.

In the Cleveland office he began work in the Iron Ore Sales Department under hard-driving George Beaumont and his trouble-shooter, Frank Armstrong. These were men of opposite types: Beaumont reliable, conscientious, steady as a rock; and Irish-born Armstrong impulsive, humorous, and engaging, gifted with a ready tongue and boundless vitality. Frank Armstrong had come to the company in 1899, beginning employment at the Buffalo dock; he knew the widespread operations of the firm. He was ready with the right word or gesture for any occasion, or nearly any. In later years he liked to tell of a time when he was caught off balance. One noon in the Western Reserve Building he found himself in the elevator with Samuel Mather. In an unusually conversational mood the older man said, "Going to lunch, Armstrong?"

"Yes, Mr. Mather."

"Well, walk along with me."

"Yes, Mr. Mather."

"Tell me something interesting, Armstrong."

At that demand, Frank Armstrong ruefully remembered, he was as blank as an office boy. They walked for a block and parted in silence.

Under these men Elton Hoyt 2nd learned the iron-ore business. Each spring he went to Philadelphia, took a suite at the Bellevue-Stratford and gathered the Pennsylvania furnacemen. He gave them his tonnages and analyses—the Bessemer, non-Bessemer, magniferous, and silicious ores—and took their orders. This scattered business, the supplying of many consumers, was soon to change. The voracious demand for steel during the years of World War I brought new furnaces into production and merged many properties into consolidated organizations. The growing steel companies could not afford to rely on external sources of supply; they needed an assured flow of raw materials, under their own control. With long experience in the producing of iron ore, Pickands Mather could bring steel companies together in ownership of mines and could provide the operating and transportation service which would keep the stockpiles replenished. Elton Hoyt gave impetus to the increasing integration of the industry. He became a Pickands Mather partner, the sixth surviving member of the firm, in 1922.

As a miner has "an eye for ore" Elton Hoyt had an eye for financial structure. He could look at a financial statement and point unerringly to any soft spot. With a comprehensive memory he carried in his mind the whole range of the company's business. He saw the strategic advantages in combinations of interest and energy. So he put together the Interlake Iron Corporation in 1929, uniting the company's scattered furnace enterprises. Samuel Mather, approaching eighty, was giving his time to civic and philanthropic interests. Henry Dalton was directing the firm's affairs with banks and steel companies. Under the eyes of these veterans Elton Hoyt was assuming command of Pickands Mather. He had not Dalton's capacity for detail but he did possess the older man's comprehensive grasp of interlocked activities. And he had the qualities of vision and imagination that had characterized Colonel James Pickands and Harry Coulby. During the 1930's he had assumed increasing responsibility in the management of the Interlake fleet, and upon the death of Henry Dalton in 1939 he became president of The Interlake Steamship Company. In that year he was elected senior partner of the firm.

Though it was physically impossible for him to go underground or to climb through the beneficiation plants, Elton Hoyt was a regular and intent visitor to the company mines. He heard reports, studied diagrams and drawings. On a visit to the Bennett Mine he watched a motion picture of the work underground. He could discuss mining procedure as well as methods of accounting. A gifted speaker, ready to take up any subject at any time, he could quickly make a room full of mining or shipping men aware of their relationship to the whole range of the company's activity.

As the steel industry emerged from Depression and faced the approach of a second World War, Elton Hoyt was looked to as a leading authority in iron mining and Great Lakes shipping. When the flow of iron ore became a life line for America and the free world, Elton Hoyt went to Washington without staff or portfolio. Drawing upon his knowledge and memory, he outlined past and potential mining and shipping operations so that officials were convinced that iron ore could be delivered to the steel mills without military or governmental supervision. While other major industries passed into Federal control, while troops patrolled the Soo locks and barrage balloons made a protective net overhead, the ore fleet continued to be operated by the Lakes shipping industry.

As a leader in the Lake Vessel Committee and in the Iron and Steel Industry Advisory Committee of the War Production Board, Elton Hoyt saw the volume of lake-borne commerce rise from 145,000,000 gross tons in 1940 to 185,000,000 in 1944. During these years there were no shortages in the raw materials of steel. Iron ore was available when and where it was required. Not a ton of steel production was lost for lack of ore at the furnaces.

In the spring of 1954, ten months before his death, Elton Hoyt was awarded the Gary Memorial Medal. The award, created by the American Iron and Steel Institute to recognize leadership in the steel industry, was an acknowledgment of "his distinguished service to his country, to his industry, and to the free world by maintaining the steady and uninterrupted flow of essential iron ore during periods of both peace and national emergency." It was the first time the award had gone to a man outside the steel-producing industry.

At mid-century, in a surge of postwar industrial growth, Great Lakes shipyards were clamorous with construction of new freighters and a backlog of orders was piling up. In 1951 a new Interlake ship, Hull 298, which would become the *J. L. Mauthe*, was taking shape at the Great Lakes Engineering Works ship-yard at River Rouge, Michigan. To obtain additional new capacity without delay, The Interlake Steamship Company turned to salt water. On July 15, 1951, at the Sparrows Point yard of the Bethlehem Steel Company's Shipbuilding Division, the keel was laid for a new Interlake flagship. It grew rapidly as pre-fabricated sections were assembled on the ways. The 626-foot ship, with scores of pennants fluttering over her long deck, was launched on March 7, 1952. In the group of officials on the bunting-decked platform stood Elton Hoyt 2nd with Mrs. Hoyt and his sister, Mrs. John W. Cross of New York. Mrs. Cross broke the bottle of champagne over the looming bow and the *Elton Hoyt 2nd* began to move down the sloping ways. With less speed and splash than the side launchings on the Lakes, the big ship slid sternforemost into tidewater. That moment, said Elton Hoyt, brought "the greatest amount of pleasure I could ever have."

Two months later, completely rigged and equipped, the new ship was put through trial runs in Chesapeake Bay. She had a capacity of 18,000 gross tons and her 7,700-horsepower geared turbines could drive her at 16.5 miles per hour. She was oil-fired and electric-powered, including electric engines on deck and deepfreeze units and a disposal system in the galley. The old hiss and clank of steam winches and the cries of gulls swooping for refuse would not be heard on the *Hoyt*. Her bow was some-what sharper than that of the traditional Lakes freighter, and her raised poop deck astern provided quarters for the engineer-ing officers and a crew's recreation hall. She was one of three identical vessels built that year on Chesapeake Bay for the Great Lakes trade. The others, the *Sparrows Point* and the *Johnstown*, were added to the fleet of the Bethlehem Transportation Com-pany.

After her trial run, the *Hoyt* was prepared for the long tow to the Lakes. To clear the bridges on the inland waters her superstructure was removed and lashed on deck. It made a novel deck load, the pilothouse, the texas, and the after penthouse covering the first eight hatches; then the twin sections of the funnel and two more deckhouses from the after end. The spars were laid on deck; the rudder and five-bladed propeller were lashed in the hold. In fine June weather a seagoing tug took her lines and the big ship with a maintenance crew of twenty began the three-thousand-mile journey, by ocean, gulf, and river, to Lake Michigan.

It was two weeks from Baltimore to the Mississippi Delta. Below Chesapeake Bay they passed notorious Cape Hatteras in a light easterly breeze, the dead ship rolling in a long ground swell. Keeping inside the Gulf Stream, they passed down the coast and around the Florida Keys, with the crew distracted from their work by friendly shrimp boats and patterns of coral sea floor showing through fathoms of clear water. For five days they crept across the Gulf, with floating sea turtles and skittering flying fish alongside and porpoises tirelessly plunging across the bow. At night in the phosphorescent water the flying fish made streaks of light and the porpoises were luminous in the dark sea. Chief Engineer Bob Folkert rigged up a fishing tackle out of a heaving line and a hammered cargo hook. With a white rag for bait he pulled in a three-foot fish. It called up the old story of the Scottish mate who kept a trout line baited on a Canadian tugboat towing logs in Lake Superior; every morning he sold his catch to the cook and then ate it for dinner. But Bob Folkert's fish was inedible. The crew had daily swims in the Number 7 side tank, under a string of lights, where fifteen feet of cool salt water sloshed with the ship's slow roll. On deck the men went about stripped to the waist; they were brown as leather when they reached the Southwest Pass entrance to the Mississippi.

At New Orleans a big pusher "towboat," the *Tenaru River* of the American Barge lines, relieved the ocean tug. To provide a pushing pad three loaded barges, two full of gravel and one deep with sulfur, were secured alongside the *Hoyt*. With a pilot on the bow of the *Hoyt* connected by telephone with the towboat pilot seven hundred feet astern, the *Tenaru River* gave a blast of her whistle and began the long push, two weeks and 1,500 miles, to Chicago.

On the Mississippi days and nights went by, or as Huck Finn put it a century ago, "I reckon I might say they swum by, they slid along so quiet and smooth and lovely." With the towboat chuffing steadily astern the *Hoyt* crept past the storied river cities, Baton Rouge, Vicksburg, Natchez, Memphis. The crew slept on deck in the starlight and sat on the shady side of the deckhouses at noon. On levees and landings people watched the long ship pass. Not the first Lakes vessel on the river, she was following a trail blazed by the *Cliffs Victory,* a converted ocean cargo ship, which had come this way to the Lakes in 1951. But an ore carrier on the Mississippi was still a novel sight. After climbing over the *Hoyt* and looking down at the towboat, one of the crew of the *Tenaru River* remarked, "This outfit must look like an ant pushing a loaf of bread."

Of 122 bridges between New Orleans and Lake Michigan the critical clearances came on the Illinois Waterway. Beyond historic Starved Rock was the fixed span of the Marseilles highway bridge; the *Hoyt* squeezed under with thirteen inches to spare. There was a tight fit in the Lockport Lock above Joliet, but Chief Engineer Folkert reported that the *Hoyt* could have been built one foot longer and made it all right. There a Great Lakes Diesel tug relieved the pusher and the *Hoyt* moved on through the Sanitary and Ship Canal toward the towers of Chicago. On July 29 she passed under the jackknifed bridges on the Chicago River and through the Sanitary Lock into Lake Michigan.

At the South Chicago yards of the American Ship Building Company the *Hoyt*'s superstructure was raised, spars rigged, rudder and propeller fitted. She made a trial run under Captain Alfred C. Drouillard and Chief Engineer Folkert. Then with a blast of her whistle she headed north. It was an auspicious time, at the end of a major steel strike and a tie-up on the Lakes, when the *Elton Hoyt 2nd* stood under the docks at Allouez loading 18,000 tons of iron ore.

"An institution," wrote Emerson, "is the lengthened shadow of one man." As president of Erie Mining Company, Elton Hoyt took a leading part in the producing of commercial iron ore from taconite. The Erie project, involving a partnership of Bethlehem Steel Company, Youngstown Sheet and Tube, Interlake Iron Corporation, and the Steel Company of Canada, became the largest undertaking in the history of iron mining. For fifteen years Elton Hoyt pushed the program, through experiment and research, the construction of a preliminary plant, and the designing of the Erie plant to yield 7,500,000 tons annually of high grade iron-ore pellets.

In February 1955, a month before Hoyt's death, a United States Post Office was opened at Hoyt Lakes, Minnesota, and the town was officially named. Two hundred families had moved in; hundreds more were coming. Now, three years later, Hoyt Lakes is a community of over eight hundred homes and about thirty-six hundred people. It is a new American town with old English street names—Yorkshire, Suffolk, Dorchester, Devonshire. Intersections are wide enough to turn a snowplow and the curving streets are lined with houses of various design and color. Except in planning and financing, it is not a company town. Residents own their homes, paying for them in monthly installments. In their recreation hall citizens from every corner of America make their own plans and regulations. Green lawns and bright flower gardens have replaced the northern bush. The town has a shopping center, public beaches and picnic sites, and two spreading schoolhouses with acres of playground.

Hoyt Lakes is a town with the future all before it. The taconite formation extends for miles under the northern forest; the Erie plant will operate for generations, as will the Reserve Mining Company's plant at Babbitt, ten miles farther north. Before his death Elton Hoyt 2nd saw life and production come to an empty country.

CHAPTER 18

At Mid-Century

As the explorers found it, the Mesabi was generally a pine country. When the pine was cut around Pokegama Lake at the western end of the range, the loggers moved on to Cass Lake and Bemidji, and eventually to Oregon, and they took with them the song of "The Pokegama Bear," composed in the Weyerhaeuser camp by Frank Hasty in 1874. The song told how in the gray winter daybreak Morris O'Hern was building a fire in a pine stub when out popped the monstrous Pokegama Bear. O'Hern took off through the swamp, but Mike McAlpin swung his ax and laid out the bruin. That night the camp feasted on fresh meat and all that winter the loggers greased down their hair with bear oil.

Behind them on many-armed Pokegama Lake the loggers left a cutover land, which slowly grew up in birch and poplar. Sometime there could be a cut of pulpwood, if fire didn't come. No one suspected iron ore under that stumpland. Pokegama Lake lay west of the Mississippi River, outside the bounds of the old maps of the Mesabi Range. But seventy-five years after the loggers sang "The Pokegama Bear" work began on the Tioga No. 2 Mine. Brush clearing and road building were started early in 1953. Stripping and plant construction began that summer. The pit yielded a low-grade ore made profitable by new methods of beneficiation. A 2,100-foot conveyer carried ore from a crushing plant in the mine to a mill where it was concentrated by washing and heavy media separation. In June of 1955, where once Pokegama pine logs had started down the Mississippi, the first train of ore cars rolled off toward the docks at Superior.

By its nature iron mining is a process of depletion. Yet the Lake Superior ranges have remained productive longer than many men foresaw. James J. Hill, the "Empire Builder" who died in 1916, predicted that all the Lake Superior iron ore would be gone in twenty years. But as old properties were exhausted new ones have been developed, and as high-grade ores have diminished a growing technology has provided beneficiated ores to replace them. The old Bangor Mine above Biwabik is a ruin, its crumbled foundation overgrown with goldenrod and foxtail. Blueberries and raspberries ripen beside the fallen chimney; meadow larks and killdeer whistle in the grass. Then comes a rumble of blasting and the roar of Diesels beyond the meadow, where the big trucks are hauling red ore out of the Embarrass Mine.

Embarrass meant "obstacle or hindrance" to the French canoemen, and they left that hard word at various points in the north country. The Embarrass Mine had a hindrance; it lay under a lake bed. In 1943, in the first large project of its kind the waters of Syracuse Lake were pumped into a diversion canal leading from Wine Lake into Embarrass Lake. In the lake bed shovels stripped off a hundred feet of overburden and a year to the day after the beginning of the project, the Embarrass Mine shipped its first trainload of ore. Now it has gone down six hundred feet, the deepest hole on the Mesabi. The oval pit with its steep-terraced banks has attracted many visitors. Margaret Bourke-White, fascinated by its colors and contours, lingered for hours making photographs in the changing light. Another kind of interest held a group of mining engineers from Russia in the summer of 1957. At first to the Russians it looked like a holiday at the mine. Then a faint rumble drew their eyes to a toy shovel in the depths, and a string of Diesel trucks came roaring up the road. Through an interpreter they followed an explanation of the workings.

The middle years of the century saw the end of some famous mines and the beginning of others. In Gogebic County, Michigan, the Plymouth Mine, the only open pit on the range in recent years, reached the end of production in November 1952. The original stripping of the Plymouth had been done by Butler Brothers in 1915; its first ore was shipped a year later. In 1918 Pickands Mather took over its operation, and during the next thirty-five years it produced seventeen million tons of soft red hematite. Steam locomotives hauled ore cars along its benches until 1942, when a seven-hundred-foot skipway replaced them. Drainage was handled by drilling down from the pit floor to underground drifts beneath the ore body; from that depth water was pumped up to a diversion ditch on the surface. When bottom was reached at the Plymouth in 1952 the mine was four hundred feet deep.

Another famous Gogebic mine came to an end five years later. One of the first big producers on the range, the Anvil-Palms shipped its first ore in 1887. Seventy years later, in January 1957, the last skipload of ore came up, and the Anvil-Palms was history. But there was a beginning to balance that ending. Just a few miles away the Peterson Mine was opened in 1955. A combination of older properties, some in operation as early as 1884, its shaft initially went to a depth of 3,750 feet. New methods and machinery gave the old locations a new future. With the opening of the mine a ceremony was borrowed from shipbuilding tradition. At the mine collar A. D. Chisholm broke a ribboned bottle of champagne against a steel bulkhead, christening the property for his long-time friend Arthur F. Peterson, vice-president of the Bethlehem Steel Company.

In the same year the Geneva Mine at Ironwood was linked with the adjoining Newport property. By merging the two mines additional shafts were acquired without the formidable expense of excavation. In 1955 the Mauthe Mining Company, named for Board Chairman J. L. Mauthe of Youngstown Sheet and Tube, took over the two properties and Pickands Mather began operating them for their three owners, Youngstown, the Interlake Iron Corporation, and The Steel Company of Canada. The Newport Mine had been managed by Pickands Mather since 1924 when the firm took charge of the iron-ore properties formerly owned by the Brier Hill Steel Company and The Steel and Tube Company of America. The Geneva Mine had been operated since 1902 by the Oliver Iron Mining Company.

In the Menominee district a new open-pit mine was opened at Fortune Lake in 1953. An old property, it had been explored in 1915 and again in 1920 by other interests. Though a shaft was sunk 275 feet into the formation, no ore was produced in the early years. When Pickands Mather took over in 1952 the old shaft was retimbered and an underground drift was driven beneath the ore body to drain the open pit. The railroad and highway were relocated, and mining began. The first ore came up in 1953. At last Fortune Lake had justified its name.

In 1956 Pickands Mather began a first venture into iron-ore mining in Canada—the Hilton Mines, named for Board Chairman Hugh Hilton of The Steel Company of Canada, Limited, located at Bristol, Quebec, on the Ottawa River, 322 miles rail haul from the blast furnaces at Hamilton, Ontario. The property is half owned by The Steel Company of Canada and the balance owned equally by the Jones & Laughlin Steel Corporation and Pickands Mather. The ore body is a low-grade magnetite under a shallow overburden; it is easier to crush and concentrate than Minnesota taconite. The new technology carries it through twenty stages of treatment and produces a pellet with 66 per cent iron content.

Behind this collaboration of Pickands Mather with The Steel Company of Canada lay more than half a century of business ties. In 1895 the Hamilton Blast Furnace Company, predecessor to Stelco, was attempting to use Ontario ore, for which the Canadian government paid a bounty. But the ore clogged the furnaces and yielded inadequate pig iron. The frustrated furnacemen went to Cleveland and talked to Colonel Pickands about the purchase of iron ore from Lake Superior. It was the beginning of a long association.

In the twentieth century ties of business and friendship linked Henry Dalton and Robert Hobson, president of The Steel Company of Canada. The two men were unlike in many ways: Dalton staid and conservative, Hobson expansive and flamboyant—with snowy hair, mustache, and goatee he looked like showman W. F. Cody (Buffalo Bill) in his later years. But they shared vacations at fishing and shooting clubs in Quebec and they brought together a comprehensive knowledge of iron mining and steelmaking. Dalton saw the development ahead of the Canadian steel industry. He opened the way to Stelco's participation in ownership of iron mines on Lake Superior and of the Mather Collieries in Pennsylvania.

Henry Dalton had the esteem not only of Robert Hobson but of all his associates. Once at a gathering in Toronto a Canadian geologist said, "I hate to go into Henry Dalton's office."

"Why?" they asked in surprise.

"Because he is so pleasant and agreeable that I end up by giving him everything he asks for."

During the years 1926-45 The Steel Company of Canada made significant progress under the leadership of R. H. McMaster, and in that period increasing ties of business and friendship linked Stelco and Pickands Mather.

One of the men who learned the manufacture of pig iron in Pickands Mather's blast furnaces was Hugh G. Hilton, who would succeed Ross McMaster as president of Stelco. Born in Canada, he studied engineering at what is now the Case Institute of Technology in Cleveland. A stocky, broad-shouldered youth of eighteen, he worked for a season in the pioneer iron-ore beneficiating plant at Coleraine on the Mesabi. After his schooling he worked for Pickands Mather at the Federal Furnace in South Chicago and the Ella Furnace at West Middlesex, Pennsylvania. In 1917 he went to the United Furnace Company at Canton, Ohio, and two years later he joined The Steel Company of Canada as assistant superintendent of blast furnaces. Frank Armstrong tried to recall him to the Pickands Mather organization, but Stelco held on. He became president of the company in 1945. Now his firm has interests in a number of Lake Superior mines—Tioga No. 2, West Hill, Scranton, Embarrass, Newport-Geneva, Danube, Carmi-Carson Lake, Volunteer, which are under Pickands Mather operation—as well as a 10 per cent ownership of the taconite-processing Erie Mining Company.

On U. S. Highway 41, just beyond the village of Humboldt, Michigan, a crumbled foundation outcrops in the brush. It is the remains of the first beneficiation plant in the Lake Superior district, an experimental mill built by Thomas A. Edison in 1896. It was a magnetic separator: as pulverized rock passed an electromagnet iron ores were attracted to one side of a barrier and collected. Edison had bad luck in his experiments with iron ore. Before the Humboldt mill got into full operation it was destroyed by fire. The inventor built a second plant on Long Island, but soon after work began a storm blew up and washed the local ore deposit into the sea. His third attempt, a pilot plant in Rhode Island, produced several thousand tons of successfully concentrated ore. Then in New Jersey Edison built a larger concentrating plant—just as the rich Mesabi ores overwhelmed the market. Seeing that his concentrates could not compete with direct shipping ores from Minnesota, Edison converted his ore-mill machinery to the manufacture of cement, and in his laboratory he turned to the development of the fluoroscope and the kinetograph, which made the world's first motion pictures. In iron-ore concentration Edison was ahead of his time but beneficiation was inevitable. By 1956 over 40 per cent of the ore shipped from Minnesota was a concentrated product, upgraded by means of washing, jigging, heavy media, and other processes of beneficiation.

Captain Alex McDougall had startled the Lakes trade with his first whaleback freighter in 1889. In 1918 he astonished the iron-mining industry by filing suit against the Oliver Iron Mining Company for forty million dollars for alleged infringement of an ore-washing patent. The washing of iron ore is an ancient process. The old prescription for separating sand from iron ore was: "Add water and stir briskly," and the primitive method was to pour water into a bucket of ore and stir the mass with a stick so as to make the tailings run over the edge. In an experiment in 1903 some Minnesota mining men shipped some sandy ore down the Lakes where it was put through a log washer. The experiment was unsuccessful, and with the Mesabi yielding mountains of direct shipping ore there was no current need for beneficiation. However, the ores at the western end of the Mesabi were worthless without upgrading, and in 1907 the Oliver Iron Mining Company began experimenting with a concentrating plant at Coleraine; the company opened a full-scale plant there in 1910. In McDougall's suit eight years later the court found no proprietary interest in the ore-washing process. It decided in favor of the defendant, a decision later affirmed by the United States Circuit Court of Appeals.

In 1918, the year of the McDougall suit, when World War I had reached deep into the Mesabi pits, Pickands Mather began beneficiation of iron ores. The work began at the Danube plant at Bovey, Minnesota, where the ore was treated by a washing process. The next step came at the Corsica Mine near McKinley, where a crushing and washing plant went into operation in 1926. In 1931 a Pickands Mather research group in the Hibbing office began experimentation with the upgrading of lean ores. In 1942 Fred D. DeVaney joined the organization and set up a laboratory on the edge of the Scranton pit.

Research is an investment in the future; it foreshadows things to come. At mid-century Pickands Mather began a number of beneficiation projects stemming from studies in the research laboratory. In 1950 a washing and jigging plant was installed at the Biwabik Mine to upgrade the last tonnage in the historic pit. A washing plant at the Scranton Mine added 300,000 tons annually to its production of direct shipping ore. In 1953 at the West Hill Mine near Coleraine the company built a washing, heavy media, and cyclone plant, with long conveyer belts carrying crushed ore from one unit to the next. In the same year a crushing and high-density plant was installed in the Mahnomen Mine on the Cuyuna Range; it prolonged the life of a property where direct shipping ores were nearing exhaustion. In 1954 the old Bennett Mine at Keewatin was given a new future with a modern crushing and washing heavy media plant, which replaced the washing plant that had been in operation since 1939.

These same methods of beneficiation led in 1955 to the opening of the Tioga No. 2 Mine beside Lake Pokegama, beyond the supposed limits of the Mesabi Range. Research had not only prolonged the life of the Mesabi but had extended its boundaries.

In 1957 a beneficiation plant at the huge Mahoning pit began a new chapter in the saga of that famous mine. On the walls of the mine office are photographs of W. C. Agnew, the original manager for the old Mahoning Ore Co., who drove over the works in a buggy while ore was being mined by horse-drawn scrapers. In his desk Superintendent W. D. Webb has Agnew's old field notes and account books, along with a worn expense book listing

venison $2.00
butchering a cow   1.50
66 qts. blueberries 5.50
repair harness   .50

After yielding more than a hundred million tons, the fabulous Mahoning has passed its peak production. The preponderance of lean ore amid the remaining direct shipping ore requires beneficiation. Its new plant produces annually up to 500,000 tons of concentrates from low-grade material.

Before the mid-century a principal supplier of coal to Pickands Mather was the Carter Coal Company of McDowell County, West Virginia, near the Virginia border. The company had been developed by George Carter, a builder of the Clinchfield

Railroad, and it passed into the hands of his son, J. Walter Carter. During World War II the coal industry was operated by the Federal government, with a flag flying over every mine-head. After the war when the mines went back to private control J. Walter Carter, a soft-spoken but strong-minded man, disagreed with the United Mine Workers. Confronted with a levy of five cents a ton for the Union Welfare Fund, he closed the Carter Mine and its famous Olga Coal disappeared from the market.

At this point Elton Hoyt 2nd began negotiations for the purchase of the property. On November 25, 1947, the Carter Coal Company was acquired, for $26,500,000, by a combination of Youngstown Sheet and Tube, Interlake Iron, and The Steel Company of Canada. The Olga Coal Company, using the Carter trade name, was formed to operate the mine. In arranging the transaction Pickands Mather sought only the sales agency for screened coal that was available after the owning companies had met their needs for blast-furnace coking slack. The mine had a daily production of ten thousand tons of high-grade, low-volatile Pocahontas fuel.

John Rust Chandler, a native of Cleveland who had worked in the Pickands Mather Coal Department since 1931, became a partner in the firm in 1948 and head of the department. A cultivated, considerate, reflective man, he suffered from ill health which led to his retirement in 1950 and his death a year later. He was succeeded by H. P. Junod.

Henri Pell Junod came to Pickands Mather in 1923 after a far-ranging youth. Born in New York City where his father was Swiss consul-general, he had an international boyhood, divided between the United States, France, and Switzerland. Too young for United States service in World War I, he became an officer in the Royal Flying Corps of Canada. War was followed by schooling at the Massachusetts Institute of Technology, and during summer vacations he sailed in merchant ships to Europe, Africa, and Asia. On one voyage he found himself in a mutinous crew who were imprisoned in Naples, but Seaman Junod went free and was back in Boston for the fall term. A big, fast-moving man, he became a sprinter on the M.I.T. track team, where he tied the world's record for the sixty-yard dash. In 1923 he began a varied career with Pickands Mather, working at blast furnaces, coke ovens, and by-product plants, selling pig iron and coke. From management of coke sales in Chicago he came to the Coal

Department in Cleveland in 1943. He was made a partner in the firm in 1951. Active in the American Coal Sales Association for many years, he was elected to its presidency in 1958. With his direction the Coal Department entered a period of continuing growth. In addition to its Olga Coal agency the department became sales agent and Lake shipping agent for several other producers, conducting the business on docks from Lake Erie to Lake Superior and in seventeen sales locations between the Atlantic Coast and the Missouri Valley.

Since its formation in 1929 the Interlake Iron Corporation had supplied pig iron to companies in the steel, automotive, agricultural implement, electrical, and other industries. At midcentury it had some eight hundred customers. With ownership interests in seventeen iron mining companies, the Olga Coal Company, and Erie Mining Company, it had substantial sources of supply of raw materials. A capacity of more than 1,500,000 tons annually made it the world's largest producer of merchant pig iron. Interlake Steamship Company delivered its raw materials and Pickands Mather served as its sales agent.

In 1956 the historic Globe Iron Company of Jackson, Ohio, was merged with Interlake Iron. Originators of a "silvery" pig iron long used in the manufacture of open-hearth steel, Globe had a secure place in the steel industry. Behind the company lay the story of the Welsh iron industry in the Hanging Rock district of the Ohio Valley, an industry which began by accident and developed with purpose and permanence.

In 1818, when Irish workmen began digging the Erie Canal and the first Great Lakes steamship voyaged between Buffalo, Cleveland, and Detroit, six families from South Wales were floating down the Ohio in flatboats, bound for the Miami Valley above Cincinnati. At the French settlement of Gallipolis they tied their boats at the riverbank and spent the night ashore. In the morning the riverbank was empty; their craft were stolen. So they stayed, becoming the nucleus of a growing Welsh settlement in Gallia, Lawrence, Scioto, and Jackson counties. Finding bog iron and hardwood forests, Welsh ironworkers began an industry—charcoal pits smoking in the valleys and ox wagons creaking up to hillside furnaces. Two of their furnaces, the Globe and the Fulton, were brought together in the Globe Iron Company in 1873. While scores of furnaces in the region closed, Globe went on producing a high silicon pig iron for the manufacture of open-hearth steel. The furnaces shifted from local ore to Lake Superior ore, from charcoal to coke. The stacks were successively rebuilt and enlarged. But they remained in the hands of the Jones family through four generations—from patriarchal, bearded Thomas T. Jones to the present Edwin A. Jones, who in 1956 saw the Globe Iron Company with its subsidiary Globe Metallurgical Corporation become the Globe plant of Interlake Iron Corporation. Pickands Mather continued to be sales agents for its ferroalloys and its traditional silvery pig iron.

The business of selling pig iron has changed and grown since William McLauchlan pulled up his horse at the scattered foundries. Now that business is in charge of George W. Striebing, who has not only seen the changes but has directed many of them. A native of Cleveland, he began work for Pickands Mather in 1911, after four years in the freight traffic department of the New York Central System. He learned the pig-iron business from the veteran McLauchlans, father and son, succeeding them in turn. He became a Pickands Mather partner in 1942. During World War II he served on the Pig Iron Allocation Committee of the War Production Board and was Chairman of the Pig Iron Industry Advisory Committee of the Office of Price Administration.

In the Chicago area the company's pig-iron and coke sales are directed by Snelling S. Robinson. The son of a former executive of The Youngstown Sheet and Tube Company, S. S. Robinson joined Pickands Mather in 1920, following his graduation from Harvard. In the Pig Iron Sales Department he became district manager at Erie, a district under competitive pressure from the adjoining producing centers of Buffalo and the Mahoning Valley. In 1928 when Pickands, Brown and Company in Chicago needed a sales manager, Robinson went to them. Two years later, with the acquisition of Pickands, Brown by Pickands Mather, he was back in the organization with which he had begun. During World War II he was a member of the War Production Board Pig Iron Allocation Committee, vice-chairman of the Coke Committee of the Office of Price Administration, and vice-chairman of the Coke Committee Solid Fuels Administration for War. He was one of the organizers of the American Coke and Coal Chemical Institute and has been a director since its inception. He became a partner in the firm in 1948.

Seventy-five years after its founding Pickands Mather & Co. has widely scattered and far-reaching operations. Iron ore, coal, ships, docks, blast furnaces are links in the chain of activities. To acquaint its people with their own divisions and also with the broad compass of the organization, two company publications have been developed. *The Interlake Log,* first published in 1937, goes to the crews of Interlake vessels. *P. M. Iron News,* inaugurated in 1952, is a journal for the personnel of the iron mines. Reporting company plans and developments along with personal notes and seasonal features, it helps to unify men in the only company operating on all six ranges of the Lake Superior district.

CHAPTER 19

The New Fleet

AT NOON on Sunday, November 10, 1940, the Interlake steamer *William B. Davock*, downbound with coal for South Chicago, passed through the Straits of Mackinac. It was a gray day with a chilly southeast breeze. Sailors have long memories, and Captain Charles W. Allen might have recalled that this was an anniversary. Twenty-seven years before, the Big Storm had destroyed fifteen ships and taken two hundred lives on Lakes Michigan and Huron.

Beyond the Straits the *Davock* left a smudge of smoke across the sky. Four hours later the Canadian freighter *Anna C. Minch*, with grain from Port Arthur, passed the Straits. She followed the *Davock* into the gray obscurity of Lake Michigan. Neither ship was ever seen again.

The wind freshened at dusk and rose steadily through the evening. By midnight a southeast gale was blowing. It was the beginning of three days of furious and shifting winds, the longest and most cyclonic storm to lash the Lakes since November 1913. It was centered on Lake Michigan.

On Monday afternoon, November 11, the weather observer at the Ludington Coast Guard Station, halfway down the Lake Michigan shore, measured wind blasts of 100 miles an hour, shifting from southeast to southwest. That circling wind would be perilous to vessels hugging the east coast for protection. From the station tower the lookout peered through flying snow. Darkness came and the tower swayed like a storm-tossed tree. An hour before midnight the lookout was ordered down for fear it would carry away. Then came a distress call. The car ferry *City of Flint* was aground just north of the Ludington piers.

At midnight in his farmhouse two miles inland from Pentwater, Edward Astruski saw flares in the western sky. They were reddish blue, he said, and quickly gone, like skyrockets. They came from beyond the lake shore somewhere between Ludington and Pentwater. He hoped the Coast Guard had seen them. Under the cry of the wind came the lake's long thunder.

Late Tuesday afternoon, November 12, a telephone rang in the office of the Marine Department of Pickands Mather & Co. in Cleveland. A newspaper reporter was asking for a crew list of the *William B. Davock*. He had heard that a ship had foundered off Ludington and that bodies wearing *Davock* life preservers were being cast ashore.

A call to the Coast Guard at Ludington confirmed the report: both the *Davock* and the *Anna C. Minch* were missing, and bodies from both vessels had come ashore. An hour later three men from the home office took the train to Michigan. By midnight George Callahan in Cleveland had word that eleven bodies from the *Davock* had been found, of which three were not identified. At Ludington the office men made identifications and ordered burial caskets.

Five miles below Ludington the wide beach was scummed with grain from the sunken *Minch*; offshore her mast jutted from the tossing gray water. The two lifeboats of the *Davock* were found, half a mile apart, on the grain-strewn sand; they had come ashore undamaged and apparently empty. The searchers went on, finding *Davock* tarpaulins, a ladder, doors, and ring buoys. Then came word that a body had washed ashore just above Big Sable Point. It was identified as that of Frank Stanak, wheelsman of the *Davock*.

On Sunday, November 17, a week after the *Davock* had been reported from Mackinac City, two more bodies were found. One was Lawrence Gonya, the *Davock*'s steward; the other was identified as a Canadian seaman from the *Minch*. A report of spars offshore promised to be the *Davock,* but proved to be the net stakes of Ludington fishermen. An air search by a Muskegon plane uncovered nothing. On November 20 the search party returned to Cleveland with no definite knowledge of the *Davock*'s end.

Ten days later the lightkeeper at Big Sable Point found a floating body which he pulled ashore. It proved to be Frank Parker, a fireman on the *Davock*. During Christmas week three more bodies came ashore. The Interlake Steamship Company provided burial, wreaths, and markers in the Ludington Cemetery. A final body, found in April, was buried in the same plot. Divers examining the hulk of the *Anna C. Minch* found her cut in two just abaft the forward house. They surmised that in the blindness of the Armistice Day storm the *Davock* and the Canadian vessel had collided, both ships sinking before the men could launch their lifeboats. The *Davock* remains buried, with half her crew, somewhere in the deep cold water of Lake Michigan.

With loss of the *Davock* the Interlake fleet numbered forty-five vessels. No new ships had been acquired since 1929; none were needed in the long Depression years. Throughout the 1930's Great Lakes shipyards stood silent and empty. But they came to life in the 1940's when war in Europe, soon to spread around the world, required unprecedented shipments of iron ore.

The navigation season of 1944 began with a late-winter siege over the Upper Lakes. Thermometers read seventeen degrees below zero in Duluth and six below at the Soo when the big Coast Guard cutter, on March 20, began crunching through the northern straits. It was a season of urgency, stockpiles leveled at the blast furnaces and war orders mounting at the mills. The Lakes fleet was enlarged by sixteen big ships, of 15,000-ton capacity, built by the United States Maritime Commission. The Interlake company had traded seven obsolete small freighters as part of the purchase of three of the government-built vessels; they became the *Frank Armstrong, E. G. Grace,* and *Frank Purnell.* There was new capacity for the movement of a record tonnage. But the season began with hardship and reversals.

Through ice-choked channels the ships steamed northward. In the first week of April forty-five vessels were icebound in the Straits of Mackinac, while thirty-seven others inched through ice in the upper St. Marys River and Whitefish Bay. Ice jammed the narrows until the final week of April, when a massive fog closed in. With whistles moaning the fleet groped through the Lakes and rivers.

On the morning of April 27 Lake Erie was shrouded in a muffling blindness. On the *James H. Reed,* bound for Buffalo with iron ore from Escanaba, men in the pilothouse could not see their own range light astern. Fog signals sounded, a lost cry in the darkness, and the lookouts stared at nothing. Without warning came the crash and shudder.

At a crossing of courses, twenty miles off Conneaut Harbor, the *Reed* collided with the Canadian steamer *Ashcroft,* upbound and running light. The deep-laden *Reed* sank quickly. Captain Bert Brightstone was on the bridge as his ship plunged into the shrouded lake. He was trapped under the sun visor of the pilot-house, but he struggled free. He was taken aboard the *Ashcroft* with twenty of his men. Twelve others were lost. Chief Engineer Robert Fletcher, now a shore engineer in the Cleveland office, took time to pull on his pants before abandoning ship; when the survivors were put ashore he was the only one who had a wallet. A few months after the collision the hulk of the *Reed,* resting in sixty-six feet of water, was demolished with dynamite to remove any hazard to navigation.

To balance the somber beginning of the season, the year brought a long serene autumn, free from storm and cold. The last laden ships came down the Lakes in late November, their crews having seen neither ice nor snow. Since the bitter weeks of April the fleet had moved a record volume—184,000,000 tons of bulk cargo.

A plan of replacing smaller vessels with large modern carriers led to the sale of the oldest Interlake ships. Seven veteran vessels had gone to the Maritime Commission to be broken up for scrap; others went to other operators. At the end of the summer of 1945 the old freighters *Perseus* and *Canopus* were sold to the Nicholson Transit Company for use as automobile carriers. When peacetime manufacture was resumed in 1946 each of the 464-foot freighters carried five hundred motorcars on its built-up main deck.

New dimensions were coming to the iron-ore fleet. New vessels, longer, wider, deeper, were making obsolete the ships of the early 1900's. Though still seaworthy the plodding old veterans were at an economic disadvantage when bigger and faster ships came into the trade. In August of 1952 the *Elton Hoyt 2nd* joined the Interlake fleet. The next spring the giant *J. L. Mauthe* went into service. During 1953 these two vessels carried nearly a million and a half tons of iron ore.

In 1955 the company sold three 7,000-ton vessels, the *Harry R. Jones* built in 1903 and the *Calumet* and *Hemlock* built in

1907. At the same time plans were begun for a new freighter of 25,000 tons, which would replace the carrying capacity of the three veterans. This ship, the *John Sherwin,* is now in service, and a comparable vessel, Hull 302, is in early stages of construction at the River Rouge shipyard of the Great Lakes Engineering Works.

A policy of modernization called for new ships and also for the renovation of older vessels, increasing their speed and efficiency. In thirteen postwar years the company spent nearly twenty million dollars on fleet improvements. In 1957, after five years of service, the *Elton Hoyt 2nd* was lengthened by seventy-two feet, increasing its capacity to 21,000 tons. The added section, fitted into the middle of the hull, had a capacity of 2,500 tons, equal to the entire cargo hold of the *V. H. Ketchum,* which had been a giant in her time.

As vessels grew in size, speed, and efficiency the men in pilothouse and engine room carried greater responsibility. Inevitably they lost some of the picturesqueness that marked the captains and engineers of a more leisurely time. Every fleet had its colorful characters, who no doubt grew more colorful in the light of memory. Some of them came from the Lake towns—Bay City, Marine City, Port Huron, Algonac. Some came from seaport towns in Norway, Denmark, and Scotland, with years on salt water before they sailed the Lakes. Some were cautious men, with records marked by prudence and safety; some were impatient, veterans of storm and stress. Some of them were gruff and some were genial; some silent and some loquacious; but all of them were devoted to their ships. During the winter season they carried a steamer's photograph as they carried a picture of wife and family during the navigation season.

Captain C. H. Woodford, called "Cord" by all his colleagues, was a huge, stout, watchful man, cautious as a spinster, always looking out for bad luck and bad weather. While master of the *Joseph Sellwood* in the early 1920's he devised a life belt for the use of deck hands when cleaning a hatch shelf. The belt was attached to a cable which clamped onto the side rail; a man could not fall far with a Woodford belt around him. Equally concerned for his ship, Captain Woodford kept an anxious eye on the barometer and on a threatening horizon. When he saw a black sky coming he made for shelter. Just the reverse was Captain Jimmy Lowes, weather-beaten, jovial, imperturbable.

He would rather put out in a gale, his men said, than in a calm. He had come over to Interlake with the Mitchell fleet in 1916. His impatience was balanced by steady judgment and cool nerve. In many strenuous seasons he never lost time for his ship or the company.

Jaunty and formal in a derby hat and a little black bow tie, Captain Lewie Stone of Vermilion, Ohio, always looked dressed for a meeting. But he was plagued by severe attacks of hay fever and asthma. Sometimes on the Lower Lakes he would lie on deck, gasping for breath, but as soon as the ship reached the Soo he was fit again. On Lake Superior he was hardy as an Indian.

For years on the *Henry G. Dalton* Captain Stone had an Irish deck hand who agreed with everything he said. One morning in a gale on Lake Superior they met halfway down the main deck.

"Good morning, Pat," the captain shouted.

"Good morning, Captain," Pat replied.

Holding on to his derby, the captain roared, "Not much wind this morning, is there?"

"You're right, sir," Pat cried, "but what little there is is blowing like blazes, sir."

When the wind built up and the seas crashed over, Captain Stone thought about his colleague who took shelter every time the barometer fell. Steadying himself in the pilothouse, he remarked to the mate: "I don't know where Woodford is, but I wish I was with him." He had the same dry comment when he brought in the last vessel at the end of a stormy November. "Late fall sailing is all right," he told the men in the office. "But I don't like this winter sailing."

Some of the fleet captains sailed every trip past their boyhood homes; others had come from the far side of the world. Arnold Evanson and Martin Ness were born in Norway. James Larsen and big Sig Matson came from Copenhagen. From Canada came James B. Lyons, who began his career before the mast in grain schooners, and Walter McNeill, who first went on the Lakes in 1893 as a deck hand in a lumber schooner in order to get to the Chicago World's Fair.

The newer captains were a different cut, looking, dressing, and talking like businessmen ashore though highly skilled in their marine profession. Not typical, because there is no type, but representative is Captain H. Chesley Inches, alert, precise, scholarly, a short, spry, wiry man, redolent of cigars, with a trim gray mustache and blue eyes glinting behind his rimless gold spectacles. He was a captain of quiet authority and cool, careful judgment. In twenty-three years of command, he never put a ship in the yards for damage or lost an hour's time in accidents.

Loss of time is a modern master's worry, as loss of his ship haunted a captain of sixty years go. Captain Inches was so conscious of time that he once bought a two-wheeled scooter powered by a one-cylinder gasoline engine. He took it aboard ship on the pantry tackle. In port, while other captains trudged through the dockyards and waited for streetcars, Captain Inches made quick trips to the shop and the offices. At Ashtabula the dockmen found some old lead letters and numbers in the storeroom. They made him a long license number, painted red, and attached it to the toolbox. On the long dock he would scoot between strings of railroad cars, missing them by inches.

During twenty-three years as an Interlake shipmaster, Captain Inches commanded the *Saturn,* the *Neptune,* the *Amasa Stone,* the *Henry G. Dalton,* and the *Frank Armstrong.* Every ship, he insists, has a personality, and the captain comes to know it like a living thing. In 1943 he brought out the 621-foot *Armstrong,* taking it away from the shipyard, giving it the freedom of open water. "There is a great satisfaction," he says, "in being the first master of a vessel. It is not secondhand but *your own,* like breaking a horse to a saddle. And no matter how many other captains sail it in years to come, it is *your* vessel, as long as you live."

Every captain could tell stories—of the legendary Mormon pirates on Beaver Island, of ships frozen in the ice of the St. Marys and the final dash of the grain fleet before the expiration of insurance rates at the end of November. But Captain Inches knew the Lakes with a seaman's experience and a scholar's study. Long a collector of marine records and photographs, he was one of the founders of the Great Lakes Historical Society in the 1940's. He has contributed to its quarterly, *Inland Seas,* and has added some of his own scale models of historic vessels to its museum.

The new fast ships, running from the Lower Lakes to Lake Superior ports in two and a half days, are in port every third night, or a part of it. Yet the crews rarely go ashore. Loading is prompt and rapid; a ship costing six million dollars cannot stand idle in the dock. Within a few hours lines are cast off, the whistle roars, and a vessel is under way again. Even during the somewhat longer discharge of coal the men generally remain aboard. With television in the recreation room and a bumboat alongside, a sailor has no need to go ashore.

In the 1920's three Kaner brothers in Duluth-Superior began a ship peddling business. Up the ladder they climbed with a bulging pack on their shoulders. While the crew gathered round they spread their stock on a hatch cover—tobacco, candy, chewing gum, toilet articles, magazines, newspapers, socks, and handkerchiefs. No sale was too small for their business; they would climb back up the ladder to sell a tardy coal passer a box of cough drops or a package of gum. Their business grew with the tightened loading schedules. Now, instead of three bulging packs the brothers have three supply boats that churn across the harbor with shelves full of seamen's goods.

Television comes and goes—in the middle of a program—on a ship under way. The Duluth signal fades out a couple of hours after a vessel clears the harbor, and there is a blank screen in the long reach of Lake Superior. On the Lower Lakes the signals overlap—Milwaukee, Chicago, Gary; Detroit, Toledo, Cleveland, Erie, Buffalo. Meanwhile in the recreation room the off-watch men have books and magazines, checkers, chess, cribbage, and pinochle. Forty years ago there were marathon poker games in the engine room and sporadic crap games on deck. Semiprofessional gamblers came aboard in November, working a trip as deck hand or coal passer while they cleaned up on the crew's last paydays. Now, encouraged by a marine mail savings plan, the men end the season with money for the winter ashore.

Forty years ago the Lakes seamen were largely impermanent, shifting from ship to ship and lounging on the waterfront between assignments. Now the crews are made up of steady workmen. More than half of the nine hundred unlicensed men in the Interlake ships collect a bonus for completing the season. Many of them stay with the fleet year after year. They have good pay and good working conditions, abundant food and comfortable quarters. Instead of the old littered and crowded bunkroom they have privacy and order.

For licensed and unlicensed men the Lake Carriers Association offers winter schools of navigation and engineering. Junior officers are annually reviewed and rated by the company officials.

In past years when the Interlake fleet numbered fifty vessels, a committee of twelve captains, dubbed the "Twelve Apostles," discussed their junior officers. Now, in a two-day meeting at the end of the season, captains' and engineers' committees of eight evaluate their men on a point system.

Since 1945 management of the Interlake fleet has been in charge of G. W. Callahan, a veteran of the company's Marine Department. The son of a long-time marine editor of the *Cleveland Plain Dealer,* George Callahan has lived with Lake shipping all his life. His first job, in 1916, was on the Erie dock at Cleveland, ten hours a day checking the balance scale on the old Brown electric clamshell that scooped up five tons at a time. After terms as assistant vessel agent at Duluth and as assistant manager of the Dock Department in Cleveland, he opened a Marine Department office in Chicago in 1930. In Cleveland he served as assistant manager of the company's Marine Department from 1937 until 1945, when he succeeded George S. Kendrick as manager. He became vice-president of The Interlake Steamship Company in 1955. At that time the company had fewer ships than in 1913 but three times the earlier carrying capacity.

During the summer of 1957 workmen at the Toledo yards of the American Ship Building Company swarmed over the huge steel skeleton of Hull 192. It was built in dry dock, a new practice on the Lakes. As the ship was longer than the graving dock the bow section was added after the hull had been floated and moved to the dock face. With a length of 710 feet, a breadth of 75 feet, and a molded depth of 27 feet, it cost about eight million dollars, nearly thirty times the cost of the biggest freighters of fifty years ago. But its 25,000-ton capacity, at a speed of 16.5 miles an hour, would carry as much cargo as an entire fleet in the 1890's. It is now in service as the *John Sherwin.*

John Sherwin had come to Pickands Mather & Co. on January 1, 1942, from a vice-presidency in The Cleveland Trust Company; he had been in the Cleveland banking business since his graduation from Yale in 1923. Chosen by Elton Hoyt 2nd, he was brought into immediate Pickands Mather partnership, the only partner to come in directly from outside. He soon made himself familiar with the operation of iron mines, ships, docks, and furnaces, and became widely known and respected in the iron and steel industry. Upon the death of Elton Hoyt 2nd in 1955, he was made senior partner of Pickands Mather & Co. and president of The Interlake Steamship Company. As the firm's senior managing partner he followed three predecessors, Samuel Mather, Henry Dalton, and Elton Hoyt 2nd. In addition to many business directorships, he is a director of the American Iron and Steel Institute and of the Lake Carriers Association. He is president of the Board of Trustees of the Cleveland Clinic Foundation.

In the company's accounting and financial policies John Sherwin relies heavily on the broad experience of Elmer C. Brunner, who was made comptroller of the firm in 1942. When he had joined Pickands Mather in 1916, E. C. Brunner was assigned to a typewriter, which lay outside his talents. Accounting was another matter; he had a natural capacity there. He made order out of the complexity of the financial operations of many participating companies. Elton Hoyt, seeing his capacity for financial analysis, relied on him for special tasks. In the late 1920's E. C. Brunner furnished the facts and figures for the Interlake Iron consolidation. He made analyses which formed a basis for integrating the furnace properties and which prepared for the acquisition of Pickands, Brown & Company. In charge of the Accounting Department since 1942, he became a partner in 1951. His experience in years before the divisional separation of departments has given him an understanding of the range and complexity of the business. As treasurer of The Interlake Steamship Company he has been close to every development in the new fleet.

Ten or twelve thousand tons was a big cargo until World War II. The increase to twice that volume is not accomplished merely by lengthening ships from six hundred to seven hundred feet. It is the result of widening and deepening the carriers, and is made possible by the deepening of channels. Additional inches of channel mean additional hundreds of tons of cargo in every vessel.

In the spring of 1957 a dynamite blast in the Detroit River started a project to deepen the Amherstburg Channel to twenty-seven feet. This was the beginning of a Federal program to open the inland seas to the shipping of the oceans. The western Great Lakes are linked by 130 miles of channels. These connecting waters will be deepened to a uniform twenty-seven feet, in line with the St. Lawrence Seaway. That channel will allow the passage of deep-draft ocean vessels and of new Lake freighters carrying 25,000 tons of cargo.

At the old iron-ore loading ports—Marquette, Escanaba, Ashland, Superior-Duluth, Two Harbors—red cargo still pours from high docks into steamers' holds. But the new ships will steer into new harbors, on Lake Superior and at the tidal mouth of the St. Lawrence. They will load a new cargo, billions of grapelike pellets, man-made from the taconites of Minnesota and the deposits of Labrador. So begins a new chapter in an age-old industry.

CHAPTER 20

Operation Hardrock

This rock is widely spread over the whole length of the
Mesabi and being different from anything found else-
where and peculiar to this horizon of the Taconic, has
been called *Taconyte* by the writer.
—N. H. WINCHELL, 1892

W HEN State Geologist Winchell explored the rough Mesabi
country in the 1890's he found an extensive body of ancient, pre-Cambrian rocks containing 20 to 35 per cent iron.
He might have named the formation for himself, but he called
it the "Taconic Strata," borrowing a name from Massachusetts
where two hundred years ago iron ore was burned in charcoal
furnaces on the slopes of the Taconic Mountains. Taconic iron
went into the cannon for the Revolution.

The word was appropriate to the Mesabi; in the Indian
tongue it meant "wild land" or "forest wilderness." When he
moved the name to Minnesota, Winchell did not know that his
word *taconite* would become a term of challenge and promise in
years to come.

Taconite is the mother rock of the Mesabi. It lies in a great
band, 110 miles from east to west, of varying widths up to two
miles wide, and from five hundred to seven hundred feet thick.
During the ancient process of geologic folding and upheaval,
with the percolating waters leaching away the silica, the iron
content was enriched at certain points in the range. In the
twentieth century these rich pockets became the site of open-pit
mines; now they are pocked out in the long band of taconite
like nibblings in a giant loaf of bread. Around and beneath the
mined pits lies the whole huge body of taconite.

About halfway across the range occurs a dividing line between magnetic and nonmagnetic taconite. East of Keewatin the mother rock is magnetic, its intensity increasing as the range reaches eastward. This hematite material was converted, eons ago, into magnetite by the heat of a volcanic eruption in the eastern part of the formation. It is the magnetic rock that is now being converted into a rich furnace ore; the taconite plants are located at the eastern end of the range.

From its pockets of hematite the Mesabi has yielded in the past sixty-five years more than two billion tons of iron ore. During World War II the Hull-Rust-Mahoning pit gave up a hundred million tons, more iron ore than the entire production of any foreign country. After the war its output declined sharply. Meanwhile, other open pits, producing since the beginning of the century, have become exhausted. No important new discoveries have been made, and there is little likelihood of finding rich new deposits.

As the rich ore bodies were mined, men saw a prospect of ghost towns on the Mesabi, like Cripple Creek and Leadville in the scarred valleys of Colorado. An alternative was to find an increasingly efficient means of concentrating increasingly low-grade ores. That technology has added years of productivity to older mines and has revived abandoned locations. But the low-grade ores, too, are limited. A lasting mining industry in Minnesota would require the extracting of iron from the mother rock. Taconite exists in staggering quantities, billions of tons, the geologists estimate, and the costs will govern how much of it is to be mined. If iron ore could be profitably produced from the mother rock, the industry could go on with no foreseeable ending.

The iron locked in taconite had tantalized men for many years. In 1915 the Mesabi Syndicate began experiment with samples of rock from the eastern end of the range. It was a sanguine group, headed by C. D. Jackling and including Horace V. Winchell, a son of the geologist who named the taconite strata. In 1916 they set up a pilot plant in Duluth, taking over the property of an old lumber company on the lake shore. For three years they wrestled with the problem of machinery that would crush the resistant rock and gather its particles of iron. Their crude ore came from a remote pit called the Sulphur Mine, seventeen miles north of the old wilderness station of Mesaba. It was near Peter Mitchell's test pit, the first excavation ever made in the great range.

In 1920 the newly formed Mesaba Iron Company moved the operation from Duluth to the mine; they built a mill and a shack settlement in the woods. With great expectations they named their town Argo, for the myth of Jason and the Golden Fleece, until they found that the magic name had been preempted by a village in southern Minnesota. Then they called their settlement Babbitt, for Judge K. R. Babbitt, a mining company lawyer of New York City. In 1920 the town of Babbitt consisted of fifteen houses, a big frame bunkhouse, a star-shaped mess hall, and a community building that doubled as a dance hall and a church. In that remote location it was hard to keep men on the job. There was a constant turnover. When the weekly train arrived from Duluth, a hundred men got off and another hundred got on.

The plant at Babbitt was designed to produce about five hundred tons of sinter a day. Actually, two hundred tons was a good day's production, and that was accomplished with difficulty. In the crushing plant the shafts broke, dust plagued men in the roll plant, couplings shattered in the fine grinding plant, and the sintering machine broke down almost every day. It was a heartbreaking operation. As a result of the formidable drilling problems and mistakes in the flow sheet, the plant design, the equipment, and the operating methods, the pioneering taconite plant closed down in 1922.

Taconite, men said, was a heartbreaker. But its challenge and promise remained. Thirty years later a new town of Babbitt, built to last for generations, grew up in the wilderness, and huge new taconite plants took shape at the eastern end of the Mesabi. The old Biwabik Mine reached the end of production in 1955, but since then the town of Biwabik, near the new taconite works, has grown and expanded. Said the president of the Biwabik State Bank, "When the mining companies are investing millions, we would be stupid not to invest a few dollars of our own to benefit from this giant that is so big some people can't see it." Taconite proved to be a life-giver.

Pickands Mather first became interested in taconite in 1931. It was a time of depression, with many mines about to be shut down. But the steel industry must look farther ahead than the next season, or even the next decade. In collaboration with Bethlehem Steel and Youngstown Sheet and Tube, Pickands

Mather worked on concentration of lean ores found in the lower and surrounding parts of direct shipping deposits. But the lean ores were limited; they offered no promise for the long future. The company turned to taconite, acquiring lands north and east of the town of Aurora, Minnesota. Drilling brought up cores of hard rock with high magnetic content, a finding confirmed by the Mines Experiment Station at Minneapolis. That was basis for an extensive exploration, systematic drilling for some sixty miles between Aurora and Nashwauk. The work was arduous and costly, but it was full of promise. During 1938-39 the crews brought up miles of drill cores. In them there was revealed, as though through a giant X ray, vast beds of taconite.

In 1940 Pickands Mather announced the forming of Erie Mining Company to acquire taconite lands and to mine iron ore from them. One of the obstacles to development of taconite had been the tax policy of the State of Minnesota, a policy which taxed mineral reserves and so hastened exhaustion of direct shipping ores. In 1941 the Minnesota legislature enacted a new and more constructive law; taconite would not be taxed in the ground but only as it was mined and concentrated. With this assurance Erie Mining Company took up new leases, from the State and private owners, on taconite lands.

In 1942 when the Battle of Britain was raging in the English skies and the ore fleet hurried down the Lakes with seventy million tons of Mesabi iron ore, Pickands Mather set up a laboratory at Hibbing to find ways to unlock the stubborn taconite. First efforts were made with a process of flotation. When this proved too costly, experiment was shifted to magnetic separation. Month after month, year after year, the tests went on. The taconite rock was crushed to various sizes and run through various processes of separation. It was hit and miss, trial and error, hope and disappointment. But out of experiment with many mechanisms came the production of efficient magnetic separators. In this task the laboratory men had the benefit of the pioneering research carried on for many years by Professor E. W. Davis, director of the Mines Experiment Station of the University of Minnesota.

One problem was to extract the minute particles of iron, many of them microscopic; another was to put them back together in a form fit for furnace consumption. The laboratory staff tried sinterizing the material into clinkers, nodulizing it into lumps, and pelletizing it into rough baked marbles about the size of a schoolboy's shooter. Pellets were the most satisfactory. They did not stick or freeze, they were free-dumping in all weather; being porous, the ore reduced readily in the blast furnace. Out of the pilot assembly in the laboratory came high-grade pellets, 64 per cent iron, black, hard, round like a pebble.

In 1946 a process was established and the company built a preliminary plant two miles north of Aurora for producing taconite pellets. Except for the primary crusher all the units were of the sizes that would be used in the commercial operation. On July 1, 1948, the plant began production. Tests of technique and equipment revealed need for changes—from steel cloth to nylon cloth in the filters, from a cylindrical to a rectangular furnace for baking the pellets. At last experiment gave way to the steady process of production—the throb and rumble of crushers and classifiers, the endless conveyer belt carrying raw taconite through a flow sheet that ended with pellets dropping into railroad cars.

Meanwhile other experiments were under way in the mining of taconite. The rock is hard enough to cut glass, too hard for conventional drills which bored slowly and required frequent changes of bit. A solution was "fusion piercing," a method developed by the Linde Air Products Company. In the jet-piercing process, kerosene is burned with oxygen in a blowpipe that rotates against the rock face. The drill burns its way in with terrific heat, and a jet of water following the flame splits off heated rock fragments. Now the heartbreaker was broken. Jet rigs drill fifteen to twenty-five feet an hour. Into holes, six inches and larger, goes blasting powder. The rock is broken into chunks, some ready for the crusher, some so large that they must be reduced by the "skull-cracker" dropped by a movable crane. In the plant the stubborn rock must be ground to the fineness of talcum powder.

By 1953 the preliminary taconite plant was producing a steady flow of concentrate and the first cargoes of pellets had gone down the Lakes. In blast-furnace stacks and open hearths the pellets proved themselves, producing more iron and requiring less coke and blast. At the end of that year Elton Hoyt 2nd announced that Erie Mining Company would construct a major taconite plant, to produce 7,500,000 tons of taconite pellets annually. The undertaking would cost over a third of a billion dollars.

At this time ownership in Erie Mining Company was shared by Bethlehem Steel with 45 per cent, Youngstown Sheet and Tube with 35 per cent, and Interlake Iron and Steel Company of Canada with 10 per cent each—Stelco having joined in 1952. Pickands Mather was in charge of operations. It was a familiar alliance. The four companies were major stockholders in mines operated by Pickands Mather on all the Lake Superior ranges.

Erie Mining Company was an undertaking on a scale that required collaboration of large interests. The men who launched it were Eugene G. Grace, Arthur B. Homer, and A. F. Peterson of Bethlehem Steel, Frank Purnell and J. L. Mauthe of Youngstown Sheet and Tube, R. W. Thompson of Interlake Iron, H. G. Hilton of Steel Company of Canada, and Elton Hoyt 2nd of Pickands Mather. The participating companies were willing to take the large risks involved in the huge financing and the complex technology of this venture to obtain a long-time supply of high-grade iron ore.

Late in 1953 work began in wild country eight miles northeast of Aurora. To a lifeless region, known only to a few trappers and woodsmen, came a rush of life. The largest iron-mining venture in history required mountains of material and equipment and thousands of workmen. Over new roads cut through the woods came trucks and tractors. A construction town with streets of trailer-houses and barracks halls sprang up in the bush. On a hill of granite, part of the ridge that marks the height of the Mesabi Range, power saws snarled through timber and machines shaped out a new terrain. Long benches of granite were carved out to fit the crushing and concentrating plants, with solid rock providing a foundation for heavy machinery. On a site of five hundred acres permanent steel buildings began to rise. Meanwhile contractors were building the town of Hoyt Lakes, six miles away, and railroad crews were laying seventy-three miles of track through the bush to Taconite Harbor where a huge dock was rising on the shore of Lake Superior.

During the four-year period of construction, beginning in 1954, an outstanding labor record was achieved by the building trades workers who clocked more than 25,000,000 man-hours with less than 15,000 man-hours lost in walkouts due to labor disputes. Both labor and management were the gainers. This record was due to the Taconite Labor Agreement which was formulated before construction began, and the fact that both parties lived up to it. Of further importance was the careful provision for the workers' living conditions in that remote country. In the trailer communities, one at the Erie plant site and another at Taconite Harbor seventy-four miles away, workers developed an enviable civic spirit. They joined volunteer fire brigades, social organizations, and service clubs. In their free time, after working hours, they built temporary churches. Seventy-five per cent of the labor force came from outside the Lake Superior district, but for a few seasons they put down roots in the wilderness. After four years of epic construction one of the labor leaders stated that the accomplishment had been "without equal in good management-labor relations for such an isolated project involving such a huge expenditure of money."

On high ground at the main plant stood a headquarters building, alternately called "Frustration Hill" and "The Pentagon." Here men faced new questions every day. There were endless problems, from the engineering stress on a concrete arch to interference on the radio intercommunication system—somehow instructions to the taconite pits were getting lost in orders from a pipe-line boss in Texas. But the questions got answered and the problems were solved. Car dumpers and dust control followed a system developed at Chuquicamata in the Chilean Andes; tailings went over the hill to a tailings dam of a type first used at Morenci in the Arizona desert. The plant began production late in 1957. At capacity the plant would consume electric power equal to that of Duluth-Superior and it would pump as much water as is used by the city of Buffalo.

The Erie plant was the result of years of teamwork extending from Cleveland to the Minnesota wilderness. A major responsibility in its development was carried by W. H. Prescott, Jr., who had come into the Pickands Mather organization in 1922, following his graduation from Williams College. Starting in the Pickands Mather mail room, he went into the Pig Iron Department and from there into the Mine Operating Department. Since 1925 he has remained in Mine Operating except for a short interval with the Dock Department. As manager of Iron Ore Mining, he handled the mining labor, taking a lead in organizing the employees representation plans for the mines and the Lakes vessels. Though not an engineer, he has worked closely with engineers and technicians. He proposed the company's initial research program and gave impetus to its first research organization. He was taken into the partnership in 1947. It has been his role to supervise the company's capital in long-range planning and investment in iron-ore projects, including a responsibility for coordination of the Erie construction project.

Now the road from Aurora leads through primitive country and comes out under a dramatic ridge where industry has made an island in the wilderness. The dark red windowless buildings stretch along the hillside. A curving road climbs up, past the grind of trucks and the rumble of railroad cars, to a crest that overlooks the woods for miles around. East and west lie the taconite pits with jet-piercing drills flying plumes of steam. A powder blast rumbles and big shovels load the rock into side-dumping railroad cars. At capacity the plant will swallow 2,700 tons of it an hour, 65,000 tons a day, nearly 25,000,000 tons a year—which will yield 7,500,000 tons of pellets.

At the crushing plant the rock goes in, jagged, hard, heavy, seemingly adamant. After four stages of crushing, each one progressively smaller, the rock is reduced to pebble size. With water added it moves on to the rod and ball mills which grind it to a black mud. Magnetic separators remove the iron particles. Thickened and then pumped to the pellet plant, with the remaining water filtered out and binding material added, the concentrate is rolled into pellets in huge, ever-revolving balling drums. Dried and hardened in the pellet furnace, the pellets go to storage bin or stockpile.

Nature took millions of years, while the earth heaved, cracked, and folded, and the patient ground water leached away the silica, to turn taconite into iron ore. In a few hours the taconite concentration process duplicates the work of nature over eons. It shows men creating a resource from primordial matter.

From the storage bin pellets pour into railroad cars for transport on the newest railroad in the United States. To acquire lands for the project, including a right of way from the Erie plant to the harbor, the Pickands Mather Legal Department handled two thousand separate descriptions of land. The route led through the Superior National Forest which is not a solid tract of land but encompasses numerous private holdings. Forest lands cannot be sold outright but can be traded, at the rate of

one acre for two in return. Over all, Erie Mining Company
acquired a total of 75,000 acres in order to obtain adequate lands.

Much of the region was swept by fire forty years ago. Now it
is grown up in spruce, birch, and poplar. Beyond the plant the
ore trains are quickly swallowed in a green silence. Hawks, blue
cranes, and killdeer fly up from the marshes; the tracks of deer,
bear, and moose are written around pink clumps of fireweed
beside the track. There is no sign of habitation, but at Milepost
10 the line crosses above another taconite railroad. Here the
Reserve Mining Company sends trainloads of crushed taconite
from Babbitt down to Silver Bay. When the two trains pass the
quaver of whistles fades over the wilderness. Beyond the black
Greenwood River the Erie line crosses the "big muskeg," where
ten miles of bog, some of it twenty-eight feet deep, was dug out
and filled with stable earth. Beaver dams make black ponds in
the creeks. The railroad crosses and recrosses twisting rivers, the
Partridge, Greenwood, Stoney (good trout fishing), and Manitou.

After forty-nine miles comes the crossing of State Highway 1,
and there is Murphy City, a small cluster of houses in the woods.
The new "city" was named for an Irish construction engineer who
died of an illness before the railroad was completed. The people
of Murphy City talk about the crop of blueberries along the railroad, the bears that rifle their garbage cans, the fishing in the
Two Islands River, and the big moose that browse on lilies in
the black pond water. They talk also about the long trains of
taconite pellets, a new link in the chain of iron.

At Milepost 62 the train plunges into a tunnel, boring for
1,800 feet through the rock escarpment that parallels the Lake
Superior shore. It comes out above a swamp where a moose,
shoulder deep in water, looks up from the lilies. It passes through
a deep rock cut and comes out to a dramatic view of the down-
sloping forest and the far bright waters of Lake Superior. After
a long loop the train pulls up on the high white cliff of the loading dock at Taconite Harbor.

Lake Superior is deep, dropping off steeply on the straight
north shore. But the Two Islands River was named for twin
islands a quarter of a mile beyond its mouth, and they provided
a harbor site. The two wooded islands made up half a breakwall, with relatively shallow water between them. The harbor
builders had a start to work from. And they had a good omen,

for according to north country tradition this was the scene of a miracle.

A century ago when there were only a few scattered Indian camps on the north shore of Lake Superior, Father Frederick Baraga carried the cross into that dark country. Small, sturdy, fearless, he made his way to remote stations in the wilderness, and through his writings in French, German, and his native Slovenian he made Lake Superior known in the universities and seminaries of Europe. In a late autumn season against the warnings of his Chippewa boatman he set out from the Apostle Islands for the north shore. All night the wind drove the bateau on its course, with the colored aurora streaming upward through the stars. With morning the wind died and a cold mist muffled the lake. Through the fog came the crash of waves on a rocky coast. The fearful boatman was trying to bring the bateau around when Father Baraga said, "Do not turn back, my son. Steer in between two islands you will see." The Indian shook his head. "We are lost, Father. There are no islands, only cliff and rock." As he spoke two dark shapes rose through the fog—two spruce-clad islands. Beyond, in quiet water, the shore opened into the mouth of Two Islands River. Leaving the bateau on the shore, the priest fulfilled his errand, baptizing the children in a Chippewa fishing camp. When they sailed back across Lake Superior the boatman crossed himself as he steered between Gull and Bear islands, which Father Baraga had seen in his revelation.

Another kind of miracle took place in 1954. Part of the mile-long harbor, sealed off with a cofferdam, was pumped dry. The floor was blasted to a smooth depth of thirty feet and the rocky shore was faced with a cement dock 2,330 feet long. The islands were joined in a solid breakwall and a quarter-mile breakwater was built out at right angles from the shore. Cap rocks as big as mine cars were hauled down from a quarry on Carlton Peak, five miles east, to armor the breakwalls. When the lake was let in there was a sheltered cove on the rugged coast.

Now a train of iron-ore pellets pulls up on a dock as white as the cliffs of Dover. A wrench car moves alongside, opening the cars for dumping. A hundred-car train is emptied in about an hour; the pellets pouring into storage bins above a row of conveyer belts. Every forty-eight feet a conveyer moves out over the open hatches of an ore ship. In the lofty glass control house are panels of switches, dials, and lighted buttons. Like an organist the operator controls the power and movement that can load an average of ten thousand tons of pellets in an hour, if the ships can pump out their ballast in that time.

The name of the main entrance light recalls an incident at Duluth in the spring of 1952, when the former steamer *Elton Hoyt 2nd* was rechristened *Alex D. Chisholm*. In the stands were the children and grandchildren of A. D. Chisholm. When the official party appeared, a score of shrill voices chorused, "Here comes Big Boy!"—the grandchildren's favorite name for their grandfather. When the Big Boy Light went into service, shining out from the entrance of Taconite Harbor, the Chisholm grandchildren numbered twenty-three.

On autumn nights the aurora streams up from the dark northern sky as it did when the Chippewas revered the Big Sea Water. But there is a new brightness on the ancient shore. Beyond the entrance beacon, green, white, and red buoy lights glimmer on the water, and up against the stars steady range lights guide the long freighters in. Loaded vessels leave through the northeast exit, the harbor lights winking behind them as they steer for the Soo.

The mid-twentieth century has brought an end to reliance on direct shipping iron ores and the beginning of a new source of supply for the American steel industry. While the large taconite projects were under way in Minnesota, attention was drawn to another horizon in the North. For a generation steel men had known of the existence of iron ore in northeast Canada and for several years Pickands Mather and The Steel Company of Canada have carried on a program of exploration in the area. Recent exploration has added to previous knowledge to extend the "Labrador Trough" several hundred miles south from Ungava Bay. It outcrops intermittently in diverse grades and types of iron ore. A part of the huge trough is the Wabush area, fifty-five miles long and four miles wide, on the border of Quebec Province and Labrador.

In 1957 Pickands Mather leased a tract of five square miles, bordering Wabush Lake, where drilling indicated a deposit of more than a billion tons of hematite and magnetite with about 40 per cent iron content. It is accessible by open-pit mining, being covered with a shallow glacial drift. In the laboratory

at Hibbing a twenty-ton sample of the ore proved to be of uniform quality, with few impurities. Coarse-grained, it can be
more readily crushed than taconite: existing processes can be
used to concentrate it to ore of 65 per cent iron content and to
roll and bake it into pellets. Associated with Pickands Mather in
forming the Wabush Iron Company were The Steel Company
of Canada, Youngstown Sheet and Tube, and Interlake Iron
Corporation. The property is about forty miles west of the
Quebec, North Shore and Labrador Railway, a common carrier,
and two hundred miles north of the port of Seven Islands on the
Gulf of St. Lawrence.

In the summer of 1957 drill crews explored the Wabush Lake
deposit. After further testing of the ore and more exploration,
plans may develop for the construction of railroad and power
lines, a town and loading docks, concentrating and pellet plants.
As in the Minnesota taconite industry, only a large-scale operation could be economically practical. But it is clear that Labrador pellets can be made competitive with foreign and other
high-grade ores.

To the iron industry Labrador means both promise and
problems. All goods and materials must be transported from
distant centers. A labor force must be brought to a remote and
primitive region. The long Labrador winter, with temperatures
far below zero, will make stern demands on men and equipment. Any development will require collaboration and substantial investment from American steel companies.

When Pickands Mather & Co. was formed in 1883 iron hunters
were searching the wilderness for direct shipping ores. Now
nature's ores are less in demand than concentrates. Taconite
pellets are richer and more uniform, they reduce more readily
in the blast furnace and produce more iron with less fuel. Men
have taken a new step in the long history of iron.

After three quarters of a century there are youth and vigor
throughout the company's enterprise. From this milestone the
organization looks to the future more than to the past, although,
as this writing comes to a close in 1958, once again the iron
and steel industry is experiencing a drop in the demand for its
products, and, inescapably, iron-ore mining is feeling the effects
of recession. It has come when blast-furnace practice is changing
to take advantage of the increasing volume of high-grade concentrated and foreign ores and when the St. Lawrence Seaway is

about to link the inland waters with tidal shores. These compound the problems of the present but also offer challenging opportunities. There are new means of producing high-grade iron ore, new ferroalloys for the manufacture of better steel, fast new vessels for moving ever-greater cargoes. In all directions a prospect lies ahead and the horizon is bright.

ACKNOWLEDGMENTS

In tracing this record of three quarters of a century of industrial enterprise in the Great Lakes area, I have had the assistance of a number of persons and institutions. Mr. George W. Cottrell, admiralty lawyer, of Mentor, Ohio, gave me vivid impressions of men and events in the Great Lakes shipping industry since 1900. Captain H. C. Inches of Westlake, Ohio, generously shared with me his extensive knowledge of Great Lakes history and tradition. Mrs. Constance Mather Bishop of Novelty, Ohio, and Mr. Philip R. Mather of Boston helped me to an understanding of the character of their father, Samuel Mather, and his early associates. Mr. H. S. Pickands of Gates Mills, Ohio, gave me the use of family records and papers, as did Mr. Donald S. Boynton of Chicago. On the Lakes and the iron ranges I had the benefit of information from men of long and varied experience in the ships, mines, laboratories, and offices.

The literature of the iron-ore industry is various and extensive. In addition to regional, county, and local histories, I have drawn upon the volumes of the *Lake Superior Mining Institute*, the files of *Skilling's Mining Review*, and *Inland Seas*, the reports of the Lake Carriers Association, and the trade journals of the iron industry. Librarians have been generous with assistance; I am especially indebted to Miss Donna Root and Miss Agnes Hansen of the Cleveland Public Library, Miss Ruth O'Malley of the Duluth Public Library, Miss Phyllis Rankin of the Peter White Memorial Library at Marquette, and Mrs. Carroll Paul and Mr. Kenyon Boyer of the Marquette Historical Society. I had efficient and generous help from the Newberry Library and the John Crerar Library in Chicago and the Chicago Historical Society.

For special items of information I am indebted to Mr. Victor F. Lemmer of Ironwood, Michigan, Mr. Joseph E. Bayliss of Sault Sainte Marie, Michigan, Mr. David N. Skillings of Duluth, Mr. George Kendrick of Cleveland, Mr. Seymour Wheeler of Chicago, Mr. A. F. Peterson, vice-president of the Bethlehem Steel Company, and Mr. Hugh Hilton, president of The Steel Company of Canada, Limited. I am grateful for assistance from Mr. Oliver J. Burnham of the Lake Carriers Association and from Mr. John Horton and Mr. Ernest Kirkwood of the Cleveland-Cliffs Iron Company.

From the outset I have had the fullest co-operation and assistance of Mr. John Sherwin and his colleagues in the Pickands Mather partnership.

WALTER HAVIGHURST

Oxford, Ohio
June, 1958

Index

Acme Steamship Company, 70, 99
Adkins, Heney, 158, 159
Agnew, W. C., 188
Allen, Charles W., 193
American Ship Building Company, 94, 180, 201
American Solvay Process Company, 152
American Steel Barge Company, 47, 70, 91, 92, 94, 179
Armstrong, Frank, 71, 152, 157, 175, 176, 186
Armstrong, Jack, 52, 104, 105, 107
Ashtabula and Buffalo Dock Company, The, 170
Aspin, Robert, 95
Astruski, Edward, 194
Ayer, Frederick, 55

Babbitt, K. R., 206
Bacon, Don H., 44
Baker, Newton D., 159, 160
Balkan Mining Company, 108
Bancroft Iron Company, 19, 21
Baraga, Father Frederick, 29, 213
Bawden, Gus, 132
Beaumont, George, 48, 175
Bennett, H. M., 77, 78
Bessemer Steamship Company, 94, 96
Bethlehem Steel Company, 98, 100, 101, 126, 160, 167, 168, 178, 180, 184, 206, 209
Bianco, Joe, 131
Bond, Frank Lewis, 129

Bool, Samuel E., 44, 157, 172
Boston Coal, Dock and Wharf Company, 96
Boynton, Charles T., 147, 148
Boynton, Donald S., 158
Breen, Bartley, 104
Breen, Thomas, 104
Breitung, Edward, 27, 43, 107-08
Brier Hill Steel Company, 101, 171, 184
Brightstone, Bert, 196
Brooks, T. B., 53, 103
Brown, Fayette, 17
Brown, Harvey S., 17
Brown, W. G., 79
Brown, William Liston, 23, 94, 154
Brunner, Elmer C., 161, 202
Buell, John L., 104
Burnham, Daniel H., 41
Burton, John E., 57
By-Products Coke Corporation, 153, 154

Caldwell, C. D., 153, 154, 158
Callahan, George W., 101, 194, 201
Cambria Iron Company, 38
Cameron, George D., 152
Carnegie, Andrew, 96
Carnegie Brothers and Company, 105
Carter, George, 188
Carter, J. Walter, 189
Carter Coal Company, 188, 189
Cartwright, Peter M., 101, 102
Castle, W. B., 172

Chandler, John Rust, 189
Chandler Iron Company, 43
Chicago Shipbuilding Company, 86
Chinn, William P., 73, 74, 75, 79, 81, 135
Chisholm, A. D., 58, 62, 135, 143, 168, 169, 172, 184, 214
Chisholm, A. D., Jr., 143
Chisholm, Donald M., 143
Clarkson Coal Mining Company, 151
Cleveland-Cliffs Iron Company, 26, 139, 152, 171
Cleveland Iron Mining Company, 9, 10, 17, 19, 23, 32, 34, 35
Cleveland Steamship Company, 99
Colby, Charles L., 91, 92
Collins, Edward K., 22
Collins Iron Company, 22
Consolidated Iron Mines, 93, 106
Coulby, Harry, 48, 65-73 pass., 96, 97, 102, 154, 157, 158, 159, 176
Credner, Hermann, 52, 103
Cross, Mrs. John W., 178
Curry, Solomon S., 137

Dalliba, James H., 47
Dalton, Henry, 38-42 pass., 48, 49, 71, 92, 96, 142, 153, 157, 171-76 pass., 185
Davis, E. W., 207
Davis, Theodore M., 64
Dear, R. B., 77
Detour Dock Company, 93
DeVaney, Fred D., 187
Drouillard, Alfred C., 180

Eaton, Cyrus S., 140, 171
Edison, Thomas A., 186, 187
Elwood, Isaac, 147
Ely, S. P., 49
Ericson, Ed, 129
Erie Mining Company, 127, 180, 181, 186, 207, 208, 209, 211, 212
Essen Coal Company, 42, 145, 151
Evanson, Arnold, 198

Fairfax, John, 48, 49
Fay, George A., 64
Federal Furnace Company, 150, 153
Federal Steel Company, 96, 148
Fitch Iron Company, 106
Fletcher, Robert, 196
Folkert, Bob, 179, 180

Gallagher, Bill, 124
Gary, E. H., 70, 96
Gates, John W., 147, 148
Gay, Stephen R., 22
Gibson, Matthew, 105
Gibson, Thoburn, 105
Gilchrist Transportation Company, 99, 113
Glidden, Joseph, 147
Globe Iron Company, 145, 190, 191
Globe Metallurgical Corporation, 191
Gogebic Powder Company, 40
Gonya, Lawrence, 194
Goodwin, Helen, 21
Grace, Eugene G., 209
Great Lakes Engineering Works, 178, 197
Green, John, 142
Gutch, Paul, 113, 114

Hamilton Blast Furnace Company, 185
Hanna, Mark, 50, 61
Hanna, Seville, 50
Hanna Company, M. A., The, 35, 49, 56, 92, 111, 116, 121
Hansen, Hans C., 118, 170, 171
Hanson, William G., 109
Hardenburgh, L. M., 125
Harvey, L. D., 22
Haskins, Marion Louise, 23
Hasty, Frank, 182
Hay, John, 67, 68
Hayes Mining Company, 55
Hazard, Rowland, 152, 153
Hemlock River Mining Company, 105
Henry, George, 155
Hibbing, Frank, 78
Higgins, Jerry, 142
Hill, James J., 78, 183
Hilton, Hugh G., 185, 186, 209
Hobson, Robert, 185
Homer, Arthur B., 209
Hoyt, Colgate, 91
Hoyt, Elton, 2nd, 95, 137, 138, 154, 157, 158, 161, 169, 174-81 pass., 189, 201, 202, 208, 209
Hoyt, Elton, III, 142
Hoyt, James Humphrey, 91, 94, 95
Hulst, N. P., 104, 105, 130
Hulst, Mrs. N. P., 130

Huron Barge Company, 70, 88, 92, 96

Huyck, F. B., 98

Illinois Steel Company, 43, 86, 95, 96, 146

Inches, H. Chesley, 198, 199

Interlake Company, 89, 96, 99

Interlake Iron Corporation, 154, 155, 158, 176, 180, 184, 189, 190, 191, 209, 215

Interlake Steamship Company, The, 71, 99, 101, 102, 112, 113, 114, 139, 142, 154, 155, 169, 175, 176, 177, 178, 190, 192, 193, 195, 196, 198, 199, 200, 201, 202

Iroquois Iron Company, 150, 151

Jackling, C. D., 205

Jackson, Herbert C., 138, 172

Jackson, James, 118

James Pickands & Co., 19, 25, 49, 143

Jobe, William H., 105

Johnson, Bill, 133

Joliet Steel Company, 43, 146

Jones, Edwin T., 191

Jones, Thomas T., 191

Jones & Laughlin Steel Corporation, 185

Jopling, Alfred, 27

Jopling, James E., 77

Junod, Henri Pell, 189

Kelley, "Mick," 169

Kelley, William, 126

Kendrick, George S., 142, 201

Kendrick, Harry Dalton, 142

Kerbitz, George, 58

Kidder, Alfred V., 26

Knott, Proctor, 76

Lackawanna Steamship Company, 70, 98, 99

Lackawanna Steel Company, 98, 101, 155, 160

Lake Superior Powder Company, 19

Lake Superior Ship Canal Company, 51, 55, 103, 107

Lang, Charlie, 31

Langford, Dick, 37, 54, 64

Larsen, James, 198

Lawrence, Charles Edwin, 105, 106, 108, 109, 110

Leith, Andy, 110, 111

Lieberthal, A., 59

Linde Air Products Company, 208

Livingstone, William, 116

Longyear, John M., 27, 54, 55, 77, 78, 107

Lowes, Jimmy, 197

Lyons, James B., 198

McAlpin, Mike, 182

McCaskill, John, 75, 78

McComber Iron Company, 19

McDonald, Squeaky Tom, 61

McDougall, Alex, 70, 91, 187

McKeehan, Homer H., 159

McLauchlan, Jay Chandler, 141, 157, 158

McLauchlan, William, 38, 42, 49, 144, 145, 150, 151, 152, 155, 191

McMaster, Ross H., 186

McNeill, Walter, 198

Mahoning Ore Co., 188

Maki, Rini, 131

Mallman, John, 47

Marquette Iron Company, 19

Martinson, George, 134

Mastodon Iron Company, 108

Mather, Amasa Stone, 46, 136-40 pass.

Mather, Flora Stone, 161

Mather, Increase, 30

Mather, Katherine L., 139

Mather, Livingston, 139

Mather, Philip, 125, 138, 139, 140

Mather, Richard, 30

Mather, Samuel, 29-36 pass., 40, 41, 46, 47, 48, 51, 54, 67, 68, 72, 93, 96, 101, 119, 134, 137, 139, 140, 141, 145, 148, 156-61 pass., 171, 175, 176

Mather, Samuel Livingston, 22, 23, 30, 33

Mather, Timothy, 30

Mather, William Gwinn, 30, 139, 140, 152, 171

Mather Iron Company, 93

Matson, Sig, 90, 198

Mauthe, J. L., 209

Mauthe Mining Company, 54, 184

Maynard, Darius Gardner, 20, 21

Menominee Iron Company, 23

Mesaba Iron Company, 206

Mesaba Steamship Company, 70, 98, 99
Metropolitan Land and Iron Company, 137
Midvale Steel and Ore Company, 138
Milwaukee Coke and Gas Company, 155
Milwaukee Iron Company, 104
Minnesota Exploration Company, 43
Minnesota Iron Company, 43, 44, 45, 47, 75, 93, 96, 106, 146
Minnesota Steamship Company, 47, 70, 86, 88, 90, 92, 96
Miracle, George, 37
Mitchell, Peter, 47, 205
Moen, Philip, 148
Moore, Nat, 54, 55
Morcom, Elisha, 44
Morgan, J. P., 96
Morse, Jay Collins, 17-24 pass., 29, 32-39 pass., 42, 43, 44, 47, 50, 95, 96, 145, 146, 147
Morse, Mrs. Jay Collins, 42
Mueller, Frederick, 36, 37
Munger, Charles H., 58, 77, 79, 81, 125, 132, 135
Murray, Robert, 79
Murray, William Parmalee, 42, 49, 152, 172

Ness, Martin, 198
Newport Mining Company, 168
Nicolay, John, 67
Norrie, A. Lanfear, 37, 54, 64
North Chicago Rolling Mills Company, 43, 146
North Shore Coke and Chemical Company, 155

O'Brien, Mike, 60
Odanah Iron Company, 58, 106
Oglebay, Norton & Co., 35, 56
O'Hern, Morris, 182
Ohio Iron and Steel Co., 42, 145
Olga Coal Company, 189, 190
Oliver, Henry W., 94, 151
Oliver Iron Mining Company, 56, 93, 105, 137, 184, 187
Olson, Bob, 131
O'Neill, Paddy, 58
Outhwaite, John, 23

Parker, Frank, 194
Peavey Steamship Company, 70
Pelardy, Amos, 38
Pendleton, George, 31
Pengilly, John, 121
Penokee and Gogebic Development Company, 38, 39
Perry Furnace Company, 154
Perry Iron Company, 150
Petersen, Peter A., 89
Peterson, Arthur F., 168, 184, 209
Pewabic Mining Company, 105
Pickands, Brown & Co., 23, 43, 94, 146, 148, 153, 154, 158, 190, 202
Pickands, Caroline, 25, 26
Pickands, Caroline Martha (Outhwaite), 24, 28
Pickands, Henry S., 15, 16, 22, 23, 24, 43, 50, 94, 146, 154
Pickands, Henry S. (son of Col. James Pickands), 49, 50, 141, 142, 154, 157, 158
Pickands, Col. James, 15-18 pass., 22-29 pass., 32, 33, 34, 36, 38, 47-50 pass., 92, 154, 176
Pickands, Rev. James D., 24
Pickands, Jay Morse, 49, 50, 141
Pickands, Joseph, 49, 141
Pickands, Van Cleve & Co., 22
Pittsburgh Coal Company, 92, 151
Pittsburgh Steamship Company, 70, 71, 92, 93, 94, 96, 97
Pitz, Charles, 98
Portage Coal & Dock Company, 143
Porter, H. H., 145
Posey, North Albert, 43
Prescott, W. H., Jr., 210
Provident Coal Company, 151, 152
Provident Steamship Company, 70, 99
Pumpelly, Raphael, 37, 51, 52, 53, 54, 61, 64, 103, 107
Purnell, Frank, 209

Rankin, Carroll Watson, 26
Reid, Whitelaw, 68
Republic Iron Company, 106
Republic Steel Corporation, 56, 150, 171
Reserve Mining Company, 181, 212
Roberts, Harry, 40
Robinson, Snelling S., 191

Rockefeller, John D., 92, 93, 94, 96, 106

Roleau, Joe, 20, 21

Rominger, C., 55

Root, Frank, 85, 86, 87

Ross, Myron, 57

Royce, Josiah, 110

Royce, Stephen, 110, 111

Rule, George, 123, 124

Savroni, Joe, 122

Schlesinger, Ferdinand, 61, 62

Scott, A. J., 109

Sellwood, Joseph, 38, 40, 45, 64, 75, 77

Selmy, Jack, 122

Sherwin, John, 157, 172, 201, 202

Sherwood, W. L., 92

Solvay, Ernest, 151

South Washburn Mining and Smelting Company, 60

Spear, Mrs. Frank B., 28

Stanak, Frank, 194

Standard Steamship Company, 99

Steel and Tube Company of America, The, 56, 62, 101, 168, 171, 184

Steel Company of Canada, Limited, The, 152, 180, 184, 185, 186, 189, 209, 214, 215

Stevens, J. D. H., 59

Stone, Amasa, 33, 39, 46, 67, 68

Stone, Clara, 68

Stone, Flora Amelia, 32-33

Stone, George, 43

Stone, Lewie, 198

Striebing, George W., 172, 191

Struthers Furnace Co., 42

Stuntz, George R., 43

Sullivan, Michael, 142

Tarleton, Leslie, 136

Taylor Iron Co., 29

Teller, George, 108

Thomas, Morris, 77

Thompson, J. R., 61

Thompson, R. W., 209

Toledo Furnace Company, 148, 150, 154

Tower, Charlemagne, 43

Union Iron and Steel Company, 145

Union Steel Company, 43, 145, 146

United Alloy Steel Corporation, 150

United Furnace Company, 150, 186

United States Steel Corporation, 61, 70, 96, 106, 138, 147, 148, 160

United Steel Company, 150

Van Hise, C. R., 61, 77

Van Orden, Matt, 60

Verona Mining Company, The, 47, 106, 107

Wabush Iron Company, 215

Wakefield, George M., 64

Washburn & Moen Manufacturing Company, 147, 148

Webb, W. D., 188

Wellman, Samuel T., 45

Wetmore, Charles W., 91, 92

Wheeler, C. P., 158

Wheeler, Seymour, 158

Wheeler Furnace Co., 42, 145

White, Peter, 20, 22, 27

Whitney, E. O., 115, 116, 118

Williams, Harrison, 62

Winchell, Horace V., 205

Winchell, N. H., 204

Winston-Dear Company, 77

Wolvin, A. B., 70, 106

Wood, James R., 54

Woodford, C. H., 197

Woolson, Constance Fenimore, 33

Wright, Frederick Eugene, 26

Young, William, 107

Youngston Iron Sheet and Tube Company, The, 145

Youngstown Sheet and Tube Company, The, 62, 101, 102, 135, 140, 151, 154-55, 160, 167, 168, 171, 172, 180, 184, 189, 191, 206, 209, 215

Youngstown Steamship Company, 102

Zenith Furnace Company, 150, 154, 172

ABOUT THE AUTHOR

Walter Havighurst, born in Appleton, Wisconsin, in 1901, graduated from the University of Denver, studied for a year at King's College, University of London, and received his master's degree from Columbia University. A member of the Department of English at Miami University, Oxford, Ohio, since 1928, he is now Research Professor of English there. He is the author of ten books of American regional history, among them *Upper Mississippi* (1937), *The Long Ships Passing* (1942), to which *Vein of Iron* is a companion volume, and *Annie Oakley of the Wild West* (1954). In 1947 and 1951, Mr. Havighurst received the Ohioana Library Association's Annual Award. He was also presented with an award in 1947 by the Friends of American Writers and another in 1957 by the Association for State and Local History. *The Long Ships Passing* was included in the library of 350 American books chosen by the Carnegie Corporation for presentation to libraries throughout the British Commonwealth as books best portraying the American scene and civilization. Mr. Havighurst is a member of the Ohio Historical Society, the Society of American Historians, and the Great Lakes Historical Society. With his wife, writer and frequent co-author Marion Boyd Havighurst, he has traveled extensively throughout the world.